Quilt Collection

They like to spend long afternoons cruising the antique shops, folding & unfolding, ooohing-and-aaahing over the old quilts. They love snappy red-and-white Log Cabins, soft pastel Wedding Rings & vivid patchworks. They spend happy hours at the corner craft store contemplating the calicos & homespuns... with a side-trip, of course, for Double Fudge Sundaes, heavy on the whipped cream & sprinkles!

They're the Country Friends®, three-of-a-kind who love all things country & quilted: Kate, all thumbs when it comes to sewing on buttons, can't get her hands on enough of them for crafting & collecting... Holly, who leans toward the finer things in life like stacks & stacks of homespun fabric & quilting patterns... and Mary Elizabeth, who always has at least six projects underway and another dozen in mind! And don't forget faithful old Spotty — he tags along in every chapter just to see what happens next!

The Country Friends® have pieced together a quilting adventure as enchanting as an old Friendship quilt. You're welcome to come along... there's always room for another Country Friend!

A LEISURE ARTS PUBLICATION

Quilt Collection

Content and Artwork by **Gooseberry Patch Company**

EDITORIAL TEAM
Editorial Director: Susan Frantz Wiles
Senior Editor: Linda L. Garner

ART TEAM
Art Publications Director: Rhonda Shelby
Art Imaging Director: Mark Hawkins
Art Category Manager: Lora Puls
Freelance Artist: Donna Blackford
Art Imaging Technicians: Stephanie Johnson and Mark Potter
Publishing Systems Administrator: Becky Riddle
Publishing Systems Assistants: Clint Hanson, John Rose, and Chris Wertenberger

BUSINESS STAFF
Publisher: Rick Barton
Vice President, Finance: Tom Siebenmorgen
Director of Corporate Planning and Development: Laticia Mull Dittrich
Vice President, Retail Marketing: Bob Humphrey
Vice President, Sales: Ray Shelgosh
Vice President, National Accounts: Pam Stebbins
Director of Sales and Services: Margaret Reinold
Vice President, Operations: Jim Dittrich
Comptroller, Operations: Rob Thieme
Retail Customer Service Managers: Sharon Hall and Stan Raynor
Print Production Manager: Fred F. Pruss

friendship is the golden thread that ties the heart of all the world.
– JOHN EVELYN 1620–1706 –

International Standard Book Number 1-57486-343-6

10 9 8 7 6 5 4 3 2 1

Contents

Fireside Quilts

When the days turn brisk and chilly and the nights become longer, it's the perfect time to settle in beside the fire and stitch a warm, cozy quilt. Let the beautiful autumn colors be your inspiration as you select fabrics to re-create this antique Trip Around the World quilt...it's sure to be a cherished heirloom!

Trip Around the World Quilt, page 12.

Acorn Lap Throw, page 14.

If the thought of sewing a full-size quilt seems a little intimidating to you, try your hand at a smaller project like this cozy appliquéd lap quilt. You'll soon be ready to take on larger projects!

"Listen! The wind is rising, and the air is wild with leaves. We have had our summer evenings, now for October eves!"

— Humbert Wolfe

Acorn Wreath, page 17; Acorn Mantel Scarf, page 18.

Create a cozy sitting area around the hearth…or even on the front porch! Toss comfy pillows on the chairs, drape a warm quilt over the couch and cover the mantel with a colorful scarf. Invite friends over to pop popcorn and play favorite board games…a great way to enjoy a chilly fall evening.

Acorn Block Pillow, page 19; Trip Around the World Pillow, page 20.

Other items to arrange on your mantel for fall: beeswax candles, copper stars, bittersweet and a twig basket filled with pears, apples, gourds and mini pumpkins.

"Here's to October…frost-kissed apples, the wild-as-the-wind smell of hickory nuts and the nostalgic whiff of that first wood-smoke."

— Ken Weber

Around the World Table Mat, page 21.

Remember coming home to a snack of milk & cookies? Make sweet memories with your own kids…greet them after school with acorn-shaped sugar cookies decorated with icing and sprinkles! You'll add a nostalgic feeling to the table when you make our scaled-down version of the Trip Around the World quilt pattern…it's just the right size for a colorful table mat.

Autumn leaves of russet, gold and red are pretty scattered down the center of the dining table…add a handful of acorns, too!

After·school SUGAR Cookies

7 T. BUTTER
⅓ c. SHORTENING
1 c. SUGAR
2 EGGS
1 t. VANILLA
2·½ c. ALL-PURPOSE FLOUR
1 t. BAKING POWDER
1 t. SALT

CREAM TOGETHER BUTTER, SHORTENING & SUGAR. MIX IN EGGS & VANILLA ～ BLEND WELL. MIX IN FLOUR, BAKING POWDER & SALT. DIVIDE DOUGH INTO TWO BALLS～WRAP IN PLASTIC WRAP. CHILL A MINIMUM OF ONE HOUR. ROLL DOUGH OUT TO ⅛" THICKNESS ON LIGHTLY·FLOURED SURFACE. CUT INTO DESIRED SHAPES. BAKE AT 375 DEGREES FOR SIX TO EIGHT MINUTES ON UNGREASED COOKIE SHEET. DECORATE WITH ICING AFTER BAKED & COOLED. MAKES ABOUT FOUR DOZEN COOKIES.

yummy!

When you're not busy stitching, pack your quilting supplies in a pretty craft basket...a neat, attractive way to keep everything close at hand!

"The trees are in their autumn beauty,
The woodland paths are dry,
Under the October twilight
The water mirrors a still sky."

— William Butler Yeats

Craft Keeper, page 23.

TRIP AROUND THE WORLD QUILT

(shown on pg. 6)

Finished Size: 77³/₄" x 77³/₄"

FABRICS

Yardage is based on 45"w fabric.
- green fabric for outer borders — 2¹/₂-yds
- yellow fabric for middle borders — 2³/₈-yds
- red fabric for inner borders — 2¹/₄-yds
- dark blue, medium blue, light blue, red, dark pink, medium pink, light pink, olive green, dark green, medium green, light green, and orange — ¹/₂-yd each
- dark yellow, medium yellow, light yellow, and navy — ³/₄-yd each
- fabric for backing and hanging sleeve — 5-yds
- fabric for binding — ⁷/₈-yd

Other supplies
- batting — 90" x 108"

*Refer to **Assembly Diagram**, pg. 14, as needed. See **Quilter's Basics** (pg. 241) for more in-depth basic instructions.*

CUTTING

Green:
- Cut 2 side outer borders 3" x 77¹/₄".
- Cut 2 lengthwise top/bottom outer borders 3" x 82¹/₄".

Yellow:
- Cut 2 lengthwise side middle borders 2¹/₂" x 73¹/₄".
- Cut 2 lengthwise top/bottom middle borders 2¹/₂" x 77¹/₄".
- Cut 8 2¹/₄"w strips.

Red:
- Cut 2 lengthwise side inner borders 2¹/₂" x 69¹/₄".
- Cut 2 lengthwise top/bottom inner borders 2¹/₂" x 73¹/₄".

Orange:
- Cut 1 square 2¹/₄" x 2¹/₄" for center square.

Dark blue, medium blue, light blue, red, dark pink, medium pink, light pink, olive green, dark green, medium green, light green, and orange:
- Cut 5 2¹/₄"w strips from *each* fabric.

Dark yellow, medium yellow, and navy:
- Cut 6 2¹/₄"w strips from *each* fabric.

Light Yellow
- Cut 8 2¹/₄"w strips.

PIECING

1. Sew strips together in color order shown to make Strip Set 1. Make 5 Strip Sets.

Strip Set 1 - make 5

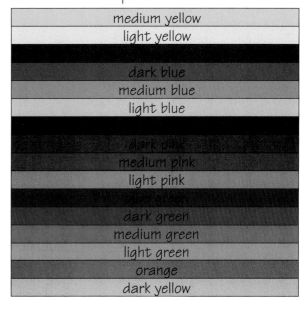

| medium yellow |
| light yellow |
| dark blue |
| medium blue |
| light blue |
| dark pink |
| medium pink |
| light pink |
| olive green |
| dark green |
| medium green |
| light green |
| orange |
| dark yellow |

2. With right sides together and matching long raw edges, sew final lengthwise seam of Strip Set to form a tube (Fig. 1). Repeat with remaining Strip Sets.

Fig. 1

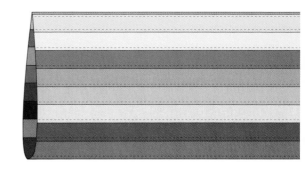

3. Referring to Fig. 2, cut across Strip Sets at 2¹/₄" intervals to make 84 circular Strip Units.

Fig. 2

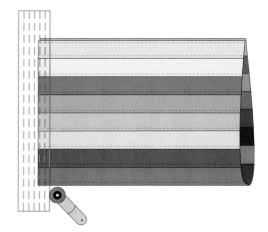

Strip Unit - make 84

4. Refer to Section diagrams to determine which color square to place at the top of each Strip Unit. Use a seam ripper to remove seam above determined top square of each Strip Unit (Fig. 3). Working from left to right on a flat surface, carefully arrange Strip Units in correct order to make each Section A. Make 4 Section A's.

Fig. 3

Section A - make 4

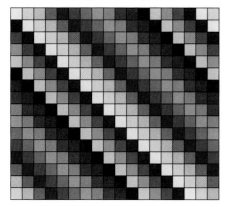

5. Carefully arrange Strip Units in correct order to make each Section B. Make 4 Section B's.

Section B - make 4

6. Sew 1 medium yellow, 2 light yellow, and 1 navy square together to make each Section C. Make 4 Section C's.

Section C - make 4

7. Use a seam ripper to remove seam above determined top of square of one strip set unit to make Section D. Make 4 Section D's.

Section D - make 4

8. Sew 1 Section C to each Section B. Sew Section A's, Section B/C's, Section D's and Center Square together to make center section of quilt top.

9. Follow **Adding Squared Borders**, pg 249, to add side, then top and bottom inner borders to center section. Repeat to add middle and outer borders to complete Quilt Top.

FINISHING

1. Mark, layer, and quilt as desired. Our quilt is hand quilted in diagonal lines across the pieced-square section and in the ditch along each border.

2. Follow **Binding,** pg. 252, to bind quilt using a 30" square of binding fabric to make $8^3/_4$-yds of $2^1/_2$"w continuous bias binding with overlapping corners.

Assembly Diagram

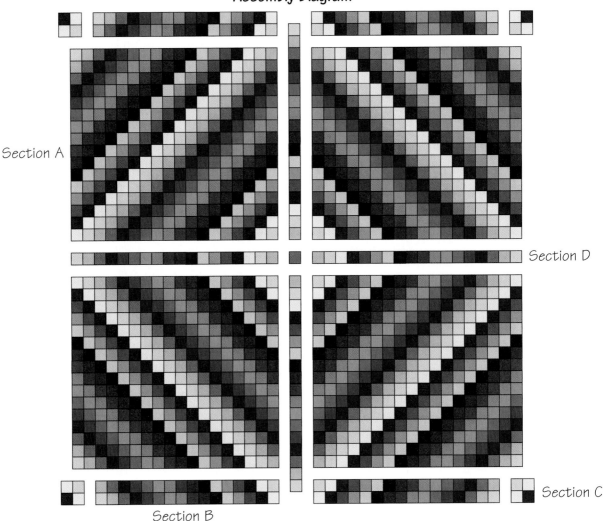

Section A

Section D

Section B

Section C

ACORN LAP THROW

(shown on pg. 7)

Finished Size: $47^3/4"$ x $47^3/4"$
Block Size: 15" x 15"

FABRICS

Yardage is based on 45"w fabric.
• light gold print — $1^1/2$-yds
• 8 different medium gold prints — 10" x 18" each
• green stripe — $3/8$-yd
• medium green print — $3/8$-yd
• dark green print — $3/4$-yd
• red print — $3/8$-yd
• 4 different black prints — 16" x 16" each
• fabric for backing and hanging sleeve — 3-yds
• fabric for binding — $1^1/2$-yds

Other supplies
• batting — 45" x 60"

*Refer to **Quilt Top Diagram** as needed. See **Quilter's Basics** (pg. 241) for more in-depth basic instructions.*

CUTTING

Light Gold Print:
• Cut 4 lengthwise strips 8"w. From these strips, cut:
 •2 borders 8" x $32^3/4"$.
 •2 borders 8" x $47^3/4"$.

Variety of medium gold prints:
• From each print, cut 2 squares 8" x 8".

Green Stripe:
• Cut 6 strips $1^1/4$"w. From these strips, cut:
 •2 strips $1^1/4$" x $15^1/2"$.
 •3 strips $1^1/4$" x $31^1/4"$.
 •2 strips $1^1/4$" x $32^3/4"$.

Medium Green Print:
• Use patterns, pg. 16, to cut:
 •20 acorn caps.
 •4 bud caps.

14

Dark Green Print:
• Follow **Making Continuous Bias Strip Binding,** pg. 252, to cut:
  • 1 square 18" x 18". From this square cut:
  • 1 bias strip 1¹/₂" x 180".
• Use pattern to cut:
  • 16 stems.

Red Print:
• Use patterns, pg. 16, to cut:
  • 20 acorns.
  • 4 buds.

Variety of Black Prints:
• Use pattern, pg. 16, to cut:
  • 4 oak leaves.

PIECING

1. Sew 4 gold print squares together to make Unit 1. Make 4 Unit 1's.

Unit 1 – make 4

2. Follow **Needle-Turn Appliqué,** pg. 248, to appliqué stems, acorn caps, acorns, and oak leaves to Unit 1's.

3. (Note: Appliqués are not shown in Steps 3-6.) Sew 2 Unit 1's and a 1¹/₄" x 15¹/₂" strip together to make Unit 2. Make 2 Unit 2's.

Unit 2 – make 2

4. Sew 2 Unit 2's and a 1¹/₄" x 31¹/₄" strip together to make Unit 3.

Unit 3

5. Sew 1¹/₄" x 31¹/₄" strips to sides. Sew remaining strips to top and bottom of Unit 3 to make Unit 4.

Unit 4

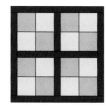

6. Sew borders to sides, then top and bottom of Unit 4 to make Unit 5.

Unit 5

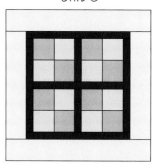

7. Matching wrong sides, fold dark green bias strip in half. Use a ¹/₄" seam allowance to sew along long edge. Centering seam, press strip. Pin bias strip and appliqués in place. Topstitch bias strip to throw along edges. Appliqué acorn, acorn caps, buds, and bud caps to border to make Quilt Top.

FINISHING

1. Mark, layer, and quilt wall hanging.

2. Follow **Making a Hanging Sleeve,** pg. 254, to attach hanging sleeve to wall hanging.

3. Follow **Binding,** pg. 252, to bind wall hanging using 6-yds of 2¹/₂"w straight-grain binding with mitered corners.

Quilt Top Diagram

Using ¼-pattern:

Fold fabric in quarters. Place heavy lines on folds of fabric. Cut along thin lines.

Stem

Acorn Cap

Acorn

Oak Leaf

Bud

Bud Cap

ACORN WREATH

(shown on pg. 8)

Wreath Size: 18" diameter
Acorn Size: 4¹/₂" x 5"

FABRICS

Yardage is based on 45"w fabric.
• 3 different green print fabrics — ¹/₄-yd each
• red print — ¹/₄-yd

Supplies
• batting — ¹/₄-yd
• grapevine wreath — 18" diameter
• assorted artificial leaves and flowers
• hot glue gun and glue sticks

CUTTING

Green Prints:
• For backing, cut 7 squares 6" x 6".
• Use pattern to cut:
  •7 acorn caps.

Red Print:
• Use pattern to cut:
  •7 acorns.

Batting:
• Cut 7 squares 6" x 6"

PIECING

1. For each acorn, place cap on top of acorn, overlapping edges ¹/₄". Zigzag stitch along the edge to hold the two pieces together.

2. Place batting square on work surface. Place backing square right side up on top of batting. Lay acorn face down on top of batting and backing. Sew around edge of acorn, leaving an opening for turning. Trim backing and batting even with edges of acorn. Clip curves.

3. Turn acorn right side out; press. Sew opening closed.

4. Follow **Mock Hand Appliqué**, pg. 249, Steps. 2 – 6, to stitch around outside edge of acorn.

5. Glue artificial leaves, flowers, and fabric acorns to wreath as desired.

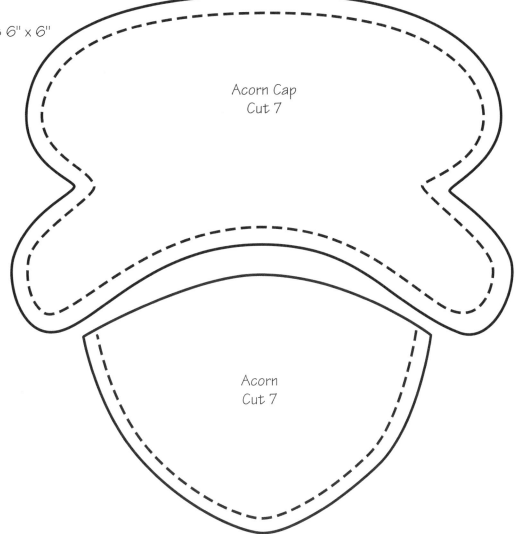

Acorn Cap
Cut 7

Acorn
Cut 7

ACORN MANTEL SCARF

(shown on pg. 8)

Finished Size: 54"w with 13½" drop
Block Size: 9½" x 9½"

FABRICS

Yardage is based on 45"w fabric.
- gold print #1 — ⅜-yd
- gold print #2 — 1¾-yds
- gold print #3 — ⅜-yd
- green print — ¼-yd
- red print — ¼-yd
- assorted black prints — ½-yd total

Refer to **Mantel Scarf Top Diagram** *as needed. See* **Quilter's Basics** *(pg. 241) for more in-depth basic instructions.*

CUTTING
Gold Print #1:
- Cut 1 square 10" x 10".
Gold Print #2:
- Cut 1 rectangle 23" x 56".
- Cut 1 rectangle 7" x 54½".
- Cut 2 squares 10⅞" x 10⅞". Cut these squares in half diagonally. Discard 1 half.
- Cut 1 square 10"x 10".
Gold Print #3:
- Cut 1 square 10⅞" x 10⅞". Cut these squares in half diagonally.
- Cut 2 squares 10"x 10".
Green Print:
- Use patterns, pg. 19, to cut:
  - 16 acorn caps.
  - 16 stems.
Red Print:
- Use pattern, pg. 19, to cut:
  - 16 acorns.
Black Print:
- Use pattern, pg. 19, to cut:
  - 4 oak leaves.

PIECING

1. Follow **Mock Hand Appliqué**, pg. 249, to appliqué stems, acorn caps, acorns, and oak leaves to 10" squares.

2. With appliquéd block turned on point, sew 1 triangle to top left side of each block to make Unit 1. Make 4 Unit 1's.

Unit 1 – make 4

3. Sew 1 triangle to top right side of 1 Unit 1 to make Unit 2.

Unit 2

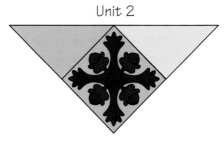

4. Sew 3 Unit 1's and Unit 2 together to make Unit 3.

Unit 3

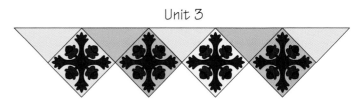

5. Trim top edge so it is straight. Trim side triangles at a right angle to the top edge.

6. Sew the 7" x 54½" strip to the top of Unit 3 to make Mantel Scarf Top.

Mantel Scarf Top Diagram

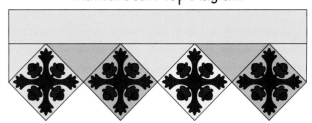

FINISHING

1. Matching right sides and long edges, stitching ¼" from edges of mantel scarf top, and leaving an opening for turning, sew mantel scarf top to remaining rectangle.

2. Trimming even with edges of mantel scarf top, trim excess fabric.

3. Turn mantel scarf right side out; press. Sew opening closed.

4. Topstitch ¼" from edges of mantel scarf.

5. Mark and quilt the block and triangle portion of the mantel scarf as desired.

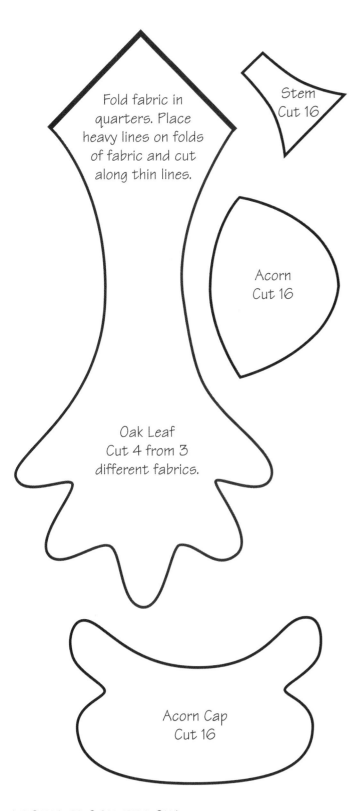

Fold fabric in quarters. Place heavy lines on folds of fabric and cut along thin lines.

Stem
Cut 16

Acorn
Cut 16

Oak Leaf
Cut 4 from 3
different fabrics.

Acorn Cap
Cut 16

- red print — $1/4$-yd
- black print — $1/2$-yd
- fabric for backing — $1/2$-yd

Supplies
- batting
- 16" pillow form

Refer to **Pillow Top Diagram** *as needed. See* **Quilter's Basics** *(pg. 241) for more in-depth basic instructions.*

CUTTING

Gold Print #1:
- Cut 2 squares 8" x 8".

Gold Print #2:
- Cut 2 squares 8" x 8".

Green Print:
- Use patterns, pg. 16, to cut:
  - 4 acorn caps.
  - 4 stems.

Red Print:
- Use pattern, pg. 16, to cut:
  - 4 acorns.

Black Print:
- Use pattern, pg. 16, to cut:
  - 1 oak leaves.

Fabric for backing:
- Cut 2 rectangles 11" x $15^1/2$".

PIECING

1. Follow **Acorn Lap Throw**, pg. 14, Step 1, to make pillow top. Follow **Mock Hand Appliqué**, pg. 249, to appliqué stems, acorn caps, acorns, and oak leaf to pillow top.

2. Mark, layer, and stipple-quilt pillow top.

3. Press 1 long side of each backing piece $1/4$" to wrong side; press to wrong side again. Stitch along fold.

4. Matching right sides and raw edges and overlapping backing pieces, sew backing to pillow top. Turn right side out. Insert pillow form.

ACORN BLOCK PILLOW

(shown on pg. 9)

Finished Size: $15^1/2$" square

FABRICS

Yardage is based on 45"w fabric.
- gold print #1 — $3/8$-yd
- gold print #2 — $3/8$-yd
- green print — $1/4$-yd

Pillow Top Diagram

19

TRIP AROUND THE WORLD PILLOW

(shown on pg. 9)

Finished Size: 12" x 20½"

FABRICS

Yardage is based on 45"w fabric.

• gold print #1 — scrap
• gold print #2 — scrap
• gold print #3 — scrap
• gold print #4 — scrap
• green print #1 — scrap
• green print #2 — scrap
• red print #1 — scrap
• red print #2 — scrap
• fabric for buttons — scraps
• fabric for backing — ½-yd

Supplies

• 12" x 16" pillow form
• 6 buttons to cover — ¾" diameter

*Refer to **Pillow Top Diagram** as needed. See **Quilter's Basics** (pg. 241) for more in-depth basic instructions.*

CUTTING

Gold Print #1:
• Cut 1 square 2¼" x 2¼".

Gold Print #2:
• Cut 4 squares 2¼" x 2¼".

Gold Print #3:
• Cut 2 strips 2⅛" x 12¾".
• Cut 2 strips 2¼" x 12½".

Gold Print #4:
• Cut 2 rectangles 5½" 24½".

Green Print #1:
• Cut 8 squares 2¼" x 2¼".

Green Print #2:
• Cut 10 squares 2¼" x 2¼".

Red Print #1:
• Cut 8 squares 2¼" x 2¼".

Red Print #2:
• Cut 4 squares 2¼" x 2¼".

Fabric for backing:
• Cut 1 rectangle 16¼" x 12½".

PIECING

1. Sew 2 red #2 squares, 2 red #1 squares, 2 green #2 squares and 1 green #1 square together to make Unit 1. Make 2 Unit 1's.

Unit 1 — make 2

2. Sew 2 red #1 squares, 2 green #2 squares, 2 green #1 squares, and 1 gold #2 square together to make Unit 2. Make 2 Unit 2's.

Unit 2 — make 2

3. Sew 2 green #2 squares, 2 green #1 squares, 2 gold #2 squares, and 1 gold #1 square together to make Unit 3.

Unit 3

4. Sew Units together to make Unit 4.

Unit 4

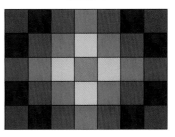

5. Sew narrow gold #3 strips to long sides of Unit 4. Sew remaining gold #3 strips to short ends of Unit 4.

6. Matching right sides and raw edges, sew Unit 4 to backing along long edges to make pillow top.

7. Matching right sides and raw edges, sew short ends of 1 gold #4 strip together to form loop. Press strip in half lengthwise; baste raw edges together. Matching right side of loop to right side of pillow top, sew loop to pillow top. Repeat with remaining gold #4 strip.

8. Insert pillow form. Follow manufacturer's instructions to cover buttons. Sew buttons to ends of pillow through all layers.

Pillow Top Diagram

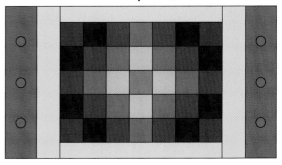

AROUND THE WORLD TABLE MAT

(shown on pg. 10)

Finished Size: 19¼" x 33¼"

FABRICS

Yardage is based on 45"w fabric.
- orange, yellow #1, yellow #2, yellow #3, green #1, green #2, green #3, green #4, red #1, red #2, red #3, gold #1, gold #2, gold #3 — ¼-yd **each**
- fabric for backing — ⅝-yd
- fabric for binding — ½-yd

Supplies
- batting — 45" x 60"

*Refer to **Assembly Diagram**, pg. 22, as needed. See **Quilter's Basics** (pg. 241) for more in-depth basic instructions.*

CUTTING

orange:
- Cut one 2¼" square for center.
- Cut one 2¼" strip.

yellow #1:
- Cut one 2¼" x 12" strip.

yellow #2 and #3:
- Cut 2 strips 2¼"w from **each** fabric. From strips, cut:
  - 2 strips 2¼" x 12" and 2 strips 2¼" x 21".

green #1, green #2, green #3, green #4, red #1, and red #2:
- Cut 2 strips 2¼"w from **each** fabric. From strips, cut:
  - 2¼" x 12" strip.
  - 2¼" x 21" strip.
  - 2¼" x 30" strip.

red #3 and gold #1:
- Cut 1 strip 2¼"w from **each** fabric. From strip, cut:
  - 2¼" x 21" strip.
  - 2¼" x 30" strip.

gold #2 and #3:
- Cut one 2¼" strip from **each** fabric.

PIECING

1. Sew 12" strips together in color order shown to make Strip Set 1. Make 1 Strip Set. Cut across Strip Sets at 2¼" intervals to make 4 Strip Units. Leave 2 Strip Units in tact to make 2 Unit 1's. From remaining Strip Units, remove seam above green #3. Discard green #3, green #4, red #1, and red #2 to make Unit 2's. Make 2 Unit 2's.

Strip Set 1 - make 1

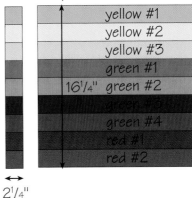

	yellow #1
	yellow #2
	yellow #3
	green #1
16¼"	green #2
	green #3
	green #4
	red #1
	red #2

2¼"

Unit 1 – make 2

Unit 2 – make 2

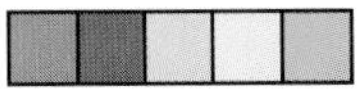

2. Sew 21" strips together in color order shown to make Strip Set 2. Make 1 Strip Set. Cut across Strip Sets at 2¼" intervals to make 8 Strip Units. From four Strip Units, remove seam above gold #1. Discard gold #1 to make Unit 3. Make 4 Unit 3's. From remaining Strip Units, remove seam above yellow #3. Discard yellow #2 to make Unit 4. Make 4 Unit 4's.

Strip Set 2 - make 1

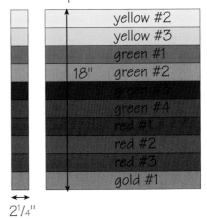

	yellow #2
	yellow #3
	green #1
18"	green #2
	green #3
	green #4
	red #1
	red #2
	red #3
	gold #1

2¼"

Unit 3 – make 4

Unit 4 – make 4

3. Sew 30" strips together in color order shown to make Strip Set 3. Make 1 Strip Set. Cut across Strip Sets at 2¼" intervals to make 12 Strip Units. From four Strip Units, remove seam above gold #3. Discard gold #3 and orange to make Unit 5. Make 4 Unit 5's. From four Strip Units, remove seam above green #2 and orange. Discard green #1 and orange to make Unit 6. Make 4 Unit 6's. From remaining Strip Units, remove seam above green #3. Discard green #1 and #2 to make Unit 7. Make 4 Unit 7's.

Strip Set 3 - make 1

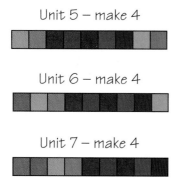

green #1
green #2
green #3
green #4
red #1
red #2
red #3
gold #1
gold #2
gold #3
orange

19³/₄"

2¼"

Unit 5 – make 4

Unit 6 – make 4

Unit 7 – make 4

4. Refer to Quarter Section diagrams to determine placement of each Unit. Working from left to right on a flat surface, carefully arrange Units in correct order. Sew Units together to make 2 Quarter Section A's and 2 Quarter Section B's.

Quarter Section A – make 2

Quarter Section B – make 2

5. Referring to **Assembly Diagram,** sew Quarter Section A's, Quarter Section B's, Units, and Center Square together to make center section of quilt top.

Assembly Diagram

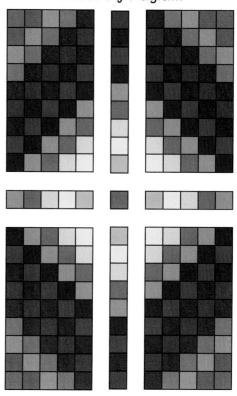

FINISHING

1. Mark, layer, and quilt as desired. Our table mat is hand quilted in diagonal lines across the pieced-square section.

2. Follow **Binding**, pg. 252, to bind quilt using an 18" square of binding fabric to make 3-yds of 2½"w continuous bias binding with overlapping corners.

CRAFT KEEPER

(shown on pg. 11 and below)

FABRICS

Yardage is based on 45"w fabric.
- gold print — ³/₈-yd
- green print — ¼-yd
- red print — ¼-yd
- black print— ³/₈-yd

Supplies
- paper-backed fusible web
- folding craft tote

CUTTING

Use Acorn Lap Throw patterns, pg. 16, and follow **Preparing Appliqué Pieces**, page 247, to make the following appliqués:

Gold Print:
- Cut 1 square 10¼" x 10¼"

Green Print:
- 4 acorn caps
- 4 stems

Red Print:
- 4 acorns

Black Print:
- 1 oak leaf

INSTRUCTIONS

1. Follow manufacturer's instructions to fuse appliqués to side of craft tote.

There is only one thing better than making a new friend and that is keeping an **old** one. ∽ Elmer G. Leterman

Autumn Harvest

Celebrate the first frost of the year with our Pumpkin Pillow and Autumn Harvest Wall Hanging. The fall colors and fun appliqué shapes make these designs a stitcher's delight!

Pumpkin Pillow, page 28.

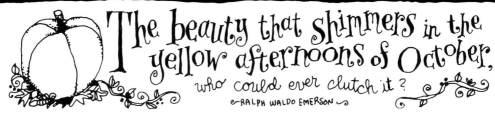

The beauty that shimmers in the yellow afternoons of October, who could ever clutch it?
~ RALPH WALDO EMERSON ~

Autumn Harvest Wall Hanging, page 29.

OH ★ MY!

Scaredy-Cats, pages 30-31.

OctobeR is good for a SCARE!

Soft-Sculpture Pumpkins, page 31.

Craft a super-easy pumpkin patch and an entire litter of lucky black kittens quicker than you can say "boo!" Just think what great party favors or hostess gifts these soft-sculpture projects would make.

What an IDEA!

PUMPKIN PILLOW

(shown on pg. 24)

Finished size: 16" square

FABRICS

- tan plaid — large scrap
- green plaid — 1/4-yd
- gold plaid — 1/8-yd
- rust print — 1/8-yd
- orange stripe for pumpkin — 10" square
- 5 different plaids or stripes for stem and leaves — scraps
- fabric for pillow back

Other supplies

- paper-backed fusible web
- embroidery floss — green
- polyester fiberfill

*Refer to **Pillow Top Diagram** as needed. See* ***Quilter's Basics** (pg. 241) for more in-depth basic instructions.*

CUTTING

Tan plaid:

- Cut 1 A — 7 1/2" square

Green plaid:

- Cut one 5 7/8"w strip. From this, cut:
  - 4 B's — Cut two 5 7/8" squares, then cut each once diagonally into 2 triangles.

Gold plaid:

- Cut one 3 1/2"w strip. From this, cut:
  - 4 C's — 3 1/2" square

Rust print:

- Cut two 3 1/2"w strips. From these, cut:
  - 4 D's — 3 1/2"x10 1/2"

PIECING

1. Sew 1 B to each edge of A to make Unit 1.

Unit 1 — make 1

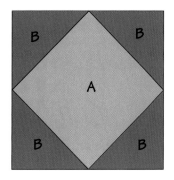

2. Sew 2 C's to each of two D's to make two Unit 2's.

Unit 2 — make 2

3. Sew remaining D's to top and bottom edges of Unit 1. Sew Unit 2's to side edges of Unit 1 to complete pillow top. Pillow top should measure 16 1/2" square.

FINISHING

1. Use large pumpkin and large stem patterns, pg. 32, and follow **Appliqué**, pg. 247, to appliqué pumpkin and stem to center of pillow top.

2. Trace leaf pattern, pg. 33, 4 times onto paper side of fusible web. Fuse web to wrong sides of leaf fabrics. Cut out pieces, then fuse to corners of pillow top. Stitch a blanket stitch by machine around edges of each leaf.

3. Use 3 strands of floss to work long running stitches on pumpkin to resemble lines on pumpkin (see photo).

4. Cut pillow back fabric same size as pillow top. Sew back and top together, leaving an opening for turning. Turn. Stuff with fiberfill; sew opening closed.

Pillow Top Diagram

AUTUMN HARVEST WALL HANGING

(shown on pg. 25)

Finished size: 22"x29"
Block size: 7" square

FABRICS
• light tan print – ¼-yd
• dark green print – ¼-yd
• orange print – ¼-yd
• gold plaid – ½-yd
• green print (for border) – ⅓-yd
• orange plaid for pumpkins – ¼-yd
• green plaid for stems – scrap
• backing – ¾-yd
• binding – ½-yd
Other supplies
• batting – 26"x32"
• embroidery floss – green

*Refer to **Wall Hanging Diagram**, pg. 30, as needed. See **Quilter's Basics** (pg. 241) for more in-depth basic instructions.*

CUTTING
Light tan print:
• Cut one 5½"w strip. From this, cut:
    • 6 C's – 5½" square
Dark green print:
• Cut three 2¼"w strips. From these:
    • Cut 14 A's – 2¼" square
    • Set aside remaining strips for Strip Set A.
Orange print:
• Cut three 2¼"w strips. From these:
    • Cut 14 A's – 2¼" square
    • Set aside remaining strips for Strip Set B.
Gold plaid:
• Cut two 3¾"w strips. From these, cut:
    • 48 B's – Cut twelve 3¾" squares, then cut each twice diagonally into 4 triangles.
• Cut two 4"w strips for strip sets.
Green print:
• Cut three 2½"w strips. From these, cut:
    • 2 top/bottom borders – 2½"x20"
    • 2 side borders – 2½"x29"

PIECING BLOCKS
1. Sew 2 gold plaid B's to each of 12 green and 12 orange A's to make 12 Unit 1a's and 12 Unit 1b's.

Unit 1a – make 12 Unit 1b – make 12

2. Sew 4 Unit 1a's to each of 3 tan print C's to make 3 Block A's. Repeat with Unit 1b's to make 3 Block B's. Blocks should measure 7½" square.

Block A – make 3 Block B – make 3

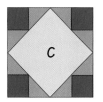 

APPLIQUÉING
1. Use small pumpkin and small stem patterns, pg. 33, and follow **Appliqué** (pg. 247) to appliqué 1 pumpkin and stem to center of each block

PIECING WALL HANGING
1. Follow **Wall Hanging Diagram**, pg. 30, to sew Blocks into rows, then sew rows together to make wall hanging center.

2. Sew 2 green strips to 1 gold plaid strip to make Strip Set A. Cut five 2¼"w Unit 2a's from strip set. Repeat with orange strips and remaining gold plaid strip to make Strip Set B and cut five 2¼"w Unit 2b's.

Unit 2a – make 5   Strip Set A

2¼"

Unit 2b – make 5   Strip Set B

 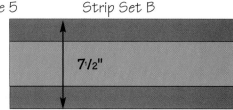

2¼"

3. Sew 1 Unit 2a and 1 Unit 2b together to make each top and bottom inner border.

Top/bottom inner border – make 2

4. Sew remaining green and orange A's, Unit 2a's and Unit 2b's together to make left and right inner borders.

Left inner border – make 1

Right inner border – make 1

5. Sew top, bottom, left, and right inner borders to wall hanging center.

6. Sew top, bottom, then side outer borders to inner borders to complete wall hanging top. Wall hanging should measure 22"x29".

FINISHING

1. Mark, layer, and quilt as desired using **Quilting Diagram** as a suggestion.

2. Use 3 strands of floss to work running stitches 1/2" from inner edge of outer border.

3. Bind wall hanging using 3-yds of 2¹/2"w bias binding.

Quilting Diagram

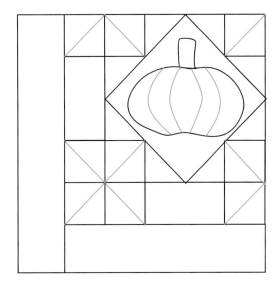

Wall Hanging Diagram

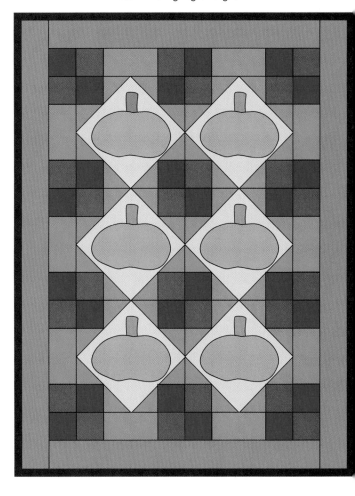

BIG SCAREDY-CAT
(shown on pg. 26)

Finished size: about 9" high

SUPPLIES
• women's black cotton/lycra tights (1 pair will make 2 cats)
• polyester fiberfill
• cardboard
• black sewing thread
• glue gun
• two 1/2" buttons for eyes
• red pearl cotton or red wool scrap for nose
• grey buttonhole twist thread
• torn fabric strip, ribbon, or seam tape for neck tie
• black wool felt – scrap

INSTRUCTIONS

1. For body, cut off one leg of tights about 7" (unstretched) from the toe.

2. Tightly stuff body with fiberfill until it is about 9" tall (tights will stretch) and about 3" in diameter.

3. Cut a 3" dia. circle from cardboard. Place cardboard into opening of body.

4. Hand baste around opening, pull thread ends to close opening over bottom of cardboard, and knot thread. Trim excess tights fabric.

5. Securely knot thread around body about 4" below toe to form head.

6. For ears, pull up a small amount of tights fabric at each end of toe seam (about ¹⁄₂") and securely knot thread around base of each gathered area.

7. Sew on buttons for eyes. Sew a small triangle of wool fabric to face for nose or use pearl cotton to work satin stitch nose and mouth.

8. For each set of whiskers, use buttonhole twist thread and follow *Fig. 1*, going down at 1 and odd numbers. Make 2 or 3 sets of whiskers.

Fig. 1

9. Tie torn fabric strip, ribbon, or seam tape around cat's neck.

10. Cut a long, skinny triangle about 9" long and 1"w at the base from felt for tail. Glue tail to bottom of cat.

SMALL SCAREDY-CAT

(shown on pg. 26)

Finished size: about 7" high

SUPPLIES

• Use same supplies as for **Big Scaredy-Cat** (pg. 30), substituting small wooden bead for red wool scrap

INSTRUCTIONS

1. For body, cut off one leg of tights about 6" (unstretched) from the toe.

2. Turn leg wrong side out. To form ears, machine stitch along top of toe as shown in *Fig. 2*. Trim

seam allowance to ¹⁄₄", turn, and tightly stuff body with fiberfill until it is about 7" tall (tights will stretch) and about 3" in diameter.

Fig. 2

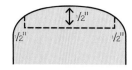

3. Follow Steps 3-5 of *Big Scaredy-Cat* instructions (this page), knotting thread 3" below top of ears to form head.

4. Follow Steps 7-10 of *Big Scaredy-Cat* instructions, using bead if desired for nose and cutting a 7" long felt tail.

SOFT-SCULPTURE PUMPKINS

(shown on pg. 27)

Finished size (each): 4", 5", or 6" high

SUPPLIES (for each)

• tracing paper
• flannel for pumpkin – ¹⁄₄-yd maximum (small pumpkin can be made with a large scrap)
• polyester fiberfill
• twig for stem – about 2" long x ¹⁄₂" dia.
• glue gun
• artificial leaves (optional)

Use a ¹⁄₄" seam allowance. Match right sides and raw edges when sewing.

INSTRUCTIONS

1. Trace desired size pumpkin section pattern (pgs. 34 – 35) onto tracing paper; cut out.

2. Use pattern to cut 6 sections from flannel.

3. Matching side edges and leaving straight edges unstitched, sew 3 sections together to make a unit. Repeat with remaining sections. Sew the units together. Do not clip curves. Turn and stuff with fiberfill.

4. Fold straight edge of opening to inside of pumpkin. Hand baste along folded edge, leaving long thread ends.

5. Glue twig into opening. Knot basting thread tightly around twig. If desired, glue artificial leaves to pumpkin.

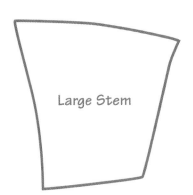

Large Stem

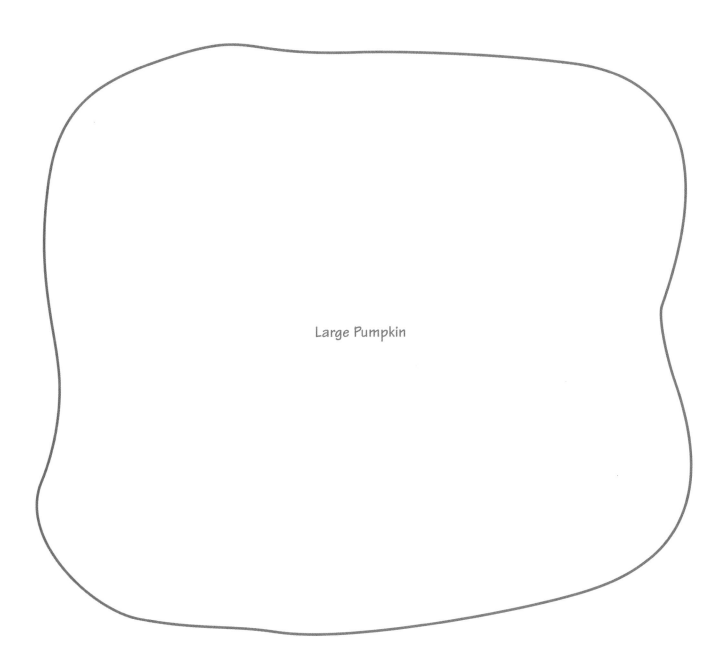

Large Pumpkin

32

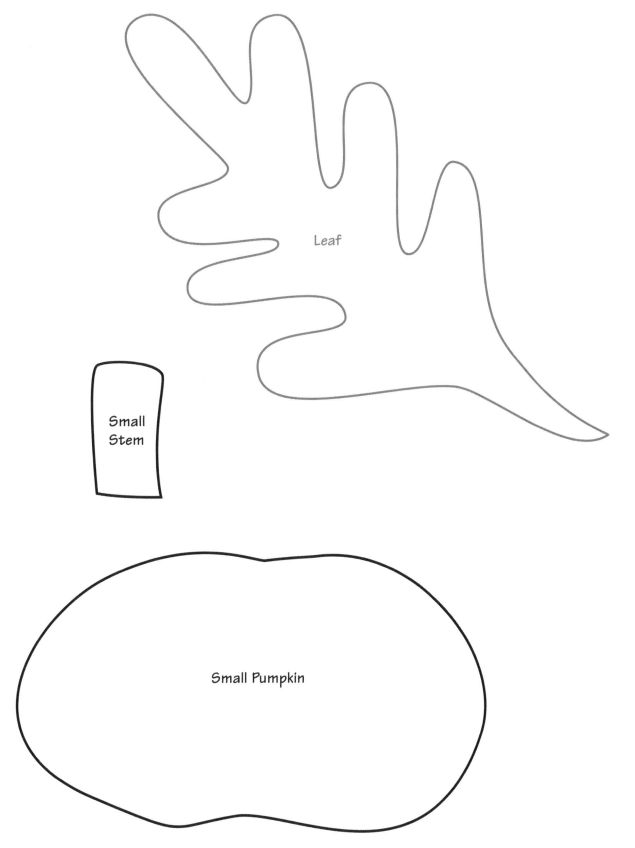

Leaf

Small
Stem

Small Pumpkin

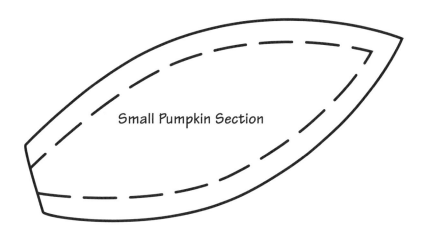

Small Pumpkin Section

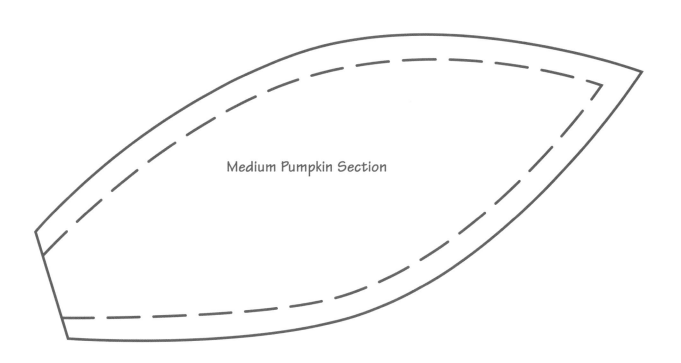

Medium Pumpkin Section

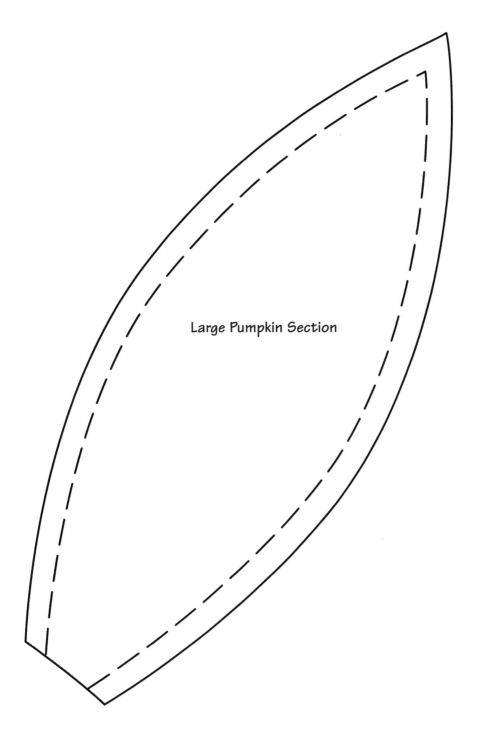

Large Pumpkin Section

35

Hen House

Feather your nest with this plucky pair! Both the wall hanging and pillow are made from warm flannel fabrics for an "eggs-tra" soft and homey touch.

Hen House Pillow, page 38.

Hen House Wall Hanging, page 38.

HEN HOUSE PILLOW

(shown on pg. 36)

Size: 17"x13"

FABRICS
- assorted plaid and striped flannels (ours uses 23 different flannels) – ½-yd total
- green striped cotton for border – ⅛-yd
- 2 print cottons for chicken appliqués – 11"x8" each
- plaid cotton for welting and backing – ¾-yd
- muslin for quilting layer – ⅜-yd

Other supplies
- batting – 20"x16"
- ½" cotton cord for welting – 1¾-yds
- polyester fiberfill

*Refer to **Pillow Top Diagram** as needed. See **Quilter's Basics** (pg. 241) for more in-depth basic instructions.*

CUTTING
Assorted flannels:
- 8 A's – 4"x5½"
- 30 B's – 1½"x2½"

Green stripe:
- top/bottom inner borders – 1"x14½"
- 2 side inner borders – 1"x12½"

PIECING
1. Sew four A's together along long edges to make each of 2 rows. Sew rows together to make pillow center.

2. Sew top, bottom, then side inner borders to center.

3. Sew all B's together along short edges to make a single strip. Cut strip into two 15½"l pieces for top/bottom outer border and two 13½"l pieces for side borders. Sew top, bottom, then side outer borders to inner border to complete pillow top. Pillow top should measure 17½"x13½".

FINISHING
1. Trace hen patterns (pgs. 40 – 41) onto paper side of web backing. Fuse web to wrong sides of cotton prints. Cut out hens, then fuse to center of pillow top.

2. Mark, layer, and quilt pillow top as desired. Our pillow top is machine quilted in the ditch along "A" seamlines (quilting does not cross over appliqués) and along inner and outer seamlines of inner border.

3. Stitch a blanket stitch by machine around edges of each hen.

4. Follow **Adding Welting to a Pillow Top** (pg. 255) and **Pillow Finishing** (pg. 255) to complete pillow.

Pillow Top Diagram

HEN HOUSE WALL HANGING

(shown on pg. 37)

Finished Size: 24"x32"
Block size: 10"x7"

FABRICS
- assorted plaid and striped flannels (ours uses 25 different flannels) – 1-yd total
- 8 cotton prints for chicken appliqués – 11"x 8" each
- plaid flannel for binding – ¼-yd
- backing – ⅞-yd

Other supplies
- batting – 28"x36"
- paper-backed fusible web

*Refer to **Wall Hanging Diagram** as needed. See **Quilter's Basics** (pg. 241) for more in-depth basic instructions.*

CUTTING

Assorted flannels:

• 32 A's – 5¹⁄₂"x4"

• 52 B's – 2¹⁄₂" square

PIECING

1. Sew 4 A's together to make each of 8 blocks. Blocks should measure 7¹⁄₂"x10¹⁄₂".

Block - make 8

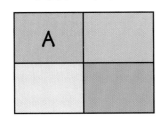

2. Sew blocks together in 4 rows of 2 blocks each to make wall hanging center.

3. Sew 10 B's together to make each top and bottom border.

Top/bottom border – make 2

4. Sew 16 B's together to make each side border.

Side border – make 2

5. Sew top, bottom, then side borders to wall hanging center.

FINISHING

1. Trace hen pattern (pg. 40) 3 times onto paper side of web, then trace reverse hen pattern (pg. 41) 5 times. Fuse web to wrong sides of cotton prints. Cut out hens, then fuse to center of each block.

2. Mark, layer, and quilt wall hanging as desired. Our wall hanging is machine quilted in a large diamond grid (quilting does not cross over appliqués).

3. Stitch a blanket stitch by machine around edges of each hen.

4. Bind wall hanging using 3¹⁄₈-yds of 2¹⁄₂"w straight-grain binding.

Wall Hanging Diagram

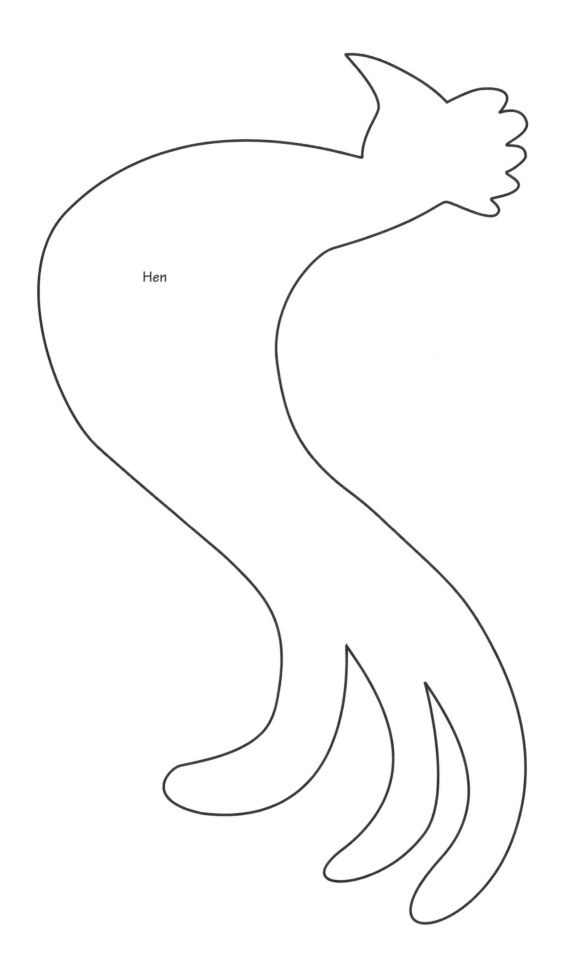

Hen

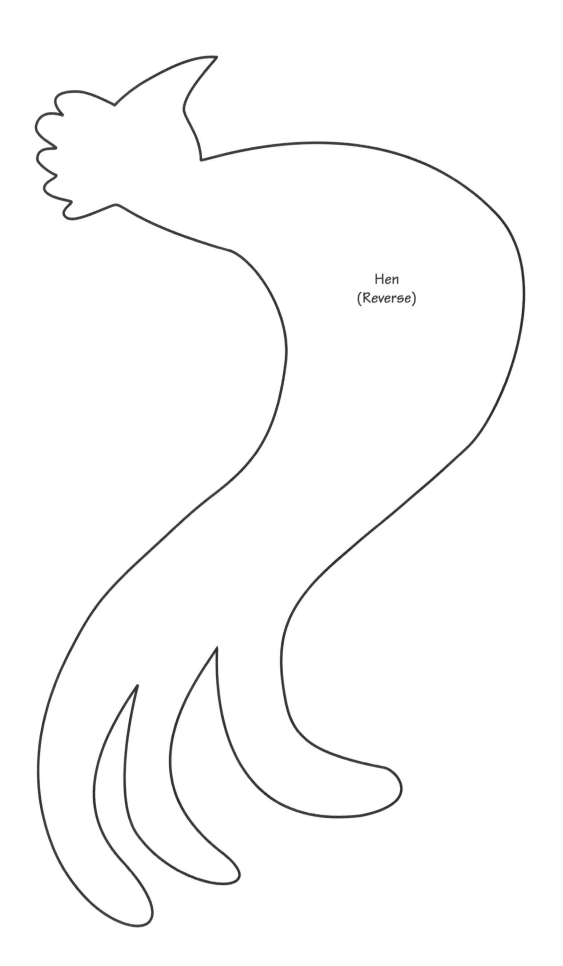

Hen
(Reverse)

Old~Fashioned

Churn Dash Wall Hanging, page 44.

The fruit derived from Labor is the Sweetest of all pleasures.
- MARQUIS DE VAUVENARGUES

Churn Dash

Churn Dash Wall Hanging, page 44.

Nothing adds warmth to a room like a handmade quilt, and you'll get double the coziness with this reversible wall hanging! Pieced in colors that were popular in the 1800's, it's quilted in a traditional pattern of repeated curves commonly known as "shells" or "Baptist fan."

CHURN DASH WALL HANGING

(shown on pgs. 42 & 43)

Finished size: 37" square

FABRICS
- maroon print – 3/8-yd
- tan print – 3/4-yd
- blue print – 1-yd
- dark maroon print – 1-yd
- brown print – 1 1/2-yds
- binding and hanging loops – 7/8-yd

Other supplies
- batting – 41" square

*Refer to diagrams as needed. See **Quilter's Basics** (pg. 241) for more in-depth basic instructions.*

CUTTING
Maroon print:
- Cut two 2 3/4"w strips. From these, cut:
  - 16 A's – 2 3/4" square
- Cut one 5 1/2"w strip. From this, cut:
  - 4 E's – 5 1/2" square

Tan print:
- Cut three 2 3/4"w strips.
  - From 1 strip, cut 4 D's – 2 3/4" square.
  - Set aside remaining 2 strips for Strip Set A's.
- Cut two 3 1/8"w strips. From these, cut:
  - 32 B's – Cut sixteen 3 1/8" squares, then cut each in half once diagonally into 2 triangles.
- Cut one 5 1/2"w strip. From this:
  - Cut 1 H – 5 1/2" square.
  - Set aside remainder of strip for Strip Set D.
- Cut one 5 7/8"w strip. From this, cut:
  - 8 F's – Cut four 5 7/8" squares, then cut in half once diagonally into 2 triangles.

Blue print:
- Cut two 2 3/4"w strips for Strip Set A's.
- Cut two 5 3/8"w strips. From these, cut:
  - 16 C's – Cut eight 5 3/8" squares, then cut each in half once diagonally into 2 triangles.
- Cut one 5 1/2"w strip for Strip Set D.
- Cut one 10 7/8"w strip. From this, cut:
  - 4 G's – Cut two 10 7/8" squares, then cut each in half once diagonally into 2 triangles.

Dark maroon print:
- Cut eleven 2"w strips for Strip Set B's and C's.
- Cut one 6"w strip. From this, cut:
  - 4 I's – 6" square

Brown print:
- Cut eleven 2"w strips for Strip Set B's and C's.
- Cut eight 2 1/2"w strips for Strip Set E's.

PIECING WALL HANGING FRONT
1. Sew 2 tan print B's to each maroon print A to make 16 Unit 1's.

Unit 1 – make 16

2. Sew 1 blue print C to each Unit 1 to make 16 Unit 2's.

Unit 2 – make 16

3. Sew 1 tan print and 1 blue print 2 3/4"w strip together to make each of 2 Strip Set A's. Cut sixteen 2 3/4"w Unit 3's from strip sets.

Unit 3 – make 16   Strip Set A – make 2

4. Sew 2 Unit 2's and 1 Unit 3 together to make each of 8 Unit 4's.

Unit 4 – make 8

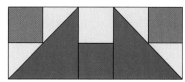

5. Sew 2 Unit 3's to each tan print D to make 4 Unit 5's.

Unit 5 – make 4

6. Sew 1 Unit 4 to each long edge of Unit 5 to make 4 Block A's. Blocks should measure 11³/₄" square.

Block A – make 4

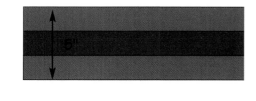

7. Sew 2 dark maroon print and 1 brown print 2"w strips together to make 1 Strip Set B. Cut eighteen 2"w Unit 6's from strip set.

Unit 6 – make 18   Strip Set B – make 1

← 2" →

8. Sew 2 brown print and 1 dark maroon print 2"w strips together to make each of 5 Strip Set C's. Cut nine 2"w Unit 7's from 1 strip set.

Unit 7 – make 9   Strip Set C – make 5

← 2" →

9. From remaining Strip Set C's, cut twelve 11³/₄"w Sashing A's.

Sashing A – make 12

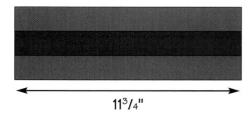

←——— 11³/₄" ———→

10. Sew 2 Unit 6's to each Unit 7 to make 9 Unit 8's.

Unit 8 – make 9

11. Sew 3 Sashing A's and 2 Block A's together to make each of 2 Row A's.

Row A – make 2

12. Sew 3 Unit 8's and 2 Sashing A's together to make each of 3 Row B's.

Row B – make 3

13. Sew Rows together to complete Wall Hanging Front. Wall hanging front should measure 36¹/₂" square.

Wall Hanging Front

WALL HANGING BACK

1. Sew 2 tan print F's to each maroon print E, then sew 1 G to each unit to make 4 Unit 9's.

Unit 9 – make 4

2. Sew 1 tan print and 1 blue print 5½"w strip together (strips are not the same length) to make Strip Set D. Cut four 5½"w Unit 10's from strip set.

Unit 10 – make 4   Strip Set D – make 1

10½"

5½"

3. Using Unit 9's, Unit 10's, and tan print H, repeat Steps 4-6 of *Piecing Wall Hanging Front* (pg. 44) to make Block B. Block should measure 25½" square.

Block B – make 1

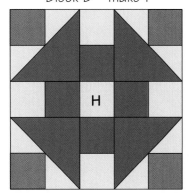

4. Sew 2 brown print 2½"w strips to each remaining dark maroon print 2"w strip to make 4 Strip Set E's. Cut four 25½"w Unit 11's from strip sets.

Unit 11 – make 4   Strip Set E – make 4

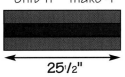 

25½"

5. Sew 1 I to each end of 2 Unit 11's to make 2 Unit 12's.

Unit 12 – make 2

6. Sew 1 Unit 11 to each side of Block B. Sew Unit 12's to top and bottom of Block B to complete Wall Hanging Back. Wall hanging back should measure 36½" square.

Wall Hanging Back

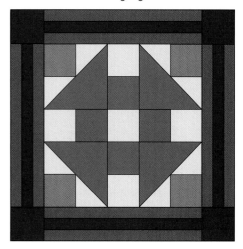

FINISHING

1. Mark, layer, and quilt as desired using Quilting Diagram as a suggestion.

2. For hanging loops, cut one 5"w strip from binding/hanging loop fabric. Fold in half lengthwise and sew long raw edges together. Turn and press. Cut five 6"l segments from sewn strip. Fold each segment in half to form a loop. Spacing evenly, baste raw edges of loops to top raw edge of wall hanging back.

3. Bind wall hanging using 4$\frac{1}{4}$-yds of 2$\frac{1}{2}$"w bias binding, making sure to catch ends of hanging loops in stitching.

Quilting Diagram

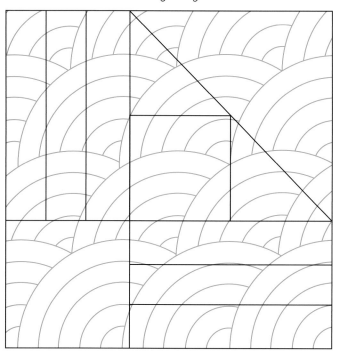

There's no place like Home

There's no place like "home sweet home," especially when it's filled with lots of cozy, country touches…ours are oh-so simple! Because the appliqués are fused in place, the wall hanging and framed piece are a snap to make, and you can sew up a whole basketful of little hearts in no time!

"Home Sweet Home" Wall Hanging, page 50.

"Home Sweet Home" Framed Piece, page 51; Stuffed Hearts, page 55.

♥I know not why, but home is dearest.♥ CICERO 106 - 43 B.C.

Do you have a collection of old buttons? Use a glue gun to easily attach some of the prettiest ones to a picture frame.

"HOME SWEET HOME" WALL HANGING
(shown on pg. 48)

Finished Size: 23¹/₂" x 24"

FABRICS

Wool felt is available in 60"w or 72"w yardage and in 9" x 12" precut pieces.
- tan felt — ³/₄-yd
- dark red felt — ¹/₄-yd
- assorted colors for appliqués — 9" x 12" pieces
- scraps of wool plaid fabric for house appliqué

Other supplies
- assorted buttons
- embroidery floss to coordinate with felt colors
- water-soluble marker
- paper-backed fusible web
- tracing paper

*Refer to **Wall Hanging Top Diagram** as needed.*

CUTTING

Tan:
- Cut 2 pieces 23¹/₂" x 24" for top and back.
- Cut 1 hanging sleeve 3" x 24".

Dark Red:
- Cut 4 borders 1" x 24¹/₂".

Assorted Colors:
Use patterns, pgs. 52 – 55, and follow **Preparing Appliqué Pieces,** pg. 247, to make the following appliqués:

- 2 large flowers
- 2 large centers
- 8 medium flowers
- 8 medium centers
- 1 small flower
- 1 small flower center
- 1 small flower center circle
- 11 large leaves
- 5 medium leaves
- 2 small leaves
- 1 tree
- 1 rabbit
- 1 large star
- 1 small star
- 1 vase
- 1 vase trim
- 1 large triangle
- 4 small triangles
- 1 heart
- 1 zigzag heart
- 2 birds
- 2 wings
- 1 gable
- 2 windows ³/₄" x 1"
- 1 roof
- 1 background 6" x 7³/₄"
- 1 house end 1¹/₄" x 2¹/₂"
- 1 house front 2¹/₂" x 3¹/₄"

INSTRUCTIONS

Use 3 strands of floss for embroidery unless otherwise indicated.

1. Cut 4 strips of fusible web 1" x 24¹/₂". Trace Border pattern, pg. 52, onto paper side of each strip, repeating along length of strip. Follow manufacturer's instructions to fuse 1 web strip to one side of each border. Cut along scalloped line. Remove paper backing.

2. Fuse side, then top and bottom borders on wall hanging top 2" from outer edges. Trim ends of borders as needed.

3. Use water-soluble marker to draw a vertical line 5¹/₄" from straight edge of each side border and a horizontal line 6¹/₄" from straight edge of top border and bottom border.

4. Layer and arrange appliqués on wall hanging top; fuse in place. Trace words, "Home Sweet Home," pg. 54, onto tracing paper. Pin paper to area above house.

5. Follow **Stitch Diagrams**, pgs. 255 – 256, to add embroidery details to appliqués and to work Running Stitch over marked lines, words, and for flower stems. Work Straight Stitches for birds' beaks. Do not add Cross Stitches to border at this time. Carefully tear away paper.

6. Matching wrong sides and raw edges, layer wall hanging top and back. Work Running Stitch along side and bottom edges. Pin hanging sleeve to back, matching top and side raw edges. Use a Running Stitch to sew all three layers together along top edge.

7. Use 6 strands of floss to work a Cross Stitch in the middle of each scallop on borders, catching bottom edge of hanging sleeve on top border.

8. Embellish with buttons as desired.

Wall Hanging Top Diagram

Stitch Diagram

"HOME SWEET HOME" FRAMED PIECE

(shown on pg. 49)

Finished Size: Fits a standard 9" x 12" frame.

FABRICS

Wool felt is available in 60"w or 72"w yardage and in 9" x 12" precut pieces.
• tan felt — 9" x 12" piece
• red felt — 9" x 12" piece
• green and gold felt for appliqués — scraps
• wool plaid fabric for house appliqué — scrap

Other supplies
• 9" x 12" frame
• 9" x 12" piece of adhesive mounting board
• 2 buttons
• embroidery floss — black, gold, and blue
• paper-backed fusible web
• hot glue gun and glue sticks
• tracing paper

CUTTING

Red:
• Cut 2 borders 1" x 12".
• Cut 2 borders 1" x 9".
• Cut 2 large flower centers, pg. 52.

Green:
• Cut 4 large leaves, pg. 53.
• Cut 2 trees, pg. 53.

Gold:
• Cut 2 large flowers, pg 52.

Assorted Colors:

Referring to **Assembly Diagram,** use patterns, pg. 53, and follow **Preparing Appliqué Pieces,** pg. 247, to make the following appliqués:
• 1 house front 2$\frac{1}{2}$" x 3$\frac{1}{4}$"
• 1 roof
• 2 windows - $\frac{3}{4}$" x 1"
• 1 house end - 1$\frac{1}{4}$" x 2$\frac{1}{2}$"
• 1 gable

INSTRUCTIONS

Use 3 strands of floss for embroidery unless otherwise indicated.

1. From paper-backed fusible web, cut two strips 1" x 9" and two strips 1" x 12". Trace Border pattern onto paper side of each strip, repeating along length of strip. Follow manufacturer's instructions to fuse 1 web strip to 1 side of each border. Cut along scalloped line. Remove paper backing.

2. Matching straight edges, fuse side, then top and bottom borders on tan felt.

3. Layer and arrange appliqués on tan felt piece; fuse in place. Trace words, "Home Sweet Home," onto tracing paper. Pin paper to area above house.

4. Follow **Stitch Diagrams**, pgs. 255 – 256, to work Running Stitch over words. Carefully tear away paper. Work Running Stitch around trees, roof, and gable. Blanket Stitch around house front and house end. Use 6 strands of floss to work a Cross Stitch in the middle of each scallop on borders. Add embroidery details to leaves, flowers, and flower centers.

5. Adhere felt piece to sticky side of mounting board.

6. Mount felt piece in frame.

7. Place flower center on top of flower. Sew button to flower center through all layers. Glue leaves and flowers to corners of frame.

Assembly Diagram

Large Flower

Large Flower Center

Vase Trim

Border

Vase

Small Triangle

Large Triangle

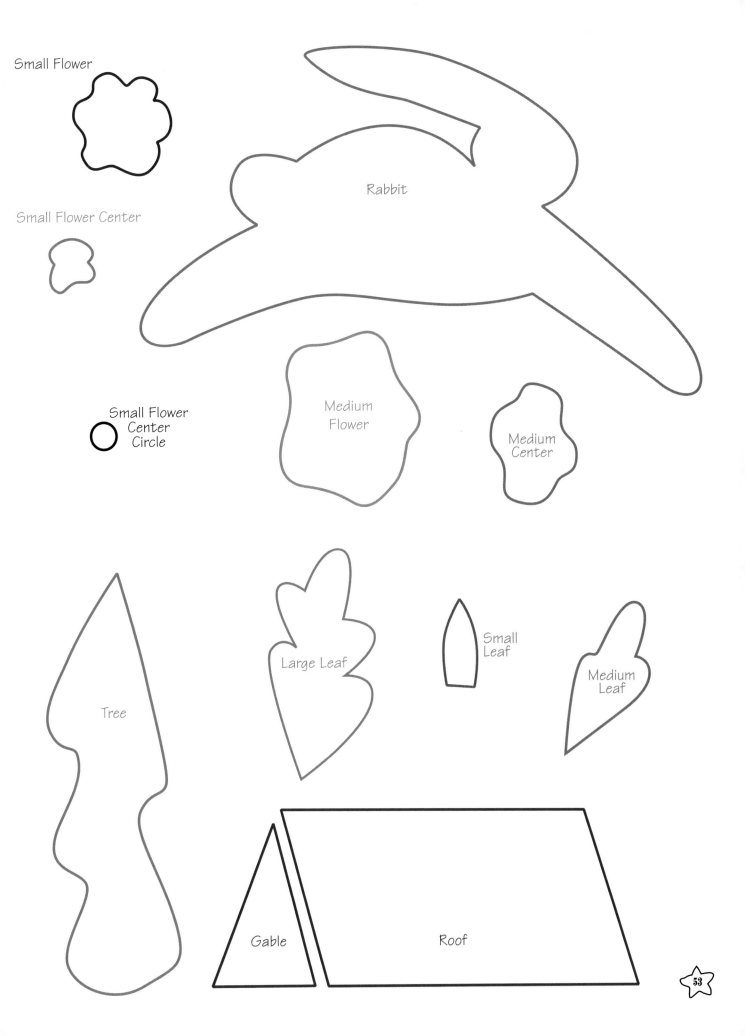

Small Flower

Small Flower Center

Rabbit

Small Flower Center Circle

Medium Flower

Medium Center

Tree

Large Leaf

Small Leaf

Medium Leaf

Gable

Roof

53

Home Sweet Home

Small Star

Bird

Wing

Wall Hanging Heart

Zigzag Heart

54

STUFFED HEARTS

(shown on pg. 49)

Finished Size: Approximately 3¹/₂" x 4¹/₂"

SUPPLIES FOR EACH HEART

Wool felt is available in 60"w or 72"w yardage and in 9" x 12" precut pieces.

• green, gold, blue, red, and white felt — scraps
• embroidery floss — black
• thick, clear-drying craft glue
• polyester fiberfill

INSTRUCTIONS

Use 3 strands of floss for embroidery unless otherwise indicated.

1. Use patterns, pgs. 53 – 55, to cut two Large Hearts, Zigzag Heart, Small Flower, Small Flower Center, Small Flower Center Circle, and 2 Small Leaves from desired colors.

2. Follow **Stitch Diagrams**, pgs. 255 – 256, to Running Stitch ¹/₂" from edge of one large heart and ¹/₄" from edge of zigzag heart. Straight Stitch detail lines on leaves. Blanket Stitch around small flower. Use Cross Stitch to stitch small flower center circle to small flower center.

3. Matching right sides and raw edges, stitch large heart front to large heart back, leaving an opening for turning. Stuff with fiberfill.

4. Glue zigzag heart to large heart front, leaves and small flower to zigzag heart, and small flower center to small flower.

Large Heart

Large Star

PATRIOTIC P·R·I·D·E

Three cheers for the red, white & blue! Show your spirit with all-American touches year 'round! You may want to just add an accent piece, like our old-fashioned sampler wall hanging…or you can redecorate an entire room!

One Nation Wall Hanging, page 60.

Patriotic Quilt, page 64; Patriotic Shams, page 65; Flag Pillow, page 66.

*S*ponge white paint all over a miniature flowerpot. When dry, add red stripes around the rim and stencil blue stars on the base, then fill with little flags...an instant burst of all-American spirit!

Hooray for the USA!

Stars and Stripes Forever!

Star Pillow, page 66.

We chose homespun prints in country shades of red, cream and blue to create the popular Dancing Star pattern on our patchwork quilt, pillow and table runner.

*"My country, 'tis of thee,
Sweet land of liberty,
Of thee I sing;
Land where my fathers died,
Land of the Pilgrim's pride,
From every mountain side
Let freedom ring."*

— Samuel F. Smith

Dancing Star Table Runner, page 70.

Dancing Star Quilt, page 69.

America is a land of wonders, in which everything is in constant motion and every change seems an improvement ... Alexis de Tocqueville

Decorate with red, white & blue for an outdoor gathering! Hang old-fashioned buntings along the porch railing and fill white baskets with red carnations, blue petunias and white daisies. Don't hide those beautiful quilts in the bedroom...drape them across your picnic table or on the backs of your rocking chair and garden swing.

ONE NATION WALL HANGING

(shown on pg. 56)

Finished Size: 23" x 32"

FABRICS

Yardage is based on 45"w fabric.

• cream print — ¼-yd
• red plaid — ¼-yd
• scraps of assorted cream prints for background
• scraps of assorted prints and plaids for appliqués and pieced squares
• fabric for backing and hanging sleeve — 1¼-yds
• fabric for binding — 1-yd

Other supplies

• batting — 45" x 60"
• heavy-duty paper-backed fusible web
• black permanent fabric marker

Refer to **Assembly Diagram** *and* **Wall Hanging Top Diagram** *as needed. See* **Quilter's Basics** *(pg. 241) for more in-depth basic instructions.*

CUTTING

Cream Print:

• Cut 1 strip 5¾"w. From this strip, cut:
  5 squares 5¾" x 5¾", then cut each twice diagonally into 20 triangles.

Red Plaid:

• Cut 1 strip 5¾"w. From this strip, cut:
  4 squares 5¾" x 5¾", then cut each twice diagonally into 16 triangles.
• Cut 2 squares 5⅜" x 5⅜", then cut each once diagonally into 4 corner triangles.

Cream Scraps:

• 1 A — 4½" x 9"
• 1 B — 4½" x 10"
• 1 C — 3" x 13½"
• 1 D — 5½" x 18½"
• 1 E — 3" x 8"
• 1 F — 3" x 11"
• 1 G — 5" x 7¼"
• 1 H — 5" x 11¾"
• 1 I — 3" x 18½"
• 1 J — 5¼" x 13½"
• 1 K — 5¼" x 5½"

Assorted Prints and Plaids:

• Cut 23 squares — 1¾" x 1¾".

Use patterns, pgs. 61 – 63, and follow **Preparing Appliqué Pieces**, pg. 247, to make the following appliqués.

• 5 stars
• 3 houses — 3" x 3⅜"
• 3 roofs
• 3 house sides
• 3 chimneys — ¾" x ¾"
• 3 doors — 1" x 2¼"
• 4 windows — 1" x 1"
• 1 tulip
• 1 tulip stem
• 1 violet
• 1 violet center
• 1 violet stem
• 1 sunflower
• 1 sunflower center
• 1 sunflower stem
• 1 flagpole — ½" x 11¾"
• 1 flag stars — 1⅞" x 2"
• 2 flag stripes — ½" x 3⅞"
• 2 flag stripes — ½" x 5¾"
• 3 tree trunks — ½" x ¾"
• 3 treetops
• 3 tree centers
• 3 tree bottoms
• 3 bodies
• 2 dresses
• 1 shirt
• 1 pants
• 1 boy hair piece
• 2 girl hair pieces
• 1 large heart
• 1 small heart

PIECING

1. Sew 8 squares together to make Unit 1. Sew 15 squares together to make Unit 2.

Unit 1 – make 1

Unit 2 – make 1

2. Sew Unit 1, Unit 2, and pieces A – K together into rows. Sew rows together, trimming short edges of Unit 2 even with raw edges of row above to make center section of wall hanging top.

3. Sew 7 triangles together to make Top/Bottom Border. Make 2 Top/Bottom Borders. Sew 11 triangles together to make Side Border. Make 2 Side Borders.

Top/Bottom Border - make 2

Side Border - make 2

4. Sew Top, Bottom, and Side Borders to center section. Sew 1 corner triangle to each corner of center section.

5. Follow manufacturer's instructions to fuse appliqués to center section to complete Wall Hanging Top.

6. Use permanent marker and dashed lines to write "One flag, one land, one heart, one hand," on wall hanging top. Write "One nation evermore!" on heart; write "Oliver Wendell Holmes" below heart.

FINISHING

1. Mark, layer, and quilt wall hanging, stitching in the ditch along seamlines.

2. Follow **Making a Hanging Sleeve**, pg. 254, to attach hanging sleeve to wall hanging.

3. Follow **Binding**, pg. 252, to bind wall hanging using 1³/₄"w straight-grain binding with mitered corners.

Wall Hanging Top Diagram

Assembly Diagram

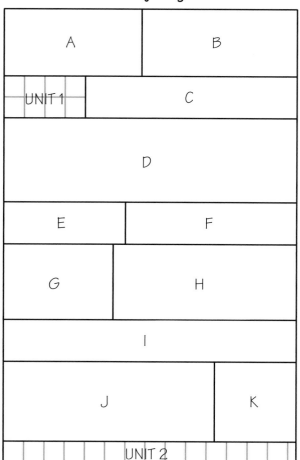

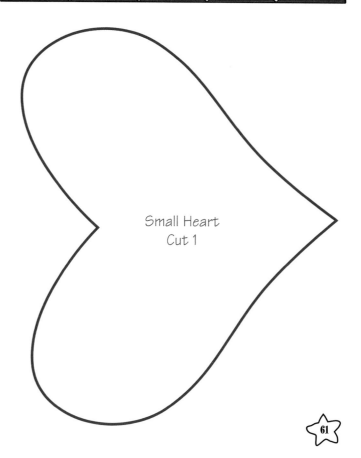

Small Heart
Cut 1

Shirt
Cut 1

Star
Cut 5

Dress
Cut 2

Pants
Cut 1

Body
Cut 3

Boy Hair Piece
Cut 1

Girl Hair Piece
Cut 2

Large Heart
Cut 1

62

Tree Top
Cut 3

Tree Center
Cut 3

Tree Bottom
Cut 3

Roof
Cut 3

Tulip
Cut 1

Violet
Cut 1

Violet
Center
Cut 1

Tulip Stem
Cut 1

Violet Stem
Cut 1

House Side
Cut 3

Sunflower
Cut 1

Sunflower
Center
Cut 1

Sunflower Stem
Cut 1

PATRIOTIC QUILT

(shown on pg. 57)

Finished Size: 75$\frac{1}{2}$" x 89"
Block Size: 10" x 10"

FABRICS

Yardage is based on 45"w fabric.
• white for borders — 2$\frac{3}{4}$-yds
• assorted white prints for squares and triangle-squares — 2$\frac{1}{2}$-yds total
• blue print for borders and sashing — 3$\frac{3}{4}$-yds
• assorted blue prints for triangle-squares — 1$\frac{3}{4}$-yds total
• red — 1$\frac{1}{8}$-yds
• fabric for backing and hanging sleeve — 5$\frac{7}{8}$-yds
• fabric for binding — 2$\frac{3}{4}$-yds

Other supplies
• batting — 81" x 96"

*Refer to **Quilt Top Diagram** as needed. See **Quilter's Basics** (pg. 241) for more in-depth basic instructions.*

CUTTING
White:
• Cut 2 top/bottom middle borders 2$\frac{1}{4}$" x 72".
• Cut 2 side middle borders 2$\frac{1}{4}$" x 89".
Assorted White Print:
• Cut 8 strips 2$\frac{3}{4}$"w. From this strip, cut: 120 squares 2$\frac{3}{4}$" x 2$\frac{3}{4}$".
• Cut 6 pieces 18" x 21" for triangle-squares.
Blue Print:
• Cut 2 top/bottom inside borders 2$\frac{1}{4}$" x 68$\frac{1}{2}$".
• Cut 2 side inside borders 2$\frac{1}{4}$" x 85$\frac{1}{2}$".
• Cut 2 top/bottom outside borders 2$\frac{1}{4}$" x 75$\frac{1}{2}$".
• Cut 2 side outside borders 2$\frac{1}{4}$" x 92$\frac{1}{2}$".
• Cut 4 long sashing strips 4" x 78".
• Cut 25 short sashing strips 4" x 10$\frac{1}{2}$".
Assorted Blue Print:
• Cut 6 pieces 18" x 21" for triangle-squares.
Red:
• Cut 2 strips 10$\frac{1}{2}$"w. From this strip, cut: 30 long sashing strips 1$\frac{1}{2}$" x 10$\frac{1}{2}$".
• Cut 3 strips 5"w. From this strip, cut: 60 short sashing strips 1$\frac{1}{2}$" x 5".

PIECING

1. To make triangle-squares, use assorted white print pieces and assorted blue print pieces and follow **Making Triangle-Squares** (pg. 243) to make 360 triangle-squares.

Fig. 1

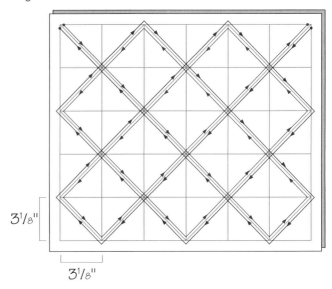

3$\frac{1}{8}$"

3$\frac{1}{8}$"

triangle-square – make 360

2. Sew 3 triangle-squares and 1 square together to make Unit 1. Make 120 Unit 1's.

Unit 1 – make 120

3. Sew 2 Unit 1's and 1 short red sashing strip together to make Unit 2. Make 60 Unit 2's.

Unit 2 - make 60

4. Sew 2 Unit 2's and 1 long red sashing strip together to make Block. Make 30 Blocks.

Block - make 30

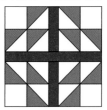

5. Sew 6 Blocks and 5 short blue sashing strips together to make Row. Make 5 Rows.

Row – make 5

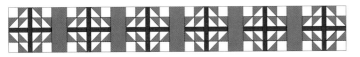

6. Sew 5 rows and 4 long blue sashing strips together to make Quilt Top.

7. Follow **Adding Squared Borders**, pg. 249, to sew top, bottom, then side inside blue borders to quilt top. Sew middle white borders, then outside blue borders to quilt top in same manner.

FINISHING

1. Mark, layer, and quilt as desired. Our quilt is hand quilted in diagonal lines across the quilt top.

2. Follow **Binding**, pg. 252, to bind quilt using $9^3/_8$-yds of $2^1/_2$"w straight-grain binding with overlapping corners.

Quilt Top Diagram

PATRIOTIC SHAMS
(shown on pg. 57)

Finished Size: 34" x 28" each

FABRICS FOR EACH SHAM
• white print — $1^5/_8$-yds
• blue striped print for trim — 1-yd

Other supplies
• white fleece — 1-yd
• fabric marking pen

CUTTING
White Print:
• Cut 1 front 35" x 29".
• Cut 2 back pieces 20" x 29".

Blue Striped Print:
We used a fabric that had a lengthwise design that created a striped effect. When cut, the design was centered in each strip.
• Centering design, cut 4 lengthwise strips $1^1/_2$"w for center trim. From these strips, cut:
  •2 top/bottom strips 27" long.
  •2 side strips 21" long.
• Centering design, cut 4 lengthwise strips $1^1/_2$"w for edge trim. From these strips, cut:
  •2 top/bottom strips 35" long.
  •2 side strips 29" long.

White Fleece:
• Cut 1 top backing 35" x 29".

INSTRUCTIONS
Use $1/_2$" seam allowances.

1. To make trim, press long edges of strips $1/_4$" to wrong side. Press ends $1/_2$" to wrong side.

2. Mark $4^1/_2$" from all edges of top. Matching outside edge of trim to mark and overlapping ends, topstitch center trim in place.

3. Matching raw edges, baste fleece to wrong side of front.

4. Press one long edge of each back piece $1/_4$" to wrong side; press $1/_4$" to wrong side again. Stitch along folded edge.

5. Sew backs to front, matching raw edges and right sides and overlapping back pieces.

6. Turn sham and press.

7. Matching outside edge of trim to edge of sham top and overlapping ends, topstitch edge trim in place.

Sham Diagram

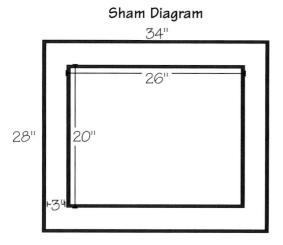

34"

26"

28"

20"

¾"

FLAG PILLOW

(shown on pg. 57)

Finished Size: 10½" x 21"

FABRICS

Yardage is based on 45"w fabric.
- 4 assorted red prints — scraps
- 3 assorted white prints — scraps
- blue print — scrap
- gold print — scrap
- fabric for backing — ³/₈-yd

Other supplies
- polyester fiberfill
- paper-backed fusible web
- clear nylon thread

*Refer to **Pillow Top Diagram** as needed. See **Quilter's Basics** (pg. 241) for more in-depth basic instructions.*

CUTTING

Red Prints:
- From each fabric, cut 1 strip 2" x 21½".

Cream Prints:
- From each fabric, cut 1 strip 2" x 21½".

Blue Print:
- Cut 1 rectangle 5¾" x 9¼"

Gold Print:
- Use Star pattern, pg. 68, and follow **Preparing Appliqué Pieces**, pg. 247, to make the star appliqué.

Backing Fabric:
- Cut 1 rectangle 11" x 21½".

PIECING

1. Alternating fabrics, sew red and white print strips together to make pillow top.

2. Press 1 short side and 1 long side of blue rectangle ¼" to wrong side.

3. Follow manufacturer's instructions to fuse appliqué to blue rectangle. Follow **Invisible Appliqué**, pg. 247, to appliqué star.

4. Matching raw edges of blue rectangle to raw edges of pillow top, topstitch rectangle in place.

FINISHING

1. Matching right sides and raw edges, sew pillow top to pillow backing, leaving an opening for turning.

2. Stuff pillow with fiberfill; sew opening closed.

Pillow Top Diagram

STAR PILLOW

(shown on pg. 58)

Finished Size: 14" square

FABRICS

Yardage is based on 45"w fabric.
- 12 assorted red and blue prints — scraps
- assorted tan prints for stars, borders, and insert — 1-yd total
- navy print for backing, lining, and ties — 1-yd

Other supplies
- polyester fiberfill
- paper-backed fusible web
- clear nylon thread

*See **Quilter's Basics** (pg. 241) for more in-depth basic instructions.*

CUTTING

Assorted red and blue prints:
• From each fabric, cut 1 rectangle 2½" x 6½".

Assorted Tan Prints:
• Use patterns, pg. 68, and follow **Preparing Appliqué Pieces**, pg. 247, to make star appliqués.
• For borders, cut 2 pieces 1⅞" x 12½".
• For pillow, cut 2 pieces 14½" x 14½".

Navy Print:
• For backing, cut 1 piece 12½" x 15¼".
• For lining, cut 1 piece 12½" x 30½".
• For ties, cut 8 pieces 1½" x 12".

PIECING

1. Sew 2 blue rectangles and 1 red rectangle together to make Unit 1. Make 2 Unit 1's.

Unit 1 – make 2

2. Sew 2 red rectangles and 1 blue rectangle together to make Unit 2. Make 2 Unit 2's.

Unit 2 – make 2

3. Sew 2 Unit 1's and 2 Unit 2's together to make Unit 3.

Unit 3

4. Sew 1 tan print border to top and bottom of Unit 3.

5. Follow manufacturer's instructions to fuse appliqués to Pillow Cover Top (Fig. 1). Follow **Invisible Appliqué**, pg. 247, to appliqué stars.

Fig. 1

6. Sew navy print backing piece to 1 border edge of Pillow Cover Top.

7. To make ties, press long edges of each tie piece ¼" to wrong side; press tie in half. Topstitch along folded edges. Refer to Fig. 2 to baste ties to pillow cover top (Note: Appliqués are not shown).

Fig. 2

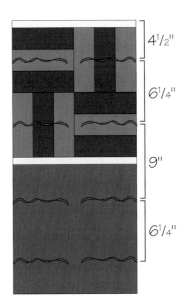

8. Press 1 short edge of pillow cover top and lining ¼" to wrong side. Matching right sides and raw edges and using a ¼" seam allowance, sew pillow cover top to lining along long edges. Turn and press.

9. With folded edges of cover overlapping raw edges of cover and forming a tube, whipstitch opening closed.

FINISHING

1. Follow **Pillow Finishing**, pg. 255, to make a knife-edge pillow.

2. Insert pillow in pillow cover; tie bows.

Star
Cut 1

Flag Pillow and Star Pillow
Star
Cut 1

Star
Cut 1

Star
Cut 1

68

DANCING STAR QUILT

(shown on pg. 59)

Finished Size: 50³/₄" x 60¹/₂"
Block Size: 12³/₄" x 12³/₄"

FABRICS

Yardage is based on 45"w fabric.
- assorted red, blue, and tan prints
- blue print for outer border — 1⁷/₈-yds
- fabric for backing — 3¹/₂-yds

Other supplies
- batting — 72" x 90"

Refer to **Quilt Top Diagram**, pg. 70, as needed. See **Quilter's Basics** (pg. 241) for more in-depth basic instructions.

CUTTING

Assorted red, blue, and tan prints:
- For each Star Block, cut:
  - 4 Strip A's — 2" x 10¹/₄".
  - 4 squares — 2" x 2".
- For each Fence Post Block, cut:
  - 12 rectangles — 2⁵/₈" x 6⁷/₈" (4 from each of 3 fabrics).
- For Borders, cut:
  - Strip B's — 1³/₄"w in random length for top/bottom inner borders.
  - Strip C's — 2¹/₄"w in random length for side inner borders.

Blue print:
- Cut 2 lengthwise strips 1³/₄" x 54³/₄" for top/bottom outer borders.
- Cut 2 lengthwise strips 1³/₄" x 64¹/₂" for side outer borders.

PIECING

1. Use patterns A-D (pgs. 71 – 73) and follow **Foundation Piecing** (pg. 245) to piece sections. Trim fabric and foundation ¹/₄" outside punched lines.

Unit 1

2. Sew 2 squares to each of 2 strips A's to make 2 Unit 2's.

Unit 2 – make 2

3. Sew Unit 1, 2 Strip A's, then 2 Unit 2's together to make Star Block. Repeat Steps 1-3 to make a total of 6 Star Blocks.

Star Block – make 6

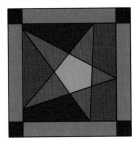

4. Sew 3 rectangles together to make each of 4 Unit 3's.

Unit 3 – make 4

5. Sew 4 Unit 3's together to make Fence Post Block. Repeat Steps 5-6 to make a total of 6 Fence Post Blocks.

Fence Post Block – make 6

6. Sew 1 Star Block and 2 Fence Post Blocks together to make each of 2 Row A's.

Row A – make 2

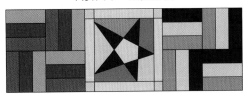

7. Sew 2 Star Blocks and 1 Fence Post Block together to make each of 2 Row B's.

Row B – make 2

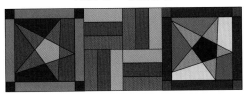

8. Sew rows together to make center section of quilt top.

9. Sew Strip B's together to make 6 long strips $1^3/4$" x $38^3/4$". Sew 3 long strips together to make top and bottom inner borders.

10. Sew Strip C's together to make 6 long strips $2^1/4$" x 59". Sew 3 long strips together to make 2 side inner borders.

11. Sew top, bottom, then side inner borders to center section of quilt.

12. Follow **Adding Mitered Borders**, pg. 250, to sew outer borders to quilt top using mitered corners.

Quilt Top Diagram

FINISHING

1. Layer backing (right side up), quilt top (right side down), then batting. Stitch all layers together $1/2$" from outer edges leaving an opening for turning. Turn quilt right side out and slipstitch opening closed; press.

2. Mark and quilt as desired. Our quilt is hand quilted using an outline stitch.

DANCING STAR TABLE RUNNER
(shown on pg. 58)

Finished Size: $14^3/4$" x 51"
Block Size: $12^3/4$" x $12^3/4$"

FABRICS

Yardage is based on 45"w fabric.
• assorted red, blue, and tan prints
• blue print for outer border and backing — $1^5/8$-yds

Other supplies
• batting — 45" x 60"

Refer to **Table Runner Top Diagram** *as needed. See* **Quilter's Basics** *(pg. 241) for more in-depth basic instructions.*

PIECING

1. Follow Steps 1-5 of Dancing Star Quilt, pg. 69, to make 2 Star Blocks, 1 Fence Post Block, and 4 Unit 3's.

2. Sew 2 Unit 3's together to make each of 2 Half Fence Post Blocks.

Half Fence Post Block — make 2

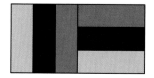

3. Sew 2 Star blocks, 1 Fence Post Block, and 2 Half Fence Post Blocks together to complete center section of table runner top.

4. Cut 2 lengthwise strips $1^3/4$" x $13^1/4$" and 2 lengthwise strips $1^3/4$" x 54" for borders.

5. Sew borders to table runner top using mitered corners.

Table Runner Top Diagram

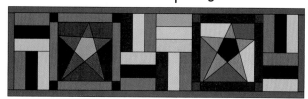

FINISHING

1. Layer backing (right side up), table runner top (right side down), then batting. Stitch all layers together $1/2$" from outer edges leaving an opening for turning. Turn table runner right side out and slipstitch opening closed.

2. Mark and quilt as desired. Our table runner is hand quilted using an outline stitch.

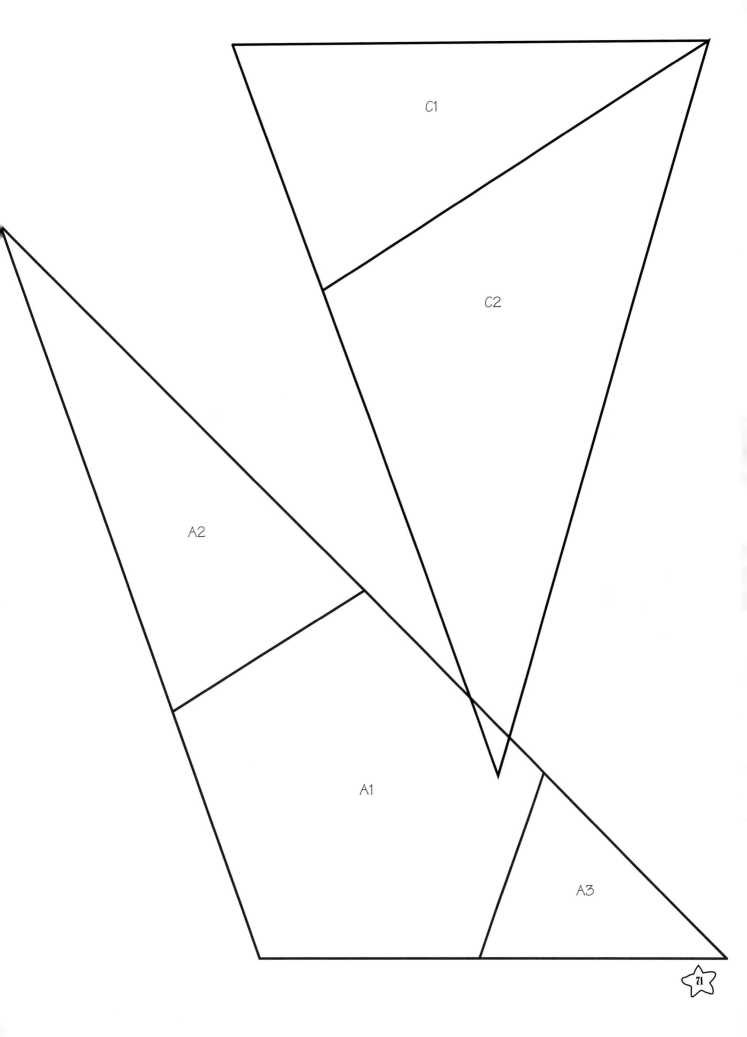

C1

C2

A2

A1

A3

71

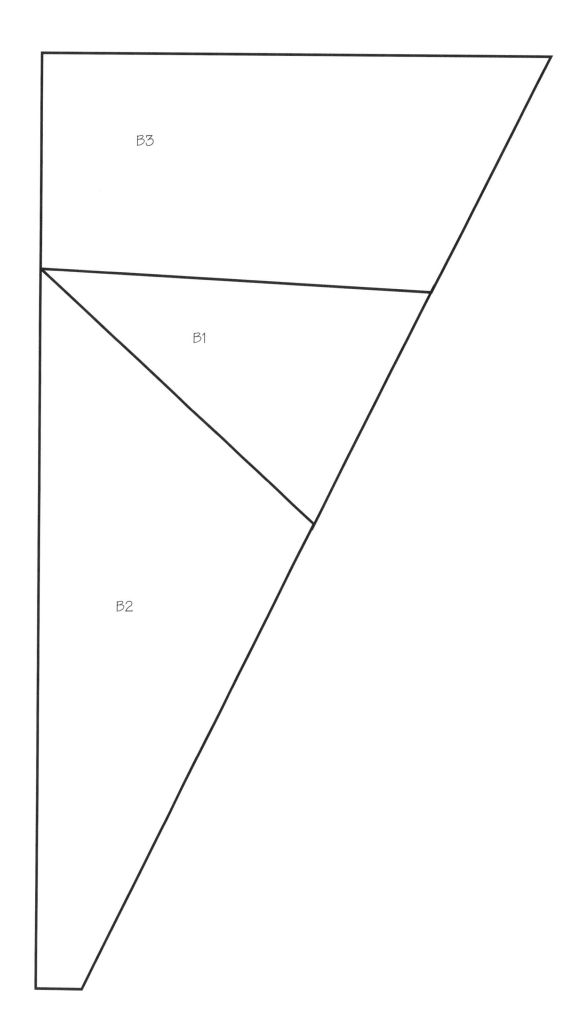

B3

B1

B2

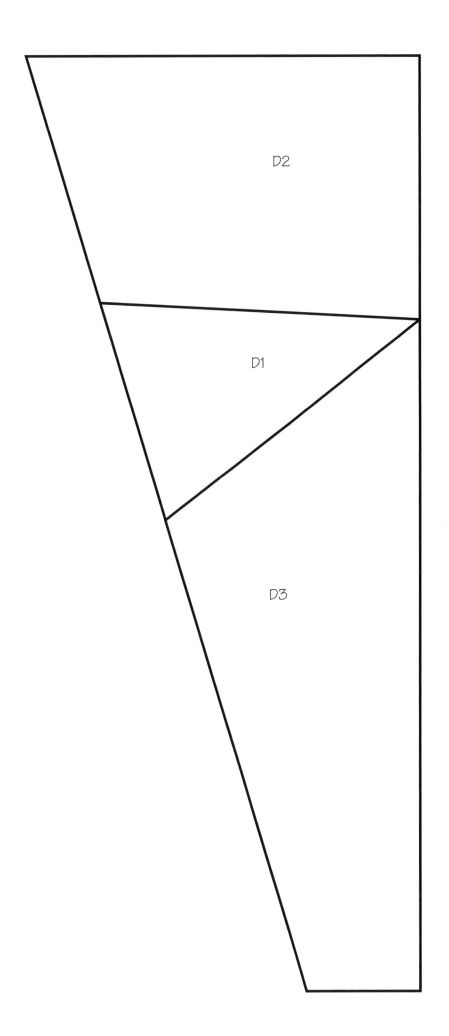

D2

D1

D3

COZY CABINS

Log cabins and quilts have gone together since the earliest days of the American pioneers. These patchwork pieces are all based on the traditional Log Cabin quilt block, and the embroidered pillow reminds us that home is a state of mind!

The stars shine bright on my little Arkansas home

Cozy Cabin Pillow, page 80.

Cabin Fever Wall Quilt, page 80.

...warm and toasty.

Gather your favorite collectibles and place them near this colorful wall hanging for a display that's uniquely you!

Pineapple Variation Wall Hanging, page 87.

Use contrasting colors to give your stitchery extra pizzazz...like in these Log Cabin pieces! Whether your fabric choices are country or contemporary, these designs will bring cabin coziness to your home.

Log Cabin Table Mat, page 86.

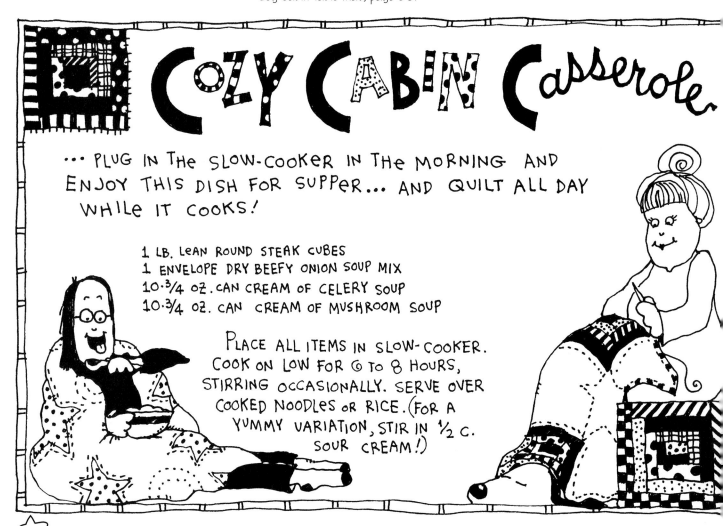

COZY CABIN Casserole

... PLUG IN THE SLOW-COOKER IN THE MORNING AND ENJOY THIS DISH FOR SUPPER... AND QUILT ALL DAY WHILE IT COOKS!

1 LB. LEAN ROUND STEAK CUBES
1 ENVELOPE DRY BEEFY ONION SOUP MIX
10·3/4 OZ. CAN CREAM OF CELERY SOUP
10·3/4 OZ. CAN CREAM OF MUSHROOM SOUP

PLACE ALL ITEMS IN SLOW-COOKER. COOK ON LOW FOR 6 TO 8 HOURS, STIRRING OCCASIONALLY. SERVE OVER COOKED NOODLES OR RICE. (FOR A YUMMY VARIATION, STIR IN 1/2 C. SOUR CREAM!)

Falling Timbers Wall Hanging, page 84.

COZY CABIN PILLOW

(shown on pg. 74)

Finished size: 16"x19"

SUPPLIES
- white fabric for embroidery – 13"x16"
- striped fabric for borders and backing – ³/₄-yd
- embroidery floss – tan, dark red, dark green, yellow, blue, black
- polyester fiberfill
- tracing paper
- iron-on transfer pen

*Refer to photo for design placement and floss colors. See **Stitch Diagrams** ww(pgs. 255 – 256) if needed.*

INSTRUCTIONS
1. Trace patterns (pgs. 89-91) onto tracing paper. Use transfer pen to transfer designs to white fabric. Continue line for path to door to within 1" of left fabric edge.

2. *For the "rustic" look of our pillow, stitches were purposely worked in different lengths.* Embroider design using 3 strands of floss as follows:
- words and stars – long straight stitches
- bunny's eye – French knot
- all other lines – stem stitch

3. Cut two 3"x16" top/bottom borders and two 3"x17" side borders from striped fabric.

4. Using a ¹/₂" seam allowance, sew top, bottom, then side borders to embroidered fabric to complete pillow top.

5. For pillow back, cut striped fabric same size as pillow top.

6. Using a ¹/₂" seam allowance and leaving an opening, sew pillow top and back together. Turn right side out and stuff with fiberfill. Sew opening closed.

CABIN FEVER WALL QUILT

(shown on pg. 75)

Finished size: 37¹/₂"x51"
Block size: 6³/₄" square

FABRICS
- assorted plaids – about 3-yds total (ours uses more than 30 different plaids)
- stripe for borders – ¹/₂-yd
- plaid for binding – ¹/₂-yd
- backing – 1⁵/₈-yds

Other supplies
- batting – 42"x 56"
- tracing or typing paper
- large right-angle triangle

*Refer to **Wall Quilt Diagram**, pg. 83, as needed. See **Quilter's Basics** (pg. 241) for more in-depth basic instructions.*

CUTTING
Assorted plaids:
- Cut each fabric into 1¹/₄"w strips. (Because this project can use such a large number of fabrics, you may wish to cut strips as you piece.)

Stripe for borders:
- Cut four 1"w strips. From these, cut:
  - 2 top/bottom inner borders – 1"x27¹/₂"
  - 2 side inner borders – 1"x42"
- Cut five 1¹/₄"w strips. From these, cut:
  - 2 top/bottom outer borders – 1¹/₄"x36
  - Set aside remainder for Step 15.

PIECING
1. Use Cabin Fever Block pattern (pg. 82) and follow **Making Needle-Punch Paper Foundations** (pg. 245) to make 24 foundations.

2. For Block 1, choose 4 different plaid fabrics (2 strips each). Label fabrics 1A, 1B, 1C, and 1D. Matching labeled fabrics to letter labels on pattern, follow **Paper-Piecing for Log Cabin Blocks** (pg. 246) to complete block.

Block 1

1C

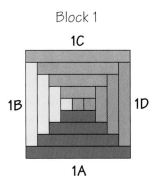

1B   1D

1A

3. For Block 2, choose 3 different plaid fabrics (2 strips each) and Fabric 1D (from Block 1). Fabric 1D now becomes Fabric 2D; label remaining fabrics 2A, 2B, and 2C. Piece block.

Block 2

2C

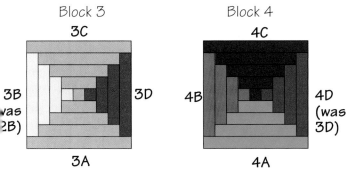

2B   2D (was 1D)

2A

4. For Block 3, choose 3 different plaid fabrics (2 strips each) and Fabric 2B. Fabric 2B now becomes 3B; label remaining fabrics 3A, 3C, and 3D. Piece block. For Block 4, repeat the same process, following block diagram for fabric placement.

Block 3   Block 4

3C   4C

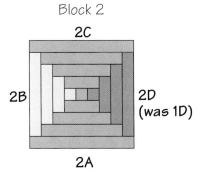

3B (was 2B)   3D   4B   4D (was 3D)

3A   4A

5. Sew Blocks together into a row, making sure the matching fabrics are placed together.

Row 1

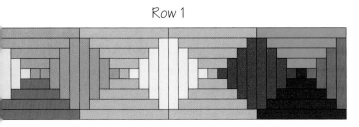

6. For Blocks 5 – 8 (blocks in row 2), follow diagrams to choose fabrics, then piece blocks. Sew blocks together into row, making sure the matching fabrics are placed together.

Block 5   Block 6

5C   6C (was 2C)

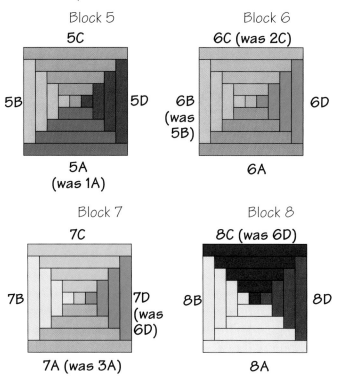

5B   5D   6B (was 5B)   6D

5A (was 1A)   6A

Block 7   Block 8

7C   8C (was 6D)

7B   7D (was 6D)   8B   8D

7A (was 3A)   8A

7. For remaining blocks and rows, repeat the same process to choose fabrics, then piece blocks. Sew blocks into rows to make a total of 6 rows. Sew rows together to make wall hanging center.

8. Sew top, bottom, then side inner borders to wall hanging center.

9. For middle border, sew several plaid strips together in random color order, adding each new strip ³/₄" from the end of the previous strip to make a strip set.

10. Referring to *Fig. 1*, align triangle with a seam to determine an accurate 45° cutting line, then trim off the uneven ends from one end of strip set.

Fig. 1

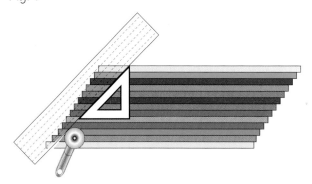

11. Aligning the 45° mark on the rotary cutting ruler (shown in pink) with a seam and aligning the 4¼" mark with the cut edge made in Step 12 (*Fig. 2*), cut across strip set at 4¼" intervals to make bias units.

Fig. 2

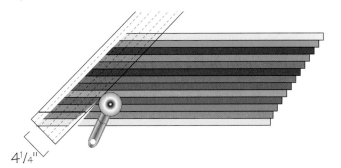

4¼"

12. Sew bias units together to form an approx. 5-yd long strip, making new strip sets as needed to achieve the correct length.

13. From this long strip, cut two 4¼"x36" top/bottom borders and two 4¼"x42" side borders. Sew side, then top and bottom borders to wall hanging center.

14. For outer border, sew remaining three striped strips together end to end, matching the stripes. Cut two 1¼"x51" side outer borders from pieced strip. Sew top, bottom, then side borders to center to complete wall hanging top.

Cabin Fever Block pattern

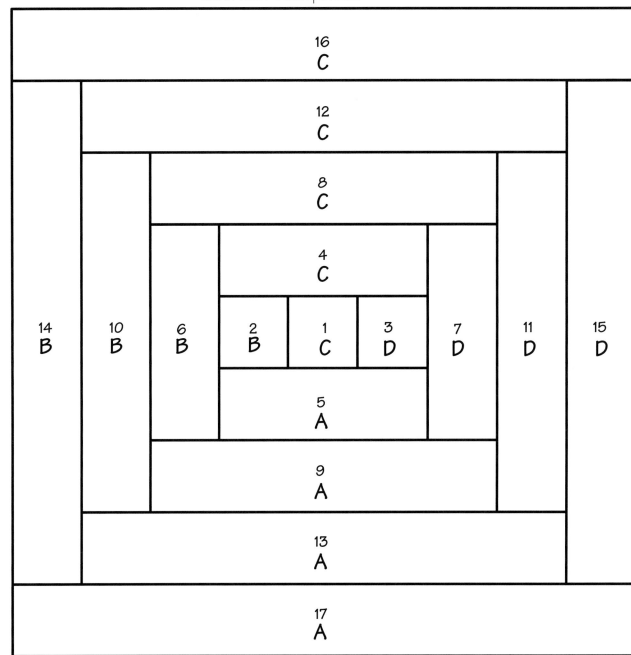

FINISHING

1. Mark, layer, and quilt wall quilt, using Quilting Diagram as a suggestion.

2. Bind quilt using 5-yds of 1¹/₂"w bias binding and a scant ¹/₄" seam allowance.

Quilting Diagram

Wall Quilt Diagram

FALLING TIMBERS WALL HANGING

(shown on pg. 79)

Finished size: 27"x39$\frac{1}{2}$"
Block size: 5$\frac{1}{2}$"x5$\frac{3}{4}$"

FABRICS
• 12 or more tan prints – scraps (largest should be at least 12"x15")
• 10 or more red prints – scraps (largest should be at least 12"x15")
• brown stripe for border – 1$\frac{1}{8}$-yds
• red plaid for binding – 18" square
• backing – 1-yd

Other supplies
• 32"x44" batting
• tracing or typing paper

Refer to **Wall Hanging Diagram** *as needed. See* **Quilter's Basics** *(pg. 241) for more in-depth basic instructions.*

PIECING

1. Use **Falling Timbers Block** pattern (pg. 90) and follow **Making Needle-Punch Paper Foundations** (pg. 245) to make 24 foundations.

2. Cut fabrics into 1"w strips. Label 2 tan fabrics as 1 and 2, following pattern. Sort remaining strips into tan and red piles. Follow **Paper-Piecing for Log Cabin Blocks** (pg. 246) to paper-piece 24 blocks, using fabrics 1 and 2 in the center each time and following **Block Diagram** for placement of tans and reds.

Block Diagram

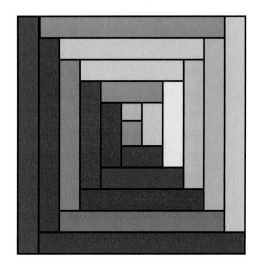

3. Sew blocks together to make 3 Row A's and 3 Row B's.

Row A – make 3

Row B – make 3

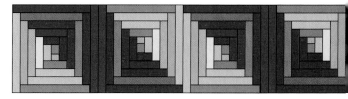

4. Sew rows together to make wall hanging center.

5. From brown stripe, cut two 2$\frac{3}{4}$"x35" side borders and two 2$\frac{3}{4}$"x27" top/bottom borders. Sew side, then top and bottom borders to wall hanging center to complete wall hanging top.

FINISHING

1. Mark, layer, and quilt wall hanging, using Quilting Diagram as a suggestion.

2. Bind wall hanging using 4-yds of 2$\frac{1}{2}$"w bias binding.

Quilting Diagram

LOG CABIN TABLE MAT

(shown on pg. 78)

Finished size: 21"x21³/₄"
Block size: 5¹/₂"x5³/₄"

FABRICS

- *12 or more tan prints – scraps (largest should be at least 12"x15")*
- *10 or more red prints – scraps (largest should be at least 12"x15")*
- brown plaid for border – ¹/₂-yd
- red plaid for binding – 18" square
- backing – 1 yard

Other supplies

- batting – 25" square
- tracing or typing paper

*Refer to **Table Mat Diagram** as needed. See **Quilter's Basics** (pg. 241) for more in-depth basic instructions.*

PIECING

1. Follow Steps 1 and 2 of Piecing instructions (**Falling Timbers Wall Hanging**, pg. 84) to make each of 9 blocks.

Block – make 9

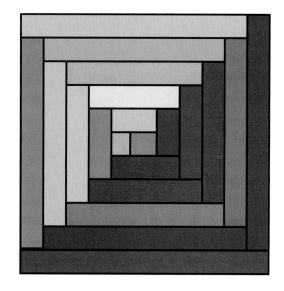

2. Sew 3 Blocks together to make each of 3 rows.

Row – make 3

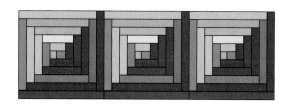

3. Sew rows together to make table mat center.

4. From brown plaid, cut two 2¹/₂"x 17" side borders and two 2¹/₂"x 21³/₄" top/bottom borders. Sew side, then top and bottom borders to center to complete table mat top.

FINISHING

1. Mark, layer, and quilt wall hanging, using **Quilting Diagram** as a suggestion.

2. Bind quilt using 2⁵/₈-yds of 1¹/₂"w bias binding and a scant ¹/₄" seam allowance.

Table Mat Diagram

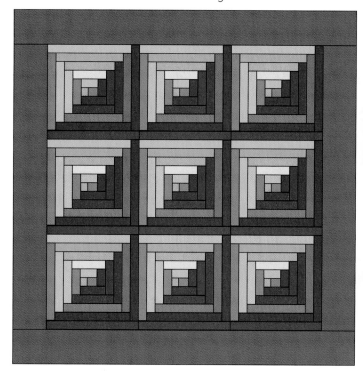

Quilting Diagram

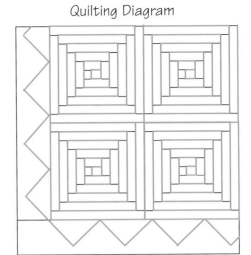

PINEAPPLE VARIATION WALL HANGING
(shown on pg. 77)

Finished size: 28" square
Block size: 5¹/₂" square

FABRICS
• red, green, brown, blue prints (at least 7 different prints of each, ranging from very dark to light in each color family) – about 3-yds total
• assorted tan prints (the more, the better) – 2-yds total
• red print and tan print for center squares – ¹/₈-yd each
• dark brown print for border and binding – ¹/₄-yd
• backing – 1-yd
Other supplies
• batting – 32" square
• tracing or typing paper

*Refer to **Wall Hanging Diagram**, pg. 88, as needed. See **Quilter's Basics** (pg. 241) for more in-depth basic instructions.*

PIECING
1. For center squares, cut one 1¹/₄"w strip each from red and tan print fabrics. Sew strips together to make a strip set. Cut thirty-two 1¹/₄"w Unit 1's from strip set. Sew two Unit 1's together to make each of 16 Unit 2's.

Unit 1 – make 32   Strip Set

 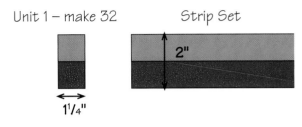

1¹/₄"

2"

Unit 2 – make 16

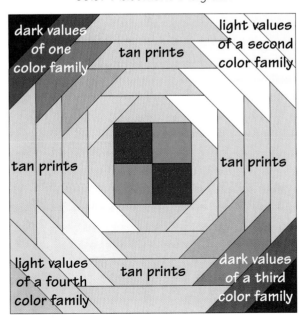

2. Use **Pineapple Variation Block** pattern (pg. 89) and follow **Making Needle-Punch Paper Foundations** (pg. 245) to make 16 foundations.

3. Center one Unit 2 on right side of each paper foundation, carefully aligning center seam lines to grey lines in center of pattern. Baste in place.

4. To choose fabric placement for blocks, sort print fabrics according to color families and from dark to light hues. When piecing, follow **Color Placement Diagram** to place color families and hues.

Color Placement Diagram

dark values of one color family

tan prints

light values of a second color family

tan prints

tan prints

light values of a fourth color family

tan prints

dark values of a third color family

5. To piece each block, cut fabric strips 1¼"w for areas 2-33 on block, and 1½"w strips for areas 34-37 and follow *Foundation Piecing for Log Cabin Blocks* (pg. 246).

6. Sew 4 Blocks together to form each of 4 Rows. Sew Rows together to make wall hanging center.

Row – make 4

7. For inner border, cut two 1"x22½" top/bottom borders and two 1"x23½" side borders. Sew top, bottom, then side borders to wall hanging center.

8. For outer border, cut several 1"w strips from tan prints and light values of red and blue prints. Sew strips together to make a strip set. Cut across strip set at 2¾" intervals to make border units.

Border Unit   Strip Set

2¾"

9. Sew border units together to form two 23½" long strips (for top/bottom borders) and two 28" long strips (for side borders), making new strip sets as needed to achieve the correct lengths.

FINISHING

1. Mark, layer, and quilt wall hanging, using Quilting Diagram as a suggestion.

2. Bind quilt using 3¼-yds of 1½"w straight-grain binding and a scant ¼" seam allowance.

Wall Hanging Diagram   Quilting Diagram

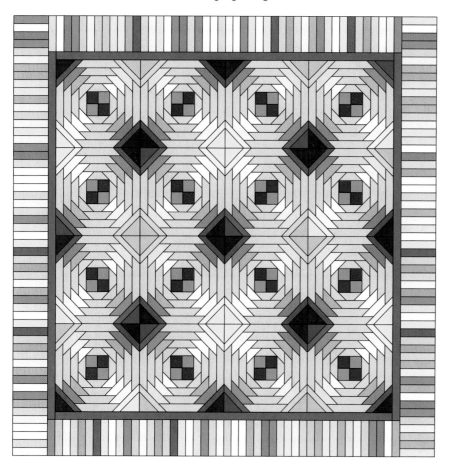

Cozy Cabin Pillow patterns

Pineapple Variation Block pattern

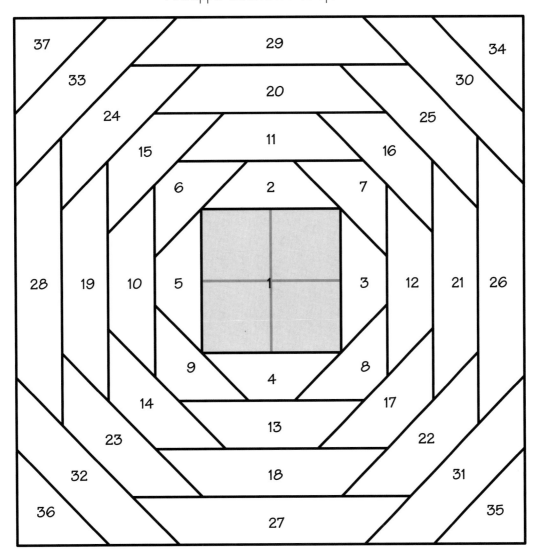

Falling Timbers Block pattern

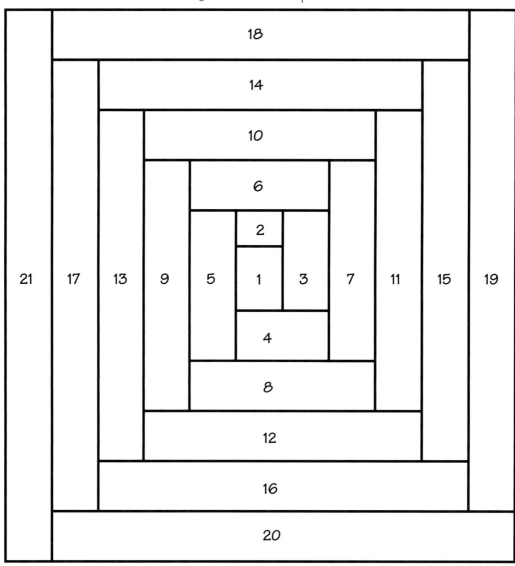

Cozy Cabin Pillow patterns (continued)

The stars shine bright on my little Arkansas Home

Cozy Cabin Pillow patterns (continued)

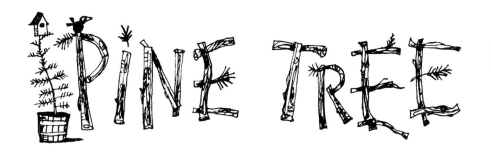

Nothing stirs our adventurous spirit like the Great Outdoors! Leisurely treks through the woods and chilly evenings spent by a crackling fire only add to the fun! Stitch together this patchwork Bear Paw wall hanging and capture those feelings…perfect for hanging anywhere you want to add a log cabin feel and a little rustic charm.

Bear Paw Wall Hanging, page 94.

BEAR PAW WALL HANGING

(shown on pg. 93)

Size: 32" square

FABRIC
- ecru print – $^3/_8$-yd
- red plaid – $^3/_4$-yd
- red print – $^3/_4$-yd
- muslin – $^1/_2$-yd
- 3 plaids for appliqués – scraps
- backing and binding– $1^3/_8$-yds

Other supplies
- batting – 36" square
- paper-backed fusible web
- clear nylon thread

Refer to **Wall Hanging Diagram** *as needed. See* **Quilter's Basics** *(pg. 241) for more in-depth basic instructions.*

CUTTING
Ecru print:
- Cut one 12" square.
Red plaid:
- Cut two $1^1/_2$"w strips. From these, cut:
  - 4 D's – $1^1/_2$" square
  - 2 side inner borders – $1^1/_2$"x12"
  - 2 top/bottom inner borders – $1^1/_2$"x14"
- Cut four $2^1/_2$"w strips. From these, cut:
  - 2 side outer borders – $2^1/_2$"x28"
  - 2 top/bottom outer borders – $2^1/_2$"x32"
Red print:
- Cut four $3^1/_2$"w strips for strip sets.
- Cut one $2^1/_2$"w strip. From this, cut:
  - 16 A's – $2^1/_2$" square
- Cut one $9^1/_2$" x 17" rectangle for triangle-squares.
Muslin:
- Cut four $1^1/_2$" strips. From these:
  - cut 16 B's – $1^1/_2$" square
  - cut 16 C's – $1^1/_2$"x$3^1/_2$"
  - Reserve remaining 2 strips for strip sets.
- Cut one $9^1/_2$" x 17" rectangle for triangle-squares.

APPLIQUÉING
1. Trace patterns (pgs. 96 – 97) onto paper backing side of web. Fuse to wrong side of appliqué fabrics. Cut out pieces, then fuse to center of ecru print square.

2. Stitch over edges of appliqués using clear thread and a small zigzag stitch.

PIECING
1. Sew side, then top and bottom inner borders to appliquéd block.

2. To make triangle-squares, use red print and muslin rectangles and follow *Fig. 1* and **Making Triangle-Squares** (pg. 243) to make 64 triangle-squares.

Fig. 1

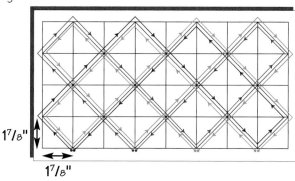

$1^7/_8$"

$1^7/_8$"

triangle-square–make 64

3. Sew 2 triangle-squares together to make each of 32 Unit 1's.

Unit 1 – make 32

4. Sew 1 muslin B and 1 Unit 1 together to make each of 16 Unit 2's.

Unit – make 16

5. Sew 1 Unit 1, then 1 Unit 2 to red print A to make each of 16 Unit 3's.

Unit 3 – make 16

6. Sew 2 Unit 3's and 1 muslin C together to make each of 8 Unit 4's.

Unit 4 – make 8

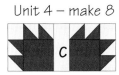

7. Sew 2 muslin C's and 1 red plaid D together to make each of 4 Unit 5's.

Unit 5 – make 4

8. Sew 2 Unit 4's and 1 Unit 5 together to make each of 4 Bear Paw Blocks. Blocks should measure 7½" square.

Bear Paw Block – make 4

9. Sew 2 red print and 1 muslin strip together to make each of 2 strip sets. Cut four 14" long Unit 6's from strip sets.

Unit 6 – make 4

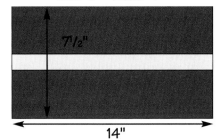

10. Sew 1 Bear Paw Block to each end of Unit 6 to make each of 2 Unit 7's.

Unit 7 – make 2

11. Sew Unit 6's to top and bottom, then Unit 7's to sides of appliquéd block to make wall hanging center.

12. Sew side, then top and bottom outer borders to wall hanging center to complete wall hanging top. Top should measure 32" square.

FINISHING

1. Mark, layer, and quilt wall hanging using **Quilting Diagram** as a suggestion.

2. Bind wall hanging using 3¾-yds of 2½"w straight-grain binding.

Wall Hanging Diagram

Quilting Diagram

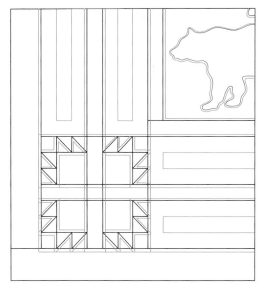

Patterns

Bear

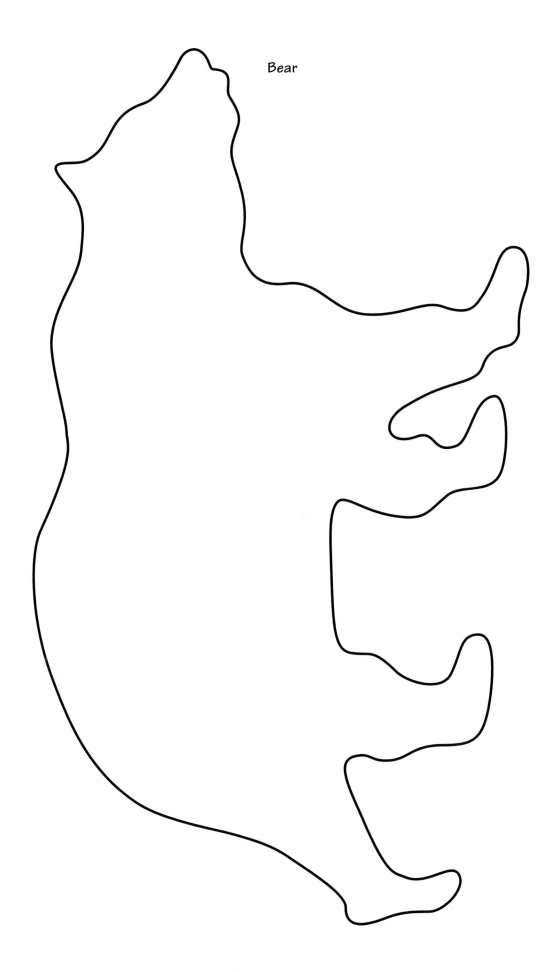

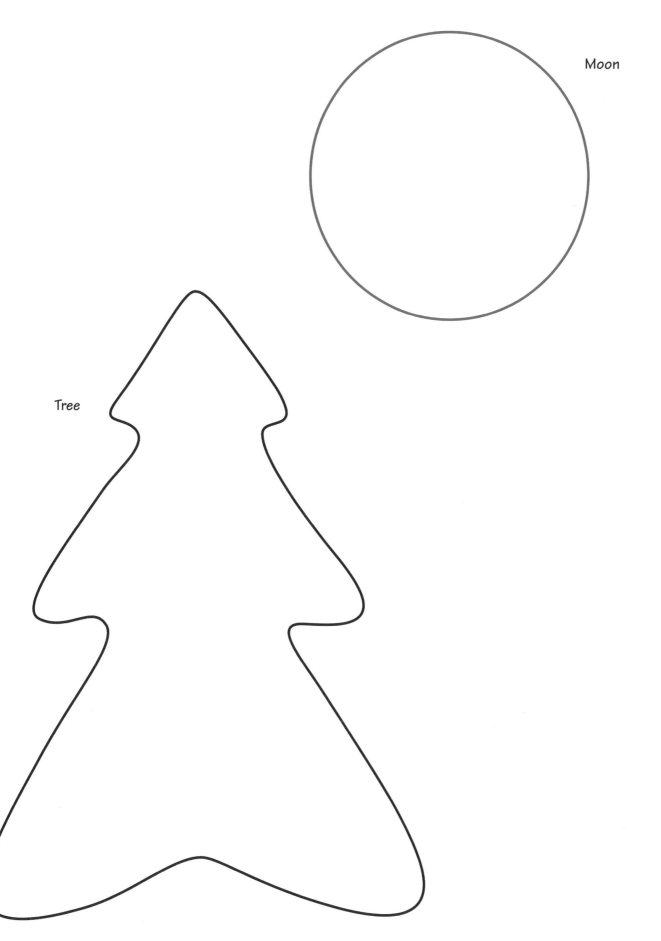

Moon

Tree

Farmhouse Christmas

Put on a pot of coffee or make yourself a cup of cocoa...then snuggle in for a quilting holiday. The Farmhouse Christmas Wall Quilt, with its three cozy cabins and starry night sky, begins our Christmas collection. Which of these festive projects will you make first?

Farmhouse Christmas Wall Quilt, page 107.

Santa Wall Hanging, page 102.

A wise old Santa greets one and all from this country wall hanging, while a purchased sweatshirt becomes a jolly Saint Nick pullover when you add bright appliqués. And of course, you'll want to make dozens of the quick-to-stitch ornaments!

Patchwork Christmas Ornaments, page 107.

Happiness makes up in height for what it lacks in length.
~Robert Frost~

Saint Nick Pullover, page 111.

SANTA WALL HANGING

(shown on pg. 100)

Finished size: 18"x 30"

FABRICS
- assorted prints for backgrounds – 3/4-yd total
- assorted red prints for stars and Santa – 1/4-yd total
- black print for boots and flagpole – 1/8-yd
- navy print for bag – 1/8-yd
- assorted green prints for trees – 1/8-yd total
- blue plaid for mittens – scrap
- navy print for border – 1/4-yd
- navy plaid for binding – 1/4-yd
- flesh-colored solid for face – scrap
- cream print for hat and cuff trim – scrap
- tan check for beard – 1/8-yd
- 2 brown plaids for tree trunks – scraps
- assorted light prints for log cabin blocks – 1/8-yd total
- assorted dark prints for log cabin blocks – 1/8-yd total
- red print for inner border and log cabin block centers – 1/8-yd
- backing – 1-yd

Other supplies
- purchased flag – at least 4 1/4"x6"
- batting – 22"x35"
- tracing or typing paper

Because the wall quilt is done in scrap, we have divided it into 5 large units for easier cutting and piecing. Refer to **Wall Hanging Diagram,** *pg. 106, as needed. See* **Quilter's Basics** *(pg. 241) for more in-depth basic instructions.*

SANTA UNIT – CUTTING
1 print for background:
- Cut two 1 1/2"w strips. From these, cut:
  - AA – 1 1/2"x20 1/2"
  - Z – 1 1/2"x6 1/2"
  - V – 1 1/2"x5 1/2"
  - D – 1 1/2"x3 1/2"
  - 2 C's – 1 1/2"x3"
  - 4 B's – 1 1/2" square
- Cut one 2"w strip. From this, cut:
  - 2 W's – 2"x3 1/2"
  - 2 K's – 2"x3"
  - R – 2"x2 1/2"
- Cut one 1"w strip. From this, cut:
  - 2 X's – 1"x3 1/4"

1 red print for Santa:
- Cut one 3 1/2"w strip. From this, cut:
  - P – 3 1/2"x4 3/4"

- Recut remainder of 3 1/2"w strip to 2"w. From this, cut:
  - S – 2"x7 1/4"
  - E – 2"x5 3/4"
  - 4 M's – 2" square
- Cut Y – 1" square

Navy print for bag:
- Cut one 1 1/2"w strip. From this, cut:
  - A – 1 1/2"x15"
  - U – 1 1/2"x13"
- Cut one 2"w strip. From this, cut:
  - J – 2"x7 3/4"
  - T – 2"x4 3/4"
  - 2 F's – 2" square
  - I – 2"x1"

Black print for boots:
- Cut 1 Q – 3"x3 1/2"

Blue plaid for mittens:
- Cut 2 H's – 1 3/4"x2"

Flesh-colored solid for face:
- Cut 1 N – 1 1/4"x3 1/2"

Cream print for hat and cuff trim:
- Cut 2 G's – 3/4"x2"
- Cut 1 O – 1"x3 1/2"

Tan check for beard:
- Cut 1 L – 3 1/2"x9 1/2"

SANTA UNIT – PIECING
1. Follow **Stitch-and-Flip Method** (pg. 243) to sew squares to ends of larger pieces to make Units.

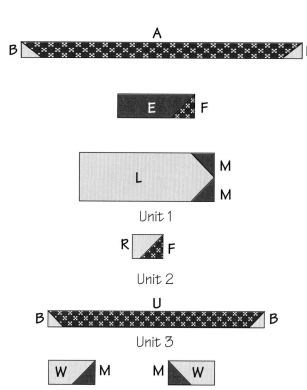

Unit 1

Unit 2

Unit 3

2. Sew remaining pieces together following diagram below to complete Santa Unit.

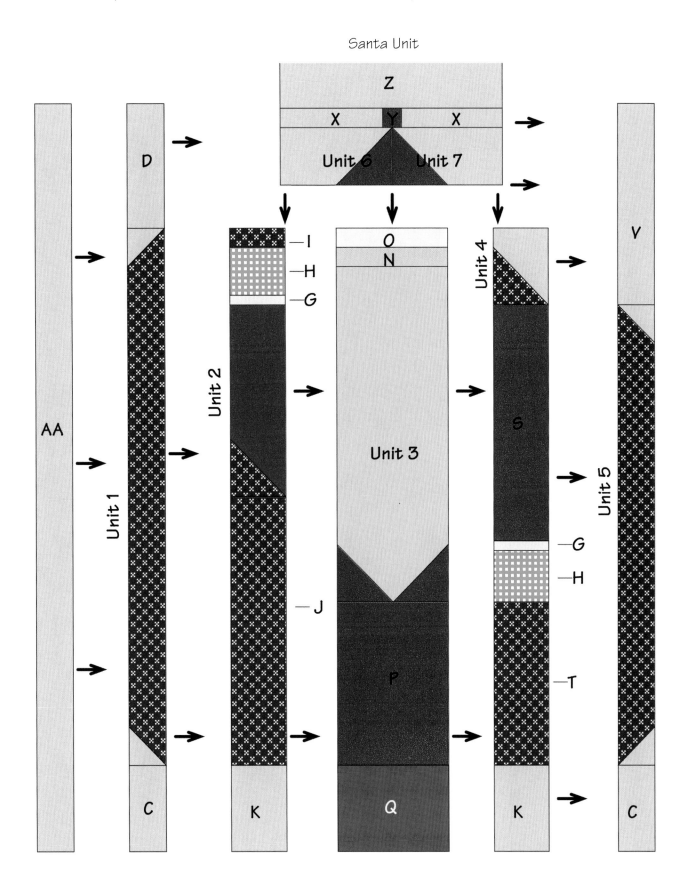

Santa Unit

FLAG AND TREE UNIT – CUTTING

Flag:
Trim to measure $4\frac{1}{4}"\times6"$.

One cream print for background:
Cut 1 E – $1\frac{1}{4}"\times6"$

Additional cream prints for background of trees:
Cut 2 A's $3\frac{1}{4}"$ square from each of 5 prints (5 pairs of A's).

A second cream print for background:
Cut 2 D's – $2\frac{1}{4}"\times2\frac{3}{4}"$

Green prints for trees:
Cut a total of 5 B's – $3\frac{1}{4}"\times6"$

One brown plaid for trunk:
Cut one C – $1\frac{1}{2}"\times2\frac{1}{4}"$

Black print for flagpole:
Cut one F – $1"\times20\frac{1}{2}"$

FLAG AND TREE UNIT – PIECING

1. Follow **Stitch-and-Flip Method** (pg. 243) to sew 2 matching cream print A's to each green print B to make a total of 5 Unit 1's.

Unit 1 – make 5

2. Sew cream D's to brown C to make Unit 2.

Unit 2

3. Sew pieces together following diagram to complete Flag and Tree Unit.

Flag and Tree Unit

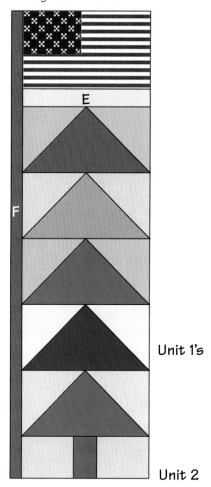

STARS UNIT – CUTTING

5 different background prints:
• From each print, cut:
  • 4 A's – $1\frac{1}{2}"$ square
  • 4 B's – Cut two $1\frac{7}{8}"$ squares, then cut each in half once diagonally into 2 triangles.

5 different red prints:
• From each print, cut:
  • 1 D – $1\frac{1}{2}"$ square
  • 4 C's – Cut two $1\frac{7}{8}"$ squares, then cut each in half once diagonally into 2 triangles.

STAR BLOCK PIECING – MAKE 5

1. Sew 1 background B and 1 red print C together to make each of 4 Unit 1's.

Unit 1 – make 4

2. Sew 2 background A's and 1 Unit 1 together to make each of 2 Unit 2's.

Unit 2 – make 2

3. Sew 2 Unit 1's and red print D together to make Unit 3.

Unit 3 – make 1

4. Sew Unit 2's and Unit 3 together to complete Block.

Block – make 1

STARS UNIT – PIECING

1. Sew Blocks together following diagram below to complete Stars Unit.

Stars Unit

LOG CABIN UNIT – CUTTING AND PIECING

1. Use Block pattern below and follow *Making Needle-Punch Paper Foundations* (pg. 245) to make 5 foundations.

2. Cut fabrics into 1"w strips. Label red print as 1. Follow *Paper-Piecing for Log Cabin Blocks* (pg. 246) to paper-piece 5 blocks, following Block Diagram for placement of lights and darks.

Block Diagram

3. Sew Blocks together to complete Log Cabin Unit.

Log Cabin Unit

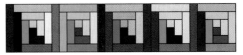

Log Cabin Block Pattern

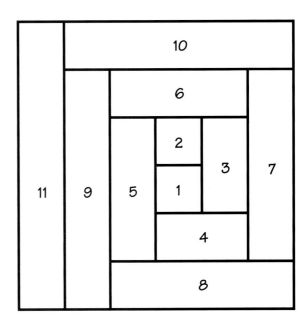

SMALL TREES UNIT – CUTTING

Green prints for trees:
• Cut a total of 5 B's – 2"x3¹/₂"

Brown plaid for trunks:
• Cut 5 C's – 1"x1¹/₂"

From <u>each</u> of 5 light prints, for background of trees:
• Cut 2 A's – 2" square
• Cut 2 D's – 1¹/₂"x1³/₄"

SMALL TREES UNIT – PIECING

1. Follow Steps 1-2 of Piecing for Flag and Tree Unit (pg. 104) to make 5 Unit 1's and 5 Unit 2's. Sew one of each unit together to make 5 Blocks.

Block – make 5

2. Sew blocks together following diagram below to complete Small Trees Unit.

Small Trees Unit

WALL HANGING FINISHING

1. Sew Santa Unit to Flag and Tree Unit. Sew Star Unit to the top, then sew Log Cabin and Small Trees Units to the bottom to make wall hanging center.

2. Cut the following borders:

Red print for inner border:
- Cut three 1"w strips. From these, cut:
  - 2 side inner borders – 1"x29½"
  - 2 top/bottom borders – 1"x16½"

Navy print for outer border:
- Cut three 1½"w strips. From these, cut:
  - 2 side inner outer borders – 1½"x30½"
- 2 top/bottom outer borders – 1½"x18½"

3. Sew side, then top and bottom inner borders to center. Repeat with outer borders.

4. Mark, layer, and quilt as desired. Our wall hanging is outline quilted around most major components of the design. Lines of quilting were added in the beard and on the leg and boots as details.

5. Bind quilt using 3-yds of 2"w straight-grain binding.

Wall Hanging Diagram

PATCHWORK CHRISTMAS ORNAMENTS
(shown on pg. 101)

SUPPLIES
- fabric scraps to piece block and for backing
- paper-backed fusible web
- tracing paper (for log cabin ornament only)
- natural-colored cotton batting
- torn strip of fabric for hanger
- button
- embroidery floss

See Quilter's Basics (pg. 241) for more in-depth basic instructions.

1. Make desired Log Cabin, Small Tree, or Star Block following the appropriate cutting and piecing instructions in *Santa Wall Hanging* instructions (pg. 102).

2. Fuse web to wrong side of block.

3. Fuse batting and backing fabric, wrong sides together.

4. Fuse block to center of fused backing and batting. Trim batting/backing to 1/4" from block.

5. Use 3 strands of floss to work a running stitch near edge of block.

6. For hanger, stitch ends of torn fabric strip to back of ornament, while stitching button to front of ornament.

FARMHOUSE CHRISTMAS WALL QUILT
(shown on pg. 99)

Finished size: 41" square

FABRICS
- cream print – 2-yds
- red print – 3/4-yd
- green print for houses – 1/4-yd
- assorted green prints for tree – scraps
- gold print – 5/8-yd
- brown print for tree trunk – scrap

Other supplies
- batting – 45" square
- template plastic
- permanent pen

Refer to Wall Quilt Diagram, pg. 111, as needed. See Quilter's Basics (pg. 241) for more in-depth basic instructions.

CUTTING
Cream print:
- Cut one 3"w strip. From this, cut:
  - 3 A's – 3"x6"
- Cut twelve 1 1/2"w strips. From these, cut:
  - 116 M's – 1 1/2"x2 1/2"
  - 116 O's – 1 1/2" square
- Cut one 3 3/8"w strip. From this, cut:
  - 6 C's – Cut three 3 3/8" squares then cut each in half once diagonally into 2 triangles.
- Cut one 2"w strip. From this, cut:
  - 2 S's – 2"x2 1/4"
- Cut one 3 1/2"w strip. From this, cut:
  - Cut 2 U's – 3 1/2"x5 1/2"
  - Recut remainder of strip to 1"w. From 1" strip, cut 2 T's – 1"x4 1/2".
- Cut five 2 1/2"w strips. From these, cut:
  - 2 long sashing strips – 2 1/2"x26 1/2"
  - 3 medium sashing strips – 2 1/2"x22 1/2"
  - 2 short sashing strips – 2 1/2"x10 1/2"
- Cut four 1 1/2"w strips. From these, cut:
  - 2 top/bottom inner borders – 1 1/2"x28 1/2"
  - 2 side inner borders – 1 1/2"x30 1/2"
- Cut four 1 3/8"w strips. From these, cut:
  - 28 Q's – 1 3/8"x4 1/2"
- Cut four 1 3/4"w strips. From these, cut:
  - 2 top/bottom outer borders – 1 3/4"x38 1/2"
  - 2 side outer borders – 1 3/4"x41"

Green scraps for tree:
- Cut a total of seven 1 3/4"x6" pieces.

Green print for houses:
- Cut one 3"w strip. Refer to *Fig. 1* and align 45° marking on the rotary cutting ruler (shown in pink) along lower right edge of strip. Cut along right side of ruler to cut end of strip at a 45° angle.

Fig. 1

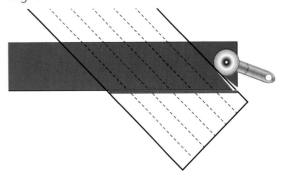

Turn cut strip 180° and align the previously cut 45° edge at the 4⅛" marking on ruler. Cut along right edge of ruler to make one G. Repeat to cut a total of 3 G's.

Fig. 2

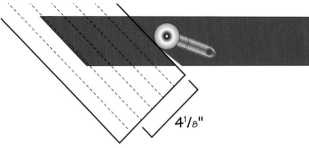

• Cut one 1¾"w strip. Label as H.

Red print:
• Cut one 1¾"w strip. From this, cut:
  • 3 B's – 1¾"x6"
• Cut one 1¾"w strip. From this, cut:
  • 3 F's – 1¾"x10½"
• Cut two 2½" strips. From these, cut:
  • 29 P's – 2½" square
• Cut one 2"w strip. Label as G.
• Cut one 2¾"w strip. Label as I.
• Cut two 1¾"w strips. From these:
  • Label 1 strip as K.
  • Cut remaining strip into six 1¾"x5½" pieces. Label each as L.
• Cut four 1½"w strips. From these, cut:
  • 2 top/bottom borders – 1½"x26½".
  • 2 side borders – 1½"x28½"
• Cut 3 D's – Cut one 6¼" square, then cut square twice diagonally into 4 triangles. Discard 1 triangle.

Gold print:
• Cut one 4¼"w strip. Label as J.
• Cut nine 1½"w strips. From these, cut:
  • 232 N's – 1½" square

Brown print:
• Cut 1 R – 2" square

PIECING – HOUSE BLOCK

1. Sew cream A's and red B's together into a strip set. Cut across strip set at 1¾" intervals to make 3 Unit 1's.

Unit 1 – make 3   Strip Set

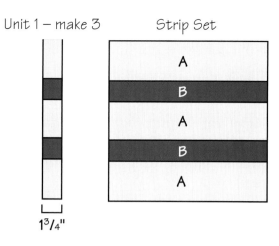

1¾"

2. Sew 2 cream print C's, 1 red print D, and 1 green print E together to make each of 3 Unit 2's.

Unit 2 – make 3

3. Sew Unit 1, Unit 2, and 1 red print F together to make each of 3 Unit 3's.

Unit 3 – make 3

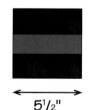

4. Sew G, H, and I strips together into a strip set. Cut across strip set at 5½" intervals to make 3 Unit 4's.

Unit 4 – make 3   Strip Set

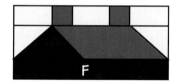

5½"

5. Sew J and K strips together into a strip set. Cut across strip set at 1¾" intervals to make 6 Unit 5's.

Unit 5 – make 6   Strip Set

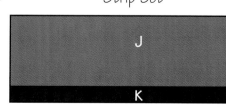

1¾"

6. Sew 1 Unit 3, 2 Unit 5's, and 2 red print L's together to make each of 3 Unit 6's.

Unit 6 – make 3

7. Sew 1 Unit 4 and 1 Unit 6 together to complete each of 3 House Blocks.

House Block – make 3

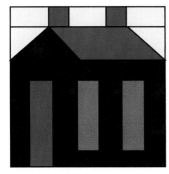

PIECING – STAR BLOCK

1. Follow **Stitch-and-Flip Method** (pg. 243) to sew 2 gold print N's to each cream print M to make a total of 116 Unit 1's.

Unit 1 – make 116

2. Sew 2 cream print O's and 1 Unit 1 together to make a total of 58 Unit 2's.

Unit 2 – make 58

3. Sew 2 Unit 1's to each red print P to make 29 Unit 3's.

Unit 3 – make 29

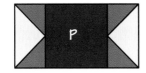

4. Sew 2 Unit 2's to each Unit 3 to make 29 Star Blocks.

Star Block – make 29

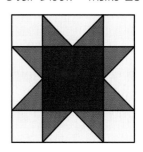

PIECING – TREE AND STAR BLOCK

1. Trace tree and background patterns (pg. 113) onto template plastic; cut out.

2. For tree, sew 7 green print rectangles together along long edges to make a strip set. Use tree template to cut one tree from the strip set.

Strip Set

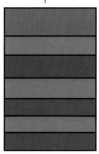

3. Use background template to cut 2 backgrounds (1 in reverse) from cream fabric.

4. Sew background pieces and tree pieces together to make Unit 1.

Unit 1

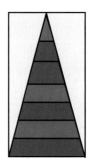

5. Sew cream S's and brown R together to make Unit 2.

Unit 2

6. Sew Unit 1 and Unit 2 together to make Unit 3.

Unit 3

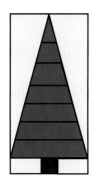

7. Sew 2 T's to side edges of one Star Block, then add U's to top and bottom to make Unit 4.

Unit 4

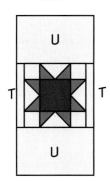

8. Sew Unit 4 and Unit 5 together to complete Tree and Star Block.

Tree and Star Block

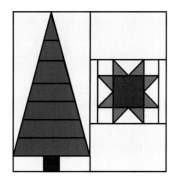

PIECING – WALL HANGING

1. Referring to **Center Diagram**, sew 2 House Blocks and 1 short sashing strip together. Sew Tree and Star Block, remaining House Block, and remaining short sashing strip together. Add medium sashing strips, then add long sashing strips to make wall hanging center.

Center Diagram

2. Sew top, bottom, then side red print borders to center. Repeat to add inner cream print borders.

3. Sew 7 Q's and 6 Star Blocks together to make each Top/Bottom Star Border. Sew to top and bottom of wall hanging.

Top/Bottom Star Border – make 2

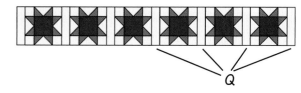

4. Sew 7 Q's and 8 Star Blocks together to make each of 2 Side Star Borders. Sew to sides of wall hanging.

Side Star Border – make 2

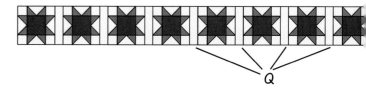

5. Add top, bottom, then side outer cream borders to complete wall hanging top.

FINISHING

1. Mark, layer, and quilt wall hanging using Quilting Diagram as a suggestion.

2. Bind wall hanging with $4^3/_4$-yds of $2^1/_2$"w bias binding.

Wall Quilt Diagram

Quilting Diagram

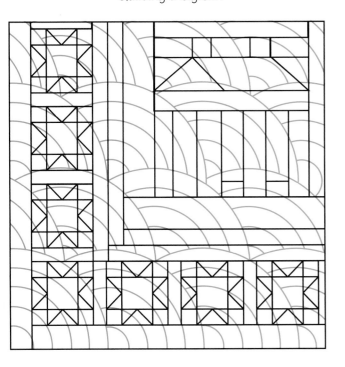

SAINT NICK PULLOVER

(shown on pg. 101)

SUPPLIES

- white sweatshirt
- red print – $1/_8$-yd
- green plaid, two brown plaids, tan print, cream print, peach solid, black solid – scraps
- lightweight fusible interfacing
- paper-backed fusible web
- clear nylon thread
- embroidery floss – red, black, and white
- red buttons

Use 3 strands of floss. **Stitch Diagrams** *are on pages 255 – 256.*

INSTRUCTIONS

1. Fuse interfacing to wrong side of light-colored fabrics.

2. Fuse web to wrong sides of all fabrics.

3. Use patterns (pg. 112) to cut hat and right arm from red print, beard from cream print, and 2 large and 1 small tree pieces from green plaid.

4. Cut remaining pieces as follows:
- tan print – $5/_8$"x3" hat trim, two $5/_{16}$" x$1^3/_8$" cuff trims
- red print – $1^3/_8$"x$5^1/_2$" left arm, 3"x$5^1/_2$" body
- one brown plaid – two 1"x$1^3/_8$" mittens
- other brown plaid – 1"x8" trunk
- peach solid – $3/_4$"x3" face
- black solid – 1"x3" boots

5. Cut cuffs and waistband from sweatshirt.

6. Arrange pieces on sweatshirt with Santa's feet even with bottom edge; fuse in place.

7. Use clear thread and a medium zigzag stitch with a medium stitch length to stitch over all raw edges of design.

8. Press bottom edge of sweatshirt under $1/_2$". Stitch in place using red floss and a running stitch.

9. Roll sleeves back desired amount. Stitch in place using red floss cross stitches. At desired intervals, use white floss to stitch buttons to sleeves, leaving floss ends at the front of the button. Stitch a button to Santa's hat.

10. Stitch red cross stitches along collar.

11. Work black French knots for eyes.

Hat/Small Tree
Piece pattern

Beard pattern

Large Tree Piece pattern

Right Arm pattern

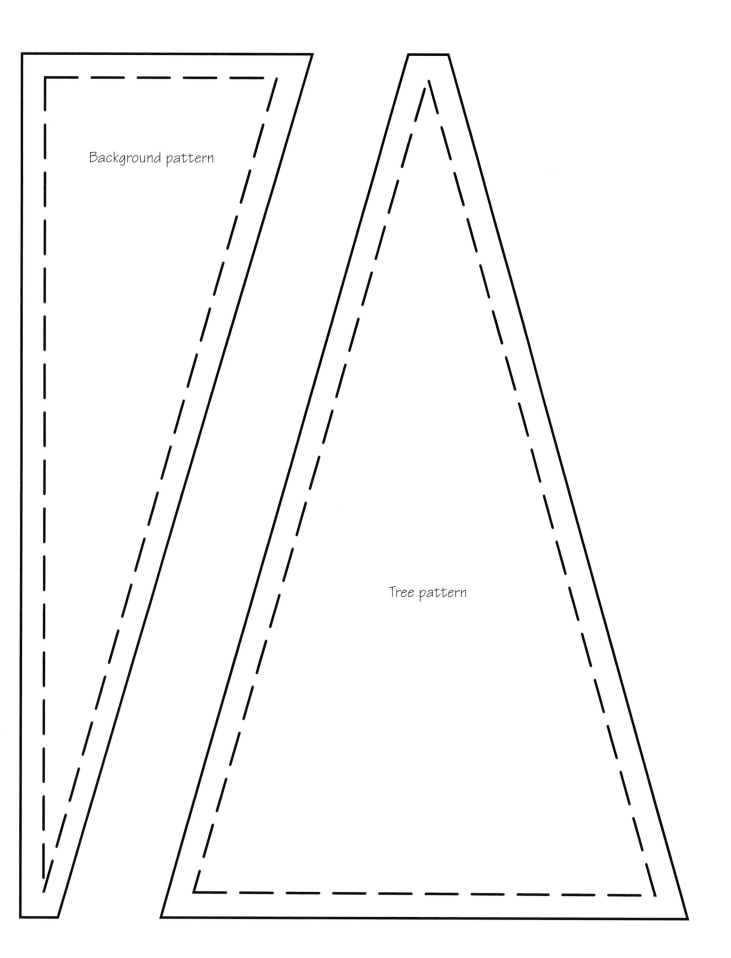

Background pattern

Tree pattern

113

Let It Snow!

If you just can't wait for the first snow of the season, you'll love our frosty friend! We made him into an appliquéd wall hanging and pillow, as well as a cuddly chenille doll.

Snowman Wall Hanging, page 116.

Chenille Snowman, page 118.

Enjoy a wintry day of play with your children! Bake and decorate cookies, make snow ice cream, build a snow fort or cut out paper snowflakes.

"Frosty, in a coat of red, with a scarf upon his head. A ball of snow from head to toe, before the springtime he must go!"

— Unknown

Snowman Pillow, page 121.

SNOWMAN WALL HANGING

(shown on pg. 114)

Finished Size: 21" x 21$\frac{1}{2}$"

FABRICS

Yardage is based on 45"w fabric.
- blue print — 1$\frac{1}{4}$-yd
- red print — $\frac{1}{4}$-yd
- assorted fabrics for appliqués
- fabric for binding — $\frac{1}{2}$-yd

Other supplies
- batting — 45" x 60"
- paper-backed fusible web
- embroidery floss — white and black
- 2 black buttons — $\frac{3}{16}$" diameter
- 3 black buttons — $\frac{1}{4}$" diameter
- white medium rickrack — 4 12$\frac{3}{4}$" lengths
- hot iron transfer pencil
- tracing paper

*Refer to **Wall Hanging Top Diagram** as needed. See **Quilter's Basics** (pg. 241) for more in-depth basic instructions.*

CUTTING
Blue Print:
- For background, cut 1 rectangle 14" x 14$\frac{1}{2}$".
- For borders, cut 2 strips 3$\frac{3}{4}$"w. From these strips, cut:
  - 2 top/bottom strips 3$\frac{3}{4}$" x 14".
  - 2 side strips 3$\frac{3}{4}$" x 21".
- For backing, cut 1 square 24" x 24".
- For hanging sleeve, cut 1 rectangle 4" x 20$\frac{1}{2}$".

Red Print:
- For trim, cut 2 strips 1$\frac{1}{4}$"w.

Assorted Fabrics for Appliqués:
- Use patterns, pg. 117, and follow **Preparing Appliqué Pieces**, pg. 247, to make the following appliqués:
  - snowman head
  - snowman body
  - nose
  - cap
  - cuff
  - pom-pom
  - scarf
  - snow
  - star

PIECING

1. Follow manufacturer's instructions to fuse appliqués to background.

2. Follow **Satin Stitch Appliqué**, pg. 248, to appliqué snow, snowman body, snowman head, nose, scarf, cap, cuff, pom-pom, and star.

3. Sew blue print borders to top and bottom, then sides of background.

4. Sew trim strips together end to end. Press each long edge of trim $\frac{1}{4}$" to wrong side. Lay trim on background along border seamlines, mitering corners and overlapping ends. Fold end to wrong side. Lay lengths of rickrack under inside edge of trim; pin in place. Topstitch trim and rickrack in place.

5. Follow manufacturer's instructions and use hot iron transfer pencil to transfer words, pg. 120, and snowflake, pg. 117, to wall hanging top. Refer to **Stitch Diagrams**, pgs. 255 – 256, to Backstitch words and snowflakes. Stitch white French Knots on ends of snowflake spokes. Stitch black French Knots for snowman's mouth. Sew buttons to snowman.

FINISHING

1. Mark, layer, and quilt. Hand quilt $\frac{1}{8}$" outside appliqués. Quilt in the ditch along outside edge of trim. Refer to **Stitch Diagrams**, pgs. 255 – 256 to randomly stitch white French Knots on wall hanging top.

2. Follow **Making a Hanging Sleeve**, pg. 254, to attach hanging sleeve to wall hanging.

3. Follow **Binding**, pg. 252, to bind wall hanging using a 15" square of binding fabric to make 2$\frac{5}{8}$-yds of 2$\frac{1}{2}$"w continuous bias binding.

Wall Hanging Top Diagram

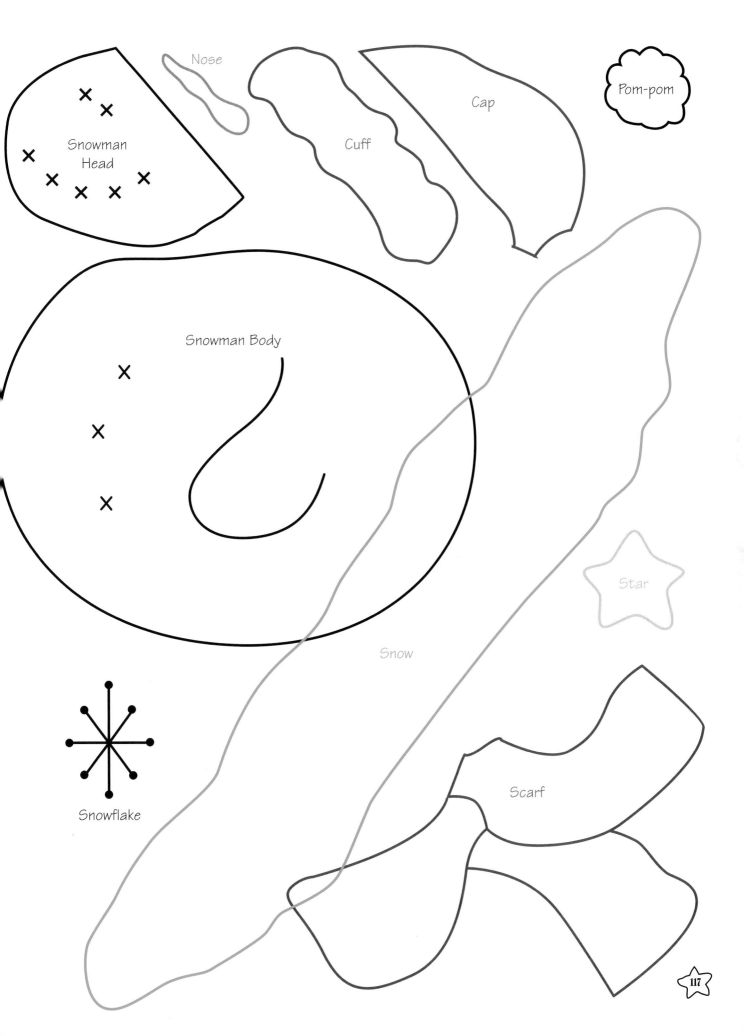

Nose

Snowman Head

Cuff

Cap

Pom-pom

Snowman Body

Star

Snow

Snowflake

Scarf

117

CHENILLE SNOWMAN

(shown on pg. 115)

Finished Size: Approximately 14" tall

FABRICS

Yardage is based on 45"w fabric.
- white chenille — $^1/_2$-yd
- green fleece — $^1/_2$-yd
- green stripe — scrap
- red print — $^1/_4$-yd
- white felt — $^1/_4$-yd
- orange felt — scrap
- 3 assorted fabrics for stars — scraps

Other supplies
- polyester fiberfill
- paper-backed fusible web — $^1/_4$-yd
- yellow paint
- paintbrush
- embroidery floss — red
- wooden stars — 1 $2^3/_4$"w and 2 2"w
- black buttons — $2^7/_{16}$" dia., $3^5/_8$" dia., and $5^5/_{16}$" dia.
- white buttons — $1^3/_4$" diameter and $2^9/_{16}$" diameter
- white medium rickrack — 2 $2^1/_2$" lengths
- red jumbo rickrack — 14" length
- red baby rickrack — 5" length
- green satin ribbon — 40" length
- orange thread for nose
- white floss for tassel — two 8" lengths
- fabric glue

CUTTING
White Chenille:
- Use patterns, pgs. 119-120, to cut 2 snowman bodies and 4 arms.
Green Fleece:
- Cut a 14" square.
Green Stripe:
- Cut a 3" x 14" piece.
- Follow manufacturer's instructions to fuse paper-backed fusible web to wrong side of fabric. Cut a $4^1/_4$" x $2^1/_2$" piece.
White Felt:
- Cut a $34^1/_2$" x 5" piece.
Orange Felt:
- Use pattern, pg. 119, to cut nose.

Match right sides and raw edges and use a $^1/_4$" seam allowance for all sewing.

INSTRUCTIONS

1. Sew 2 arm pieces together leaving straight edge open; turn. Stuff arm with fiberfill. Repeat for remaining arm pieces.

2. With arms facing in, baste arms to 1 body piece.

3. Sew $^7/_{16}$" buttons to one body piece for eyes. Sew $^5/_{16}$" buttons to body piece for mouth. Sew $^5/_8$" buttons to body. Sew body front to body back, leaving an opening for turning; turn. Stuff body with fiberfill. Sew opening closed.

4. For nose, start at one straight side and roll into nose shape. Sew final side closed. Wrap thread around nose; secure. Sew wide end of nose to face. Folding nose to one side, secure nose to face.

5. For cap, fold 14" square of fleece in half. Measure over 3" from top right corner; mark. Draw a line from mark to lower right hand corner. Sew along drawn line; trim $^1/_4$" from stitching.

6. For cuff, sew short ends of 3" x 14" green stripe piece together. Fold cuff in half lengthwise. Matching raw edges of cuff to wrong side of cap, sew cuff to cap. Fold cuff to outside. Referring to **Stitch Diagrams**, pgs. 255 – 256, and overlapping ends at seam, use floss to sew jumbo rick rack to cuff with a Running Stitch.

7. For tassel, cut white felt into $^1/_2$" x 5" pieces. Lay 1 floss length on flat surface. With strips of white felt perpendicular to floss length, stack strips on top of each other. Knot floss ends around center of strips. Smoothing strips, tie remaining floss length around top of tassel. Glue baby rick rack around top of tassel. Gather open end of cap. Glue tassel to cap over gathers.

8. For scarf, cut 2 pieces $2^3/_8$" x $27^1/_2$". Holding all ends together, trim ends at a diagonal. Cut $2^1/_2$" x $4^1/_4$" piece of green stripe fabric into thin strips approx. $^1/_8$"w. Fuse strips and glue white rick rack in parallel lines on each end of 1 scarf piece. Matching right sides and raw edges, sew scarf pieces together, leaving an opening for turning; turn. Sew opening closed.

9. For star garland, paint stars yellow. Draw around wooden stars on paper side of fusible web. Fuse web to wrong sides of star fabrics. Cut out along drawn lines. Fuse fabric stars to wooden stars. Sew through remaining buttons with yellow thread. Hot glue buttons to stars. Cut green ribbon into 1 20" length and 2 10" lengths. Knot short lengths around long length approx. 5" from ends. Hot glue knots to snowman's hands. Fold ends of ribbons in half lengthwise and trim diagonally to form "V."

Nose
Cut 1

Snowman Body
Cut 2

Arm
Cut 4

Place on fold of fabric.

Aligning grey dashed lines and arrows, trace pattern onto tracing paper. Fold fabric in half. Place blue lines along fold of fabric. Cut along solid black line.

119

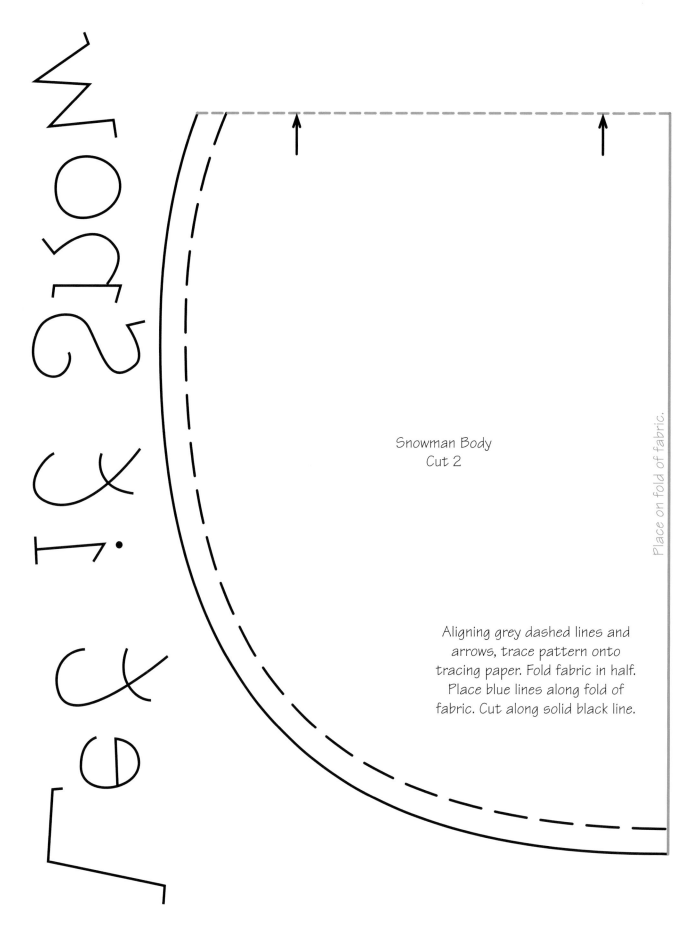

Snowman Body
Cut 2

Place on fold of fabric.

Aligning grey dashed lines and
arrows, trace pattern onto
tracing paper. Fold fabric in half.
Place blue lines along fold of
fabric. Cut along solid black line.

SNOWMAN PILLOW
(shown on pg. 115)

Finished Size: 14" square excluding flange

FABRICS
Yardage is based on 45"w fabric.
blue print — 1¼-yd
red print — ¼-yd
assorted fabrics for appliqués

other supplies
pillow form — 14" square
paper-backed fusible web
embroidery floss — white and black
2 black buttons — ³/₁₆" diameter
3 black buttons — ¼" diameter
white medium rickrack — 4 12³/₄" lengths
hot iron transfer pencil
tracing paper

Refer to **Pillow Top Diagram** as needed. See **Quilter's Basics** (pg. 241) for more in-depth basic instructions.

CUTTING
Blue Print:
For pillow front, cut 1 square 19" x 19".
For pillow back, cut 2 rectangles 12½" x 19".
For binding, cut 1 square 14" x 14".

Red Print:
For trim, cut 2 strips 1¼"w.

Assorted Fabrics for Appliqués:
Use patterns, pg. 117, and follow **Preparing Appliqué Pieces**, pg. 247, to make the following appliqués:
- snowman head
- snowman body
- nose
- cap
- cuff
- pom-pom
- scarf
- snow
- star

PIECING
1. Follow manufacturer's instructions to fuse appliqués to background.

2. Follow **Satin Stitch Appliqué**, pg. 248, to appliqué snow, snowman body, snowman head, nose, scarf, cap, cuff, pom-pom, and star.

3. Sew trim strips together end to end. Press each long edge of trim ¼" to wrong side. Lay trim on pillow top with outside edge 2½" from edges, mitering corners and overlapping ends. Fold overlapping end to wrong side. Lay lengths of rickrack under inside edge of trim; pin in place. Topstitch trim and rickrack in place.

4. Follow manufacturer's instructions and use hot iron transfer pencil to transfer words, pg. 120, and snowflake, pg. 117, to pillow top. Refer to **Stitch Diagrams**, pgs. 255 – 256, to Backstitch words and snowflakes. Stitch white French Knots on ends of snowflake spokes. Stitch black French Knots for snowman's mouth. Sew buttons to snowman.

5. For each pillow back piece, press 1 long edge ¼" to wrong side; press to wrong side again. Topstitch along folded edge.

6. Matching **wrong** sides and raw edges and overlapping pillow back pieces, baste pillow front to pillow back ¼" from edges. Topstitch along outside edge of trim.

7. Follow **Binding**, pg. 252, to bind pillow using a 14" square of binding fabric to make 2½-yds of 2½"w continuous bias binding with mitered corners. Insert pillow form.

Pillow Top Diagram

simple
Comforts

The Amish may live the simple life, but the traditional colors of their quilts show a love of drama in their fabric selections! This Amish Stripe Wall Hanging uses a quilt pattern also known as "Chinese Coins," and the center square of the vibrant miniature quilt is an easy Nine-Patch block.

Amish Stripe Wall Hanging, page 124.

Amish Friendship Bread STARTER

Make your own starter by combining one cup flour, one cup sugar and one cup of milk in a non-metal bowl. Set the starter on your counter, loosely cover with a towel, do not refrigerate. On **Day one**, <u>the day you make or receive your starter</u>, do nothing. On **Days 2, 3 and 4**, stir with a wooden spoon. Do not use a metal spoon. **Day 5** add one cup flour, one cup sugar and one cup milk; stir. **Days 6, 7, 8 and 9**, stir with wooden spoon. **Day 10** add one cup flour, one cup sugar and one cup milk; stir. To give the starter as gifts, add one cup of starter to each of 3 glass or plastic containers. You can now bake bread with the starter remaining in your bowl. Keep one container of starter for yourself and share the others with 2 friends. When sharing, be sure to give the starter instructions for keeping the starter going, along with the bread recipe. Your friends will be able to share their starter and make bread only after following the starter instructions for 10 days.

Miniature Amish Quilt, page 125.

Amish Friendship Bread

2 c. all-purpose flour
1 c. sugar
1·¼ t. baking powder
1 t. cinnamon
½ t. salt
½ t. baking soda
⅔ c. oil
3 eggs, beaten
1 t. vanilla

Sift together dry ingredients and blend well with oil, eggs and vanilla. Combine with the starter remaining in your bowl after dividing it among the three containers described in the Starter Recipe. Pour batter into two well-oiled and sugared 9"x5" loaf pans. Bake at 350 degrees for 40 to 50 minutes. Cool 10 minutes before removing from pans.

AMISH STRIPE WALL HANGING

(shown on pg. 122)

Size: 37½"x39½"

FABRIC
- black solid – 1⅛-yds
- assorted solids – 1½-yds total (our wall hanging uses 19 different solids)
- blue solid – ⅓-yd
- backing – 1½-yds
- binding – ½-yd

Other supplies
- batting – 42"x44"

Refer to **Wall Hanging Diagram** *as needed. See* **Quilter's Basics** *(pg. 241) for more in-depth basic instructions.*

CUTTING
Black solid:
- Cut four 2¾"w strips. From these, cut:
  - 4 sashing strips – 2¾"x26"
- Cut four 5½"w strips. From these, cut:
  - 2 top/bottom borders – 5½"x25½"
  - 2 side borders – 5½"x39½"

Assorted solids:
- Cut 1 or more 20"l strips from each fabric in widths varying from 1¼"w to 1¼"w.

Blue solid:
- Cut four 2¼"w strips. From these, cut:
  - 2 top/bottom inner borders – 2¼"x22"
  - 2 side inner borders – 2¼"x29½"

PIECING

1. Sew 20"l strips together in random color order to make a 26"h strip set. Cut five 3"w Unit 1's from strip set.

Unit 1 – make 5

Strip Set – make 1

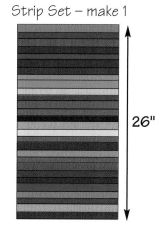

26"

3"

2. Sew Unit 1's and black sashing strips together to make wall hanging center. Center should measure 22"x26".

3. Sew top, bottom, then side blue inner borders to wall hanging center. Sew black outer borders to wall hanging in same order. Wall hanging should measure 37½"x39½".

FINISHING

1. Mark, layer, and quilt wall hanging using **Quilting Diagram** as a suggestion.

2. Bind wall hanging using 4⅜-yds of 2½"w bias binding.

Wall Hanging Diagram

Quilting Diagram

MINIATURE AMISH QUILT

(shown on pg. 123)

Size: 7" square

FABRICS
• black solid - ¼-yd (enough for piecing, backing, and binding)
• solid blue, solid green, solid red - scraps

Other supplies
• batting – 9" square

Refer to **Quilt Top Diagram** *as needed. See* **Quilter's Basics** *(pg. 241) for more in-depth basic instructions.*

CUTTING
Black solid:
• Cut one 1½"w strip. From this, cut:
    • 4 A's - 1½" square
• Cut one 1¾"w strip. From this, cut:
    • 4 borders - 1¾"x4½"

Blue solid:
• Cut 5 B's - 1½" square
• Cut 4 D's – 1¾" square

Green solid:
• Cut four 1"x3½" inner borders

Red solid:
• Cut 4 C's - 1" square

PIECING
1. Sew black A's and blue B's together to make Unit 1.

Unit 1 – make 1

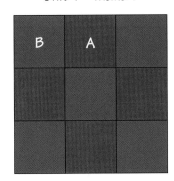

2. Sew 1 green inner border to opposite sides of Unit 1. Sew red C's to ends of remaining inner borders, then sew borders to remaining edges of Unit 1.

3. Repeat Step 2 to add black borders and blue D's to complete quilt top. Top should measure 7".

FINISHING
1. Mark, layer, and quilt as desired, using **Quilting Diagram** as a suggestion.

2. Bind quilt using 1-yd of 1¾"w bias binding and a scant ¼" seam allowance.

Quilt Top Diagram

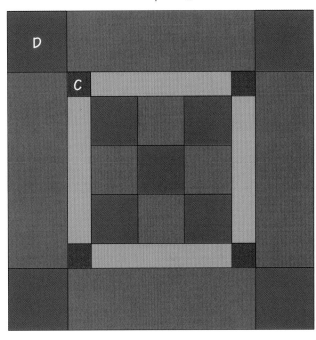

Quilting Diagram

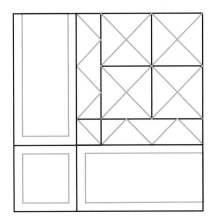

Tip•toe through the Tulips

Give your surroundings a fresh-as-springtime look with lots of pretty flowers! Shades of green and rose make a radiant star in the center of this Wild Rose Wall Hanging.

Wild Rose Wall Hanging, page 130.

Tiny Tulips Wall Quilt, page 134

Pick just a little posy or the whole bouquet…you'll love making both of these tulip quilts! The quilting patterns capture the shapes of springtime.

Tiptoe Throw, page 133.

WILD ROSE WALL HANGING

(shown on pgs. 126 – 127)

Finished size: 49" square

FABRICS
- muslin – 1²/₃-yds
- maroon print – ¹/₃-yd
- light maroon print – scraps
- ecru floral – ¹/₈-yd
- dark pink print – ¹/₄-yd
- light pink print – ¹/₃-yd
- green print – 1-yd
- light green print – 1-yd
- dark green floral for border and binding – 1³/₄-yds
- backing – 3 yds

Other supplies
- template plastic
- large right-angle triangle
- ¹/₄" bias pressing bar
- batting – 53" square

Refer to **Wall Hanging Diagram**, *pg. 132, as needed. See* **Quilter's Basics** *(pg. 241) for more in-depth basic instructions.*

CUTTING
Muslin:
- Cut one 11¹/₄"w strip. From this, cut:
  - 4 B's – Cut one 11¹/₄" square, then cut square twice diagonally into 4 triangles.
- Cut four 8¹/₂"w strips. From these, cut:
  - 2 top/bottom borders – 8¹/₂"x24¹/₂"
  - 2 side borders – 8¹/₂"x40¹/₂"
- Cut one 7¹/₂"w strip. From this, cut:
  - 4 A's – 7¹/₂" square
Maroon print:
- Cut three 1¹/₂"w strips. Cut these strips in half to make 6 short strips.
Ecru floral, dark pink print, light pink print, and green print:
- Cut two 1¹/₂"w strips from each fabric. Cut each strip in half to make 4 short strips of each.
Light green print:
- Cut two 1¹/₂"w strips. Cut each strip in half to make 2 short strips. Discard 1 short strip.
- Cut four 5"w strips. From these, cut:
  - 4 outer borders – 5"x40¹/₂"

Dark green floral:
- Cut five 5"w strips. From these, cut:
  - 4 appliqué borders – 5"x 40¹/₂"
  - 4 C's – 5" square

PIECING
1. *Refer to* **Strip Set and Unit Diagrams** *(pg. 132) for Steps 1-3.* Sew 5 strips together in the color order shown, adding each new strip 1" from the end of the previous strip to make Strip Sets A-E. Strip sets should measure 5¹/₂"h.

2. Referring to *Fig. 1*, align triangle with a seam to determine an accurate 45° cutting line, then trim off the uneven ends from 1 end of each strip set.

Fig. 1

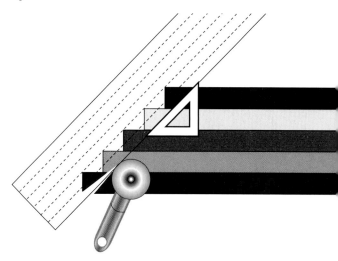

3. Aligning the 45° mark on the rotary cutting ruler (shown in blue in *Fig. 2*) with a seam and aligning the 1¹/₂" mark with the cut edge made in Step 2 (*Fig. 2*), cut across each strip set at 1¹/₂" intervals to make 8 units from each strip set.

Fig. 2

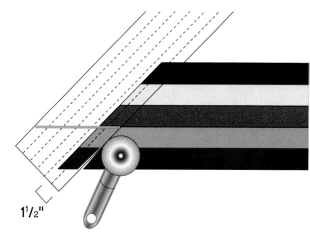

1¹/₂"

4. When making Unit 6's, refer to *Fig. 3* to match long edges of units. Seam will cross 1/4" from cut edges of fabric. Pin and stitch as shown in *Fig. 3*. Sew 1 each of Units 1-5 together to make each of 8 Unit 6's.

Fig. 3

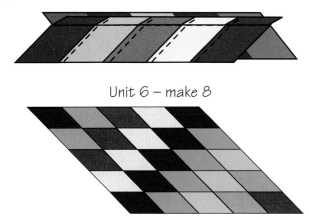

Unit 6 – make 8

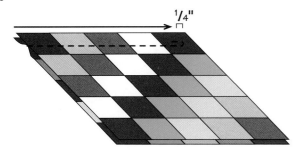

5. To make each of 4 Unit 7's, place 2 Unit 6's right sides together, carefully matching edges and seams; pin. Stitch in direction shown in *Fig. 4*, ending stitching 1/4" from edge of fabric (you may find it helpful to mark a small dot at this point before sewing) and backstitching at end of seam.

Fig. 4

Unit 7 – make 4

6. Following **Wall Hanging Diagram**, pg. 132, sew Unit 7's together to make star, ending stitching 1/4" from edges and backstitching each seam.

7. Follow **Setting in Seams** (pg. 244) to sew B's and A's to star to complete center of wall hanging. Star square should measure 24 1/2" square.

8. Sew top, bottom, then side inner borders to star square to complete center of wall hanging.

APPLIQUÉING

1. Use patterns (pg. 136) and follow **Preparing Appliqué Pieces** (pg. 247) to make the following appliqués from the fabrics listed:
• maroon print – 4 large flowers, 4 small flower centers
• light maroon print – 4 large flower centers
• dark pink print – 8 buds
• light pink print – 8 buds, 4 small flowers
• green print – 8 calyxes, 40 leaves
• light green print – 16 leaves

2. For stems, cut six 1 1/8"x 20" bias strips from green print and three 1 1/8"x 20" bias strips from light green print. Fold 1 bias strip in half lengthwise with wrong sides together; sew long edges together. Trim seam allowance to 1/8". Place bias pressing bar in 1 end of tube. Center seam and press as you move bar down length of tube. Repeat for each bias strip. Cut eight 6" lengths from light green and sixteen 6" lengths from green tubes.

3. Follow **Wall Hanging Diagram**, pg. 132, and **Needle-Turn Appliqué** (pg. 248) to appliqué all pieces to wall hanging center.

4. For outer border, trace Wild Rose Picket template (pg. 136) onto template plastic; cut out. For each dark green floral appliqué border, match template to bottom left corner of fabric and trace template, repeating pickets as needed to opposite end and ending with a seam allowance; cut out a 1/4" from drawn line. Matching long straight edges, baste appliqué borders to light green outer borders. Appliqué the zigzag edges of the pickets only.

FINISHING

1. Sew top and bottom outer borders to wall hanging.

2. Sew dark green floral C's to ends of remaining outer borders. Sew borders to side edges to complete wall hanging top. Wall hanging top should measure 49½" square.

3. Mark, layer, and quilt wall hanging, using **Quilting Diagram** as a suggestion.

4. Bind quilt using 5¾-yds of 1¾"w bias binding and a scant ¼" seam allowance.

Strip Set and Unit Diagrams

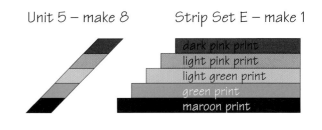

Unit 5 – make 8   Strip Set E – make 1

dark pink print
light pink print
light green print
green print
maroon print

Wall Hanging Diagram

Quilting Diagram

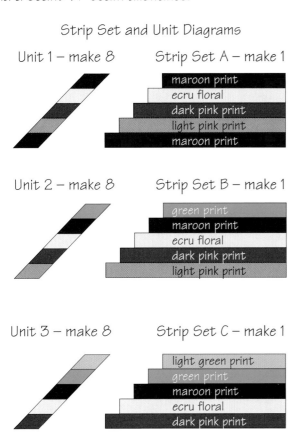

Unit 1 – make 8   Strip Set A – make 1

maroon print
ecru floral
dark pink print
light pink print
maroon print

Unit 2 – make 8   Strip Set B – make 1

green print
maroon print
ecru floral
dark pink print
light pink print

Unit 3 – make 8   Strip Set C – make 1

light green print
green print
maroon print
ecru floral
dark pink print

Unit 4 – make 8   Strip Set D – make 1

light pink print
light green print
green print
maroon print
ecru floral

TIPTOE THROW

(shown on pg. 129)

Finised size: 42"x52"
Block size: 6"x8"

FABRICS
- muslin – 2³/4-yds
- green print for border and binding – 2¹/4-yds
- 13 different pink prints – scraps
- 13 different green prints – 8" square of each
- backing – 2³/4-yds

Other supplies
- batting – 50"x62"

*Refer to **Quilt Top Diagram**, pg. 134, as needed. See **Quilter's Basics** (pg. 241) for more in-depth basic instructions.*

CUTTING
Muslin:
- Cut five 8¹/2"w strips. From these, cut:
  - 25 blocks – 6¹/2"x8¹/2"
- From the lengthwise grain of fabric, cut:
  - 2 top/bottom borders – 6¹/2"x42¹/2"
  - 2 side borders – 6¹/2"x52¹/2"

Green print for border:
- From the lengthwise grain of fabric, cut:
  - 2 top/bottom borders – 6¹/2"x42¹/2"
  - 2 side borders – 6¹/2"x52¹/2"

PIECING AND APPLIQUÉING

1. Use large tulip, stem, and leaf patterns (pg. 137) and follow **Appliqué** (pg. 247) to appliqué each of 13 blocks with 1 green stem, 2 green leaves, and 1 pink tulip.

2. Sew 3 appliquéd blocks and 2 plain blocks together to make each of 3 Row A's.

Row A – make 3

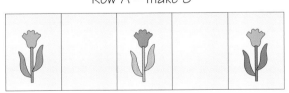

3. Sew 3 plain blocks and 2 appliquéd blocks together to make each of 2 Row B's.

Row B – make 2

4. Sew rows together to make center of quilt.

5. Follow **Adding Mitered Borders** (pg. 250) to sew muslin borders to quilt center.

6. For appliquéd border, trace Tiptoe Throw Picket template (pg. 135) onto template plastic, making sure to transfer pink and blue center lines; cut out.

7. To mark top/bottom appliquéd border, match **pink** centering line to center of 1 green print border and align straight edge of template with 1 long edge. Mark pickets, repeating as needed to ends of fabric.

8. To mark side appliquéd borders, repeat previous step, aligning **blue** mark on template to center of each border.

9. Cut out appliquéd borders. Matching long raw edges and beginning at center, appliqué the zigzag edges of the pickets to the muslin border. At each mitered corner, fold under the raw edge of the green border to match the seamline of the mitered muslin border, then blindstitch in place.

FINISHING

1. Mark, layer, and quilt, using **Quilting Diagram** as a suggestion.

2. Bind quilt using 5¹/2-yds of 1³/4"w bias binding and a scant ¹/4" seam allowance.

Quilting Diagram

Quilt Top Diagram

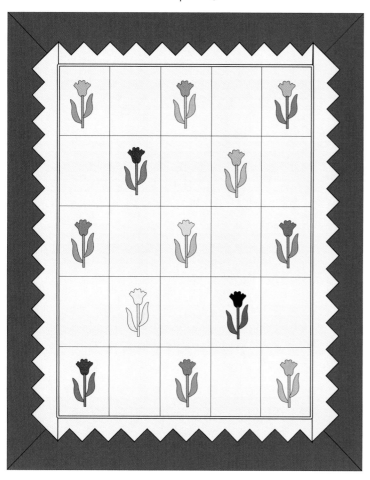

TINY TULIPS WALL QUILT

(shown on pg. 128)

Finished size: 20"x26"
Block size: 4"x6"

FABRICS
- muslin – 3/4-yd
- green print for border and binding – 3/4-yd
- 5 different pink prints – scraps
- 5 different green prints – scraps
- backing – 2/3-yd

Other supplies
- batting – 24"x32"

Refer to **Wall Quilt Diagram** as needed. See *Quilter's Basics* (pg. 241) for more in-depth basic instructions.

CUTTING
Muslin:
- Cut six 4 1/2"w strips. From these, cut:
  - 9 blocks – 6 1/2"x4 1/2"
  - 2 top/bottom borders – 4 1/2"x20 1/2"
  - 2 side borders – 4 1/2"x26 1/2"

Green print for border:
- Cut four 2 1/2"w strips. From these, cut:
  - 2 top/bottom appliqué borders – 2 1/2"x20 1/2"
  - 2 side appliqué borders – 2 1/2"x26 1/2"

PIECING AND APPLIQUÉING

1. Use small tulip, stem, and leaf patterns (pg. 137) and follow *Appliqué* (pg. 247) to appliqué each of 5 blocks with 1 green stem, 2 green leaves, and 1 pink tulip.

2. Sew 2 appliquéd blocks and 1 plain block together to make each top and bottom row.

3. Sew 2 plain blocks and remaining appliquéd block together to make center row.

4. Sew rows together to make center of wall quilt.

5. Follow *Adding Mitered Borders* (pg. 250) to sew muslin borders to wall quilt center.

6. To add appliquéd border, use Tiny Tulips Picket template and follow Steps 6-9 of *Piecing and Appliquéing* (Tiptoe Throw, pg. 133).

FINISHING

1. Mark, layer, and quilt wall quilt, using **Quilting Diagram** as a suggestion.

2. Bind quilt using 2 3/4-yds of 1 3/4"w bias binding and a scant 1/4" seam allowance.

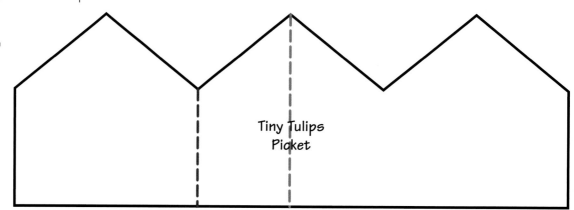

Tiny Tulips Picket

Wall Quilt Diagram

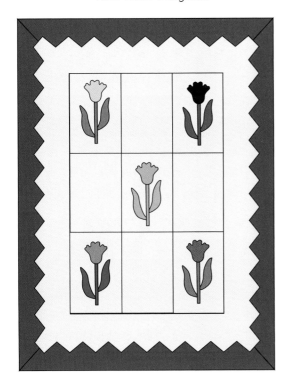

Quilting Diagram

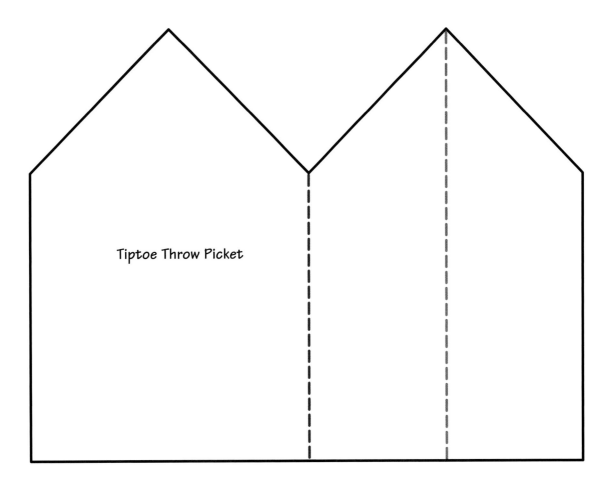

Tiptoe Throw Picket

135

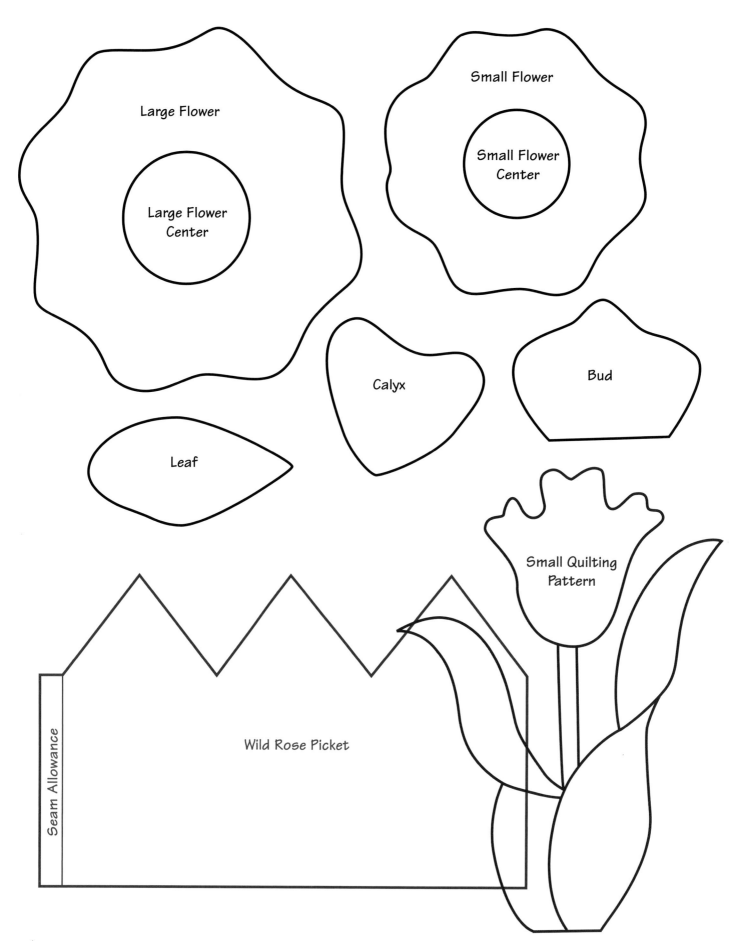

Large Flower

Small Flower

Large Flower
Center

Small Flower
Center

Calyx

Bud

Leaf

Small Quilting
Pattern

Seam Allowance

Wild Rose Picket

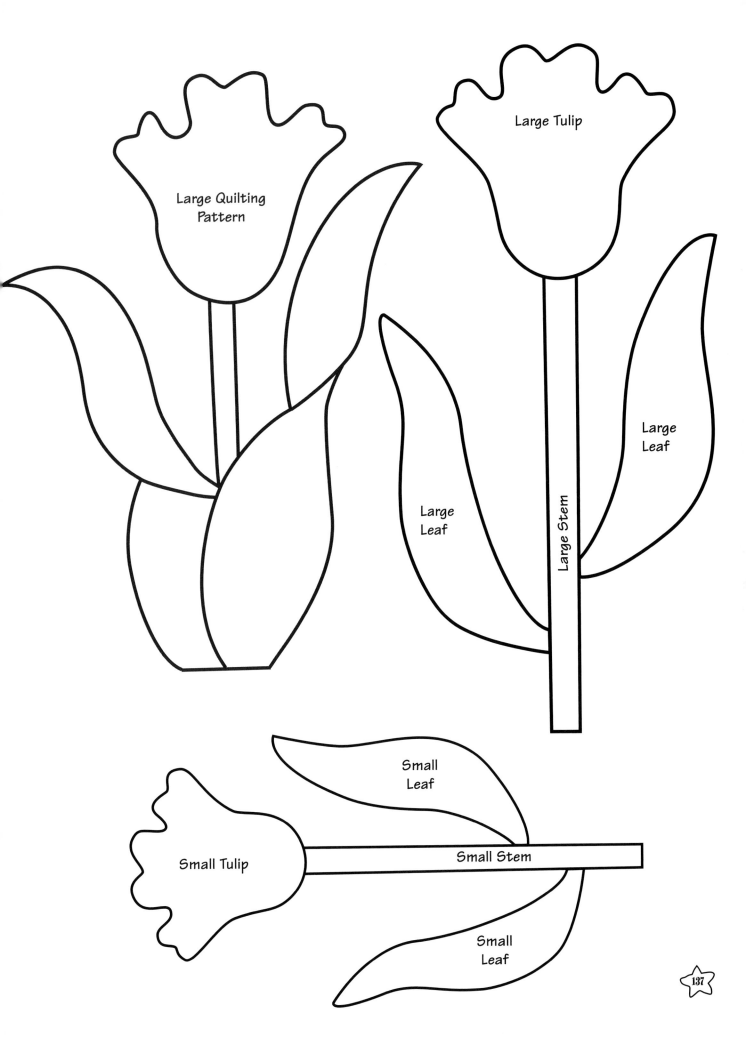

Large Quilting Pattern

Large Tulip

Large Leaf

Large Leaf

Large Stem

Small Leaf

Small Stem

Small Tulip

Small Leaf

137

Springtime Blossoms

Who can resist the appeal of a springtime garden? Come along with us and let Kate, Holly and Mary Elizabeth show you some of their all-time favorite floral patchwork patterns. Tulip fanciers will love reproducing this pretty antique coverlet...the blocks are positioned with the tulip tips together to create an intriguing design.

Tulip Quilt, page 144.

Dogwood Quilt, page 145.

One of the first flowering trees to bloom in the spring, the dogwood dots the forest with puffy clouds of pink and white. We just had to find a way to bring these beautiful blossoms indoors! Girls of all ages will enjoy our appliquéd quilt, pillow and wall hanging. Simple Nine-Patch blocks accent the corners of the wall hanging.

*F*un fact: The dogwood is the state flower or tree of
Virginia, North Carolina, New Jersey and Missouri, as
well as the official provincial flower of British Columbia.

Dogwood Pillow, page 148; Dogwood Wall Hanging, page 149.

To add a touch of spring anywhere, stitch up this trio of blossoming pillows. You could also use the patchwork blocks to make wall hangings, potholders or framed pieces...put your creative talents to work!

Dress your home for spring with fresh-cut flowers from your garden! Place vases overflowing with daffodils, lilacs and tulips on your kitchen table, mantel, stairsteps, sideboard and windowsills. You can even tuck a large basketful of flowers in an empty fireplace for a fresh springtime look!

Pot of Lilies Pillow, page 153; Grandmother's Flower Garden Pillow, page 152; Palm Leaf Pillow, page 150.

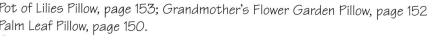

She who kneels where violets grow
a thousand secret things shall know.
-OLD FOLK RHYME

Stacked on shelves, folded over one another to show off their colors and patterns or framing a single block; quilts are fun to decorate with!

TULIP QUILT

(shown on pgs. 138 – 139)

Finished Size: 79" x 88"
Block Size: 9" x 9"

FABRICS

Yardage is based on 45"w fabric.
- white — 4-yds
- pink — 3³/4-yds
- green — 1¹/2-yds
- fabric for backing and hanging sleeve — 5¹/2-yds
- fabric for binding — 2⁵/8-yds

Other supplies
- batting — 81" x 96"

*Refer to **Quilt Top Diagram**, pg. 145, as needed. See **Quilter's Basics** (pg. 241) for more in-depth basic instructions.*

CUTTING

White:
- Cut 9 strips 1⁵/8"w. From this strip, cut:
  - 216 small squares 1⁵/8" x 1⁵/8".
- Cut 15 strips 2³/4"w. From this strip, cut:
  - 216 medium squares 2³/4" x 2³/4".
- Use template, pg. 82, and follow **Template Cutting**, pg. 242, to cut 144 triangles; cut 144 in reverse. Mark dots.

Pink:
- Cut 9 strips 5"w. From this strip, cut:
  - 72 large squares 5" x 5".
- Use template to cut 72 triangles; cut 72 in reverse. Mark dots.
- Cut 2 top/bottom borders 3¹/2" x 76".
- Cut 2 side borders 3¹/2" x 85".

Green:
- Cut 3 strips 1⁵/8"w. From this strip, cut:
  - 72 small squares 1⁵/8" x 1⁵/8".
- Use template to cut 72 triangles; cut 72 in reverse. Mark dots.

PIECING

1. Matching dots, sew 1 pink triangle and 1 white triangle together to make Unit 1. Make 72 Unit 1's. Sew 1 pink triangle and 1 white triangle together to make Unit 2. Make 72 Unit 2's.

Unit 1 – make 72   Unit 2 – make 72

2. Matching dots, sew 1 green triangle and 1 white triangle together to make Unit 3. Make 72 Unit 3's. Sew 1 green triangle and 1 white triangle together to make Unit 4. Make 72 Unit 4's.

Unit 3 – make 72   Unit 4 – make 72

3. Sew 3 small white squares and 1 small green square together to make Unit 5. Make 72 Unit 5's.

Unit 5 – make 72

4. Sew 1 medium white square, 1 Unit 1, and 1 Unit 5 together to make Unit 6. Make 72 Unit 6's.

Unit 6 – make 72

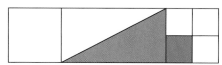

5. Sew 1 unit 3, 1 large pink square, and 1 Unit 2 together to make Unit 7. Make 72 Unit 7's.

Unit 7 – make 72

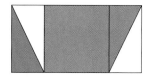

6. Sew 2 medium white squares and 1 Unit 4 together to make Unit 8. Make 72 Unit 8's.

Unit 8 – make 72

7. Sew Units 6, 7, and 8 together to make Block. Make 72 blocks.

Block – make 72

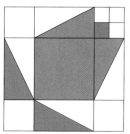

8. Sew 8 blocks together to make Row. Make 9 Rows.

Row – make 9

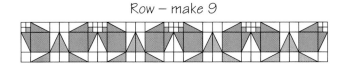

9. Sew 9 Rows together to make center section of Quilt Top.

10. Follow **Adding Mitered Borders**, pg. 250, to add borders to complete Quilt Top.

Quilt Top Diagram

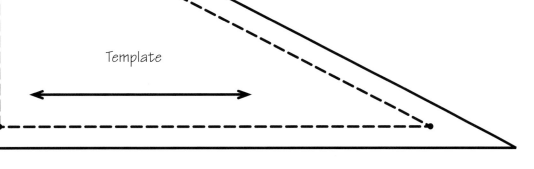

Template

FINISHING

1. Mark, layer, and quilt as desired. Our quilt is hand quilted in intersecting diagonal lines 1" apart across the center section of the quilt top and in diagonal lines $^3/_8$" apart along the borders.

2. Follow **Binding,** pg. 252, to bind quilt using $9^1/_2$-yds of 1"w straight-grain binding with overlapped corners.

DOGWOOD QUILT
(shown on pg. 140)

Finished Size: 67" x 96"

FABRICS

Yardage is based on 45"w fabric.
• cream — $6^1/_4$-yds
• light pink — $^1/_4$-yd
• pink — $^1/_2$-yd
• dark pink — $^1/_4$-yd
• yellow — $^1/_4$-yd
• green — $^3/_8$-yd
• brown — $^3/_8$-yd
• fabric for backing — $6^1/_4$-yds
• fabric for binding — 3-yds
Other supplies
• batting — 81" x 96"
• embroidery floss — pink, yellow, green, and brown

*Refer to **Quilt Top Diagram**, pg. 146, as needed. See **Quilter's Basics** (pg. 241) for more in-depth basic instructions.*

CUTTING
Cream:
• Cut two pieces of fabric 42" x 100".
Light Pink:
• Use patterns, pgs. 146 – 147, to cut the following:
  •25 petals for large flower.
  •36 petals for medium flower.
  •9 petals for small flower.

Pink:
- Use patterns to cut the following:
  - 50 petals for large flower.
  - 72 petals for medium flower.
  - 18 petals for small flower.

Dark Pink:
- Use patterns to cut the following:
  - 25 petals for large flower.
  - 36 petals for medium flower.
  - 18 petals for small flower.

Yellow:
- Use pattern to cut the following:
  - 70 flower centers.

Green:
- Use patterns to cut the following:
  - 126 leaves in any combination.

Brown:
- Use patterns to cut the following:
  - 9 each of all branches.

PIECING

Note: Use 3 strands of floss for all embroidery.

1. Referring to **Choosing and Preparing the Backing**, pg. 251, use cream fabric to assemble a 3-panel quilt top with 2 vertical seams. Fold quilt top into quarters; press to mark placement guidelines and center.

2. Refer to **Quilt Top Diagram** to pin appliqués in place.

3. Using brown floss for branches, pink floss for flowers, green floss for leaves, and yellow floss for centers, refer to **Stitch Diagrams**, pgs. 255 – 256, to Blanket Stitch appliqués to background. Use brown floss to Stem Stitch detail lines in petals, Satin Stitch tips of petals, and Straight Stitch highlights in centers. Use green floss to Stem Stitch leaf stems and detail lines in leaves.

FINISHING

1. Trim appliquéd top to 66¹/₂" x 95¹/₂". Mark, layer, and quilt as desired.

2. Follow **Binding**, pg. 252, to bind quilt using 9¹/₂ -yds of 1¹/₂"w straight-grain binding with overlapping corners.

Quilt Top Diagram

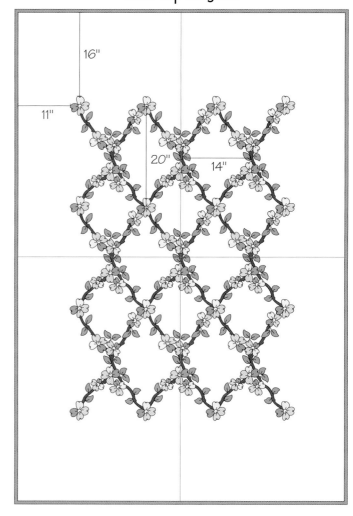

16"
11"
20"
14"

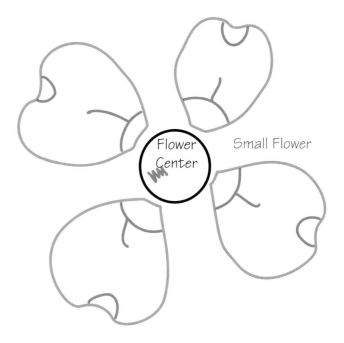

Flower Center

Small Flower

Branch

Branch

Branch

Branch

Branch

Branch

Medium Flower

Leaf

Branch

Branch

Large Flower

Branch

Leaf

Leaf

Branch

147

DOGWOOD PILLOW

(shown on pg. 141)

Finished Size: 12" x 16"

FABRICS

Yardage is based on 45"w fabric.
- cream — 1/2-yd
- light pink — 1/8-yd
- pink — 3/8-yd
- dark pink — 3/8-yd
- yellow — 1/8-yd
- green — 1/8-yd
- brown — 1/8-yd

Other supplies
- batting — 45" x 60"
- 1/4" cord
- embroidery floss — pink, yellow, green, and brown
- water-soluble fabric marking pen
- pillow form or fiberfill for stuffing

Refer to **Pillow Top Diagram** *as needed. See* **Quilter's Basics** *(pg. 241) for more in-depth basic instructions.*

CUTTING

Cream:
- Cut rectangle 10" x 15" for top.
- Cut rectangles 12 1/2" x 16 1/2" for pillow top backing and pillow backing.

Light Pink:
- Use patterns, pgs. 146 – 147, to cut:
  - 2 petals for medium flowers.
  - 1 petal for small flower.

Pink:
- Cut 2 strips 2 1/2" x 13 1/2.
- Cut 2 strips 2" x 12 1/2.
- Use patterns to cut:
  - 4 petals for medium flowers.
  - 2 petals for small flower.

Dark Pink:
- Use patterns to cut:
  - 2 petals for medium flowers.
  - 1 petal for small flower.
- Cut fabric square 12" x 12" for welting.

Yellow:
- Use pattern to cut:
  - 3 centers.

Green:
- Use patterns to cut:
  - 6 leaves in any combination.

Brown:
- Use patterns to cut:
  - 3 branches.

PIECING

Note: Use 3 strands of floss for all embroidery.

1. Fold 10" x 15" rectangle into quarters; press to mark placement guidelines and center.

2. Refer to **Pillow Top Diagram** to pin appliqués in place.

3. Using brown floss for branches, pink floss for flowers, green floss for leaves, and yellow floss for centers, refer to **Stitch Diagrams**, pgs. 255 – 256, to Blanket Stitch appliqués to background. Use brown floss to Stem Stitch detail lines in petals, Satin Stitch tips of petals, and Straight Stitch highlights in centers. Use green floss to Stem Stitch leaf stems and detail lines in leaves.

4. Trim appliquéd rectangle to 8 1/2" x 13 1/2".

5. Sew 2 1/2" x 13 1/2" strips to top and bottom of appliquéd rectangle. Sew remaining strips to sides of appliquéd rectangle.

6. Mark, layer, and quilt. Quilt in the ditch around all appliqués. Beginning with a diagonal line from corner to corner, stitch diagonal lines 7/8" apart across background and borders.

7. Follow **Pillow Finishing**, pg. 255, to make a welted pillow.

Pillow Top Diagram

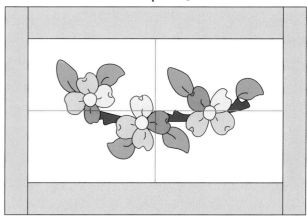

DOGWOOD WALL HANGING

(shown on pg. 141)

Finished Size: 21¹/₂ " x 21¹/₂"

FABRICS

Yardage is based on 45"w fabric.
- cream — ⁵/₈-yd
- light pink — ¹/₈-yd
- pink — ³/₈-yd
- dark pink — ¹/₈-yd
- yellow — ¹/₈-yd
- green — ¹/₈-yd
- brown — ¹/₈-yd
- fabric for binding — ¹/₂-yd

Other supplies
- batting — 45" x 60"
- embroidery floss — pink, yellow, green, and brown
- water-soluble fabric marking pen

*Refer to **Wall Hanging Diagram**, pg. 150, as needed. See **Quilter's Basics** (pg. 241) for more in-depth basic instructions.*

CUTTING

Cream:
- Cut fabric square 16" x 16" for top.
- Cut fabric square 23" x 23" for backing.
- Cut 2 strips 1¹/₂"w. Label each as A.
- Cut 2 strips 1¹/₂"w. Label as D and E.
- Cut fabric square 14¹/₂" x 14¹/₂" for binding.

Light Pink:
- Use patterns, pg. 147, to cut:
  - 2 petals for large flowers.
  - 4 petals for medium flowers.

Pink:
- Cut 4 strips 1¹/₂"w. Label two as B and two as C.
- Cut 1 strip 1¹/₂"w. Label as F.
- Use patterns, pg. 147, to cut:
  - 4 petals for large flower.
  - 8 petals for medium flower.

Dark Pink:
- Use patterns, pg. 147, to cut:
  - 2 petals for large flowers.
  - 4 petals for medium flowers.

Yellow:
- Use pattern, pg. 146, to cut:
  - 6 centers.

Green:
- Use patterns, pg. 147, to cut:
  - 9 leaves.

Brown:
- Use patterns, pg. 147, to cut:
- 6 branches.

PIECING

Note: Use 3 strands of floss for all embroidery.

1. Fold 16" square into quarters; press to mark placement guidelines and center. Using fabric marking pen, mark an 8" diameter circle in center of square.

2. Refer to **Wall Hanging Diagram** to pin appliqués in place.

3. Using brown floss for branches, pink floss for flowers, green floss for leaves, and yellow floss for centers, refer to **Stitch Diagrams**, pgs. 255 – 256, to Blanket Stitch appliqués to background. Use brown floss to Stem Stitch detail lines in petals, Satin Stitch tips of petals, and Straight Stitch highlights in centers. Use green floss to Stem Stitch leaf stems and detail lines in leaves.

4. Trim appliquéd square to 15¹/₂" x 15¹/₂".

5. Sew 1 each of strips A, B, and C together to make a Strip Set. Repeat with remaining A, B, and C. Cut across 1 strip set at 1¹/₂" intervals to make Unit 1's. Make 4 Unit 1's. Cut across strip sets at 15¹/₂" intervals to make Unit 2. Make 4 Unit 2's.

Strip Set

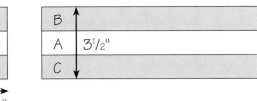

1¹/₂"

Unit 1 – make 4

Unit 2 – make 4

149

6. Sew strips D, E, and F together to make a Strip Set. Cut across strip set at 1½" intervals to make Unit 3's. Make 8 Unit 3's.

Strip Set

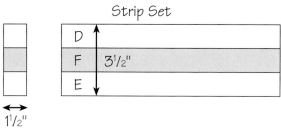

7. Sew 2 Unit 3's and 1 Unit 1 together to make a 9-patch block. Make 4 9-patch blocks.

9-Patch Block

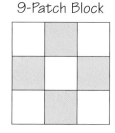

8. Sew 1 Unit 2 to each side of appliquéd square. Sew 1 9-patch block to each side of remaining Unit 2's; sew to top and bottom of appliquéd square.

FINISHING

1. Mark, layer, and quilt. Quilt in the ditch around all appliqués. Beginning with a diagonal line from corner to corner, stitch diagonal lines ⅞" apart in cream background. Quilt in the ditch along all borders.

2. Follow **Making a Hanging Sleeve**, pg. 254, to attach hanging sleeve to wall hanging.

3. Follow **Binding**, pg. 252, to bind wall hanging using a 17" square of binding fabric to make 2½-yds of 2½"w continuous bias binding with mitered corners.

Wall Hanging Diagram

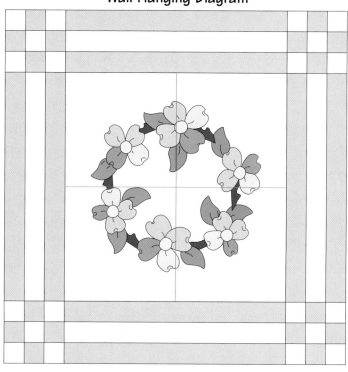

PALM LEAF PILLOW
(shown on pg. 143)

Finished Size: 14" square

FABRICS

Yardage is based on 45"w fabric.
• assorted pink, blue, yellow, green and purple prints
• white solid
• fabric for backing — ½-yd
Other supplies
• 14" pillow form

Refer to **Pillow Top Diagram**, pg. 151, as needed. See **Quilter's Basics** (pg. 241) for more in-depth basic instructions.

CUTTING

1. From each print, cut :
• 1 strip 2½"w. Randomly cut each strip in widths varying from 1½" to 4".

PIECING

1. Use patterns A and B, pg. 151, and follow **Foundation Piecing** (pg. 245) to paper piece Units A and B.

Unit A

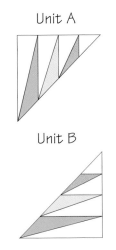

Unit B

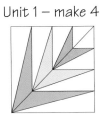

2. Sew Units together to complete Unit 1. Make 4 Unit 1's.

Unit 1 – make 4

3. Sew 4 Unit 1's together to complete Block.

FINISHING

1. For pieced borders, piece strips together to form 2 short borders 2$\frac{1}{2}$" x 10$\frac{1}{2}$" and two long borders 2$\frac{1}{2}$" x 14$\frac{1}{2}$".

2. Follow **Pillow Finishing**, pg. 255, to make a knife-edge pillow.

Pillow Top Diagram

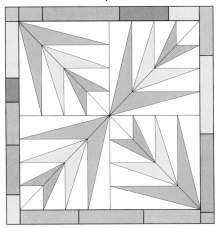

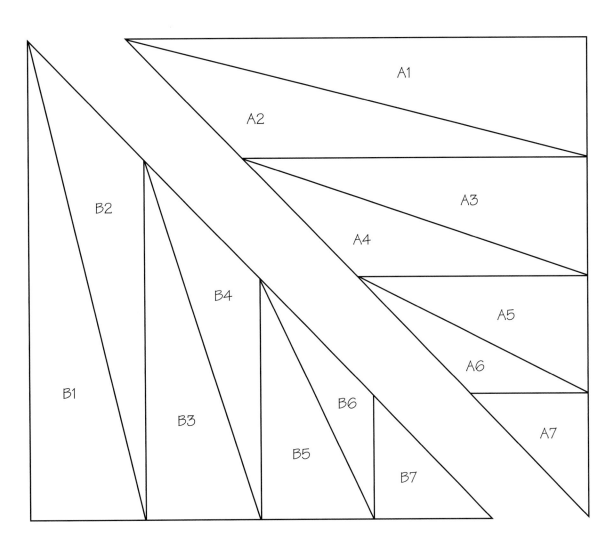

GRANDMOTHER'S FLOWER GARDEN PILLOW

(shown on pgs. 142 – 143)

Finished Size: 12" square

FABRICS

Yardage is based on 45"w fabric.
• yellow, pink, and blue prints — scraps
• white solid for background, backing and ruffle — 1-yd
• fabric for welting — ¹/₂-yd

Other supplies
• freezer paper
• ¹/₄" diameter cord
• 12" pillow form

*Refer to **Pillow Top Diagram** as needed. See **Quilter's Basics** (pg. 241) for more in-depth basic instructions.*

CUTTING

1. From freezer paper, use dashed line on pattern, pg. 153, to cut:
• 19 hexagons.
2. From each print, use solid line on pattern to cut:
• 1 yellow hexagon.
• 6 pink hexagons.
• 12 blue hexagons.
3. From white, cut:
• 2 squares 12¹/₂" x 12¹/₂" for background and backing.
• 3¹/₂"w bias strips for ruffle.

PIECING

1. Place 1 freezer paper hexagon on the wrong side of one fabric hexagon, with the waxy side of the freezer paper facing up. Use a warm, dry iron to press the seam allowances onto the paper. Repeat for remaining hexagons.

2. Matching right sides and all corners, place yellow and 1 pink hexagon together as shown in Fig. 1. Avoiding stitching through the paper, whipstitch two edges together from corner to corner along one side, backstitching at the beginning and end of the seam. Open pieces flat (Fig. 2).

Fig. 1

Fig. 2

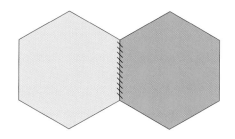

3. Continue adding pink hexagons to the yellow hexagon, one at a time, in the same manner to make Unit 1. It is not necessary to knot and clip your thread each time you reach the end of a hexagon side.

Unit 1

4. Sew a second ring of blue hexagons around Unit 1 to make Unit 2.

Unit 2

5. Remove the freezer paper from the hexagons. Following **Stitch Diagram,** pg. 255, to center and Blind Stitch Unit 2 to white background to make Pillow Top.

Pillow Top Diagram

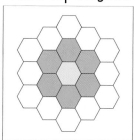

FINISHING

1. For ruffle, piece strips together to form 3¹/₂" x 120" ruffle.

2. Follow **Pillow Finishing**, pg. 255, to make a ruffled pillow with welting.

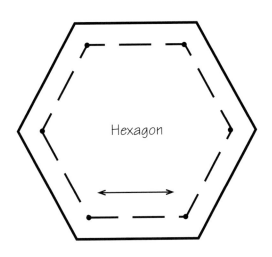

Hexagon

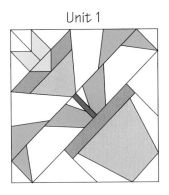

Unit 1

3. Sew 1 white triangle to each side of Unit 1 to complete Unit 2.

POT OF LILIES PILLOW

(shown on pg. 142)

Finished Size: 12" square

FABRICS

Yardage is based on 45"w fabric.
• assorted pink, blue, yellow, green and purple prints and solids
• white solid
• fabric for backing — $^3/_8$-yd
• fabric for welting — $^1/_2$-yd

Other supplies
• $^1/_4$" diameter cord
• 12" pillow form

Refer to **Pillow Top Diagram** as needed. See **Quilter's Basics** (pg. 241) for more in-depth basic instructions.

CUTTING

Purple Print:
• For Borders, cut:
  •2 strips 1$^1/_2$" x 10$^1/_2$" for side borders.
  •2 strips 1$^1/_2$" x 12$^1/_2$" for top and bottom borders.

White solid:
• For background, cut:
  •2 squares 5$^7/_8$" x 5$^7/_8$". Cut each square diagonally.

PIECING

1. Use patterns A-F, pgs. 154 – 155, and follow **Foundation Piecing** (pg. 245) to paper piece Units A-F.

2. Sew Units together to complete Unit 1.

Unit 2

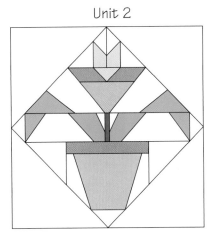

FINISHING

1. Sew side then top and bottom borders to Unit 2 to complete Pillow Top.

Pillow Top Diagram

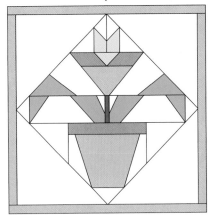

2. Follow **Pillow Finishing**, pg. 255, to make welted pillow.

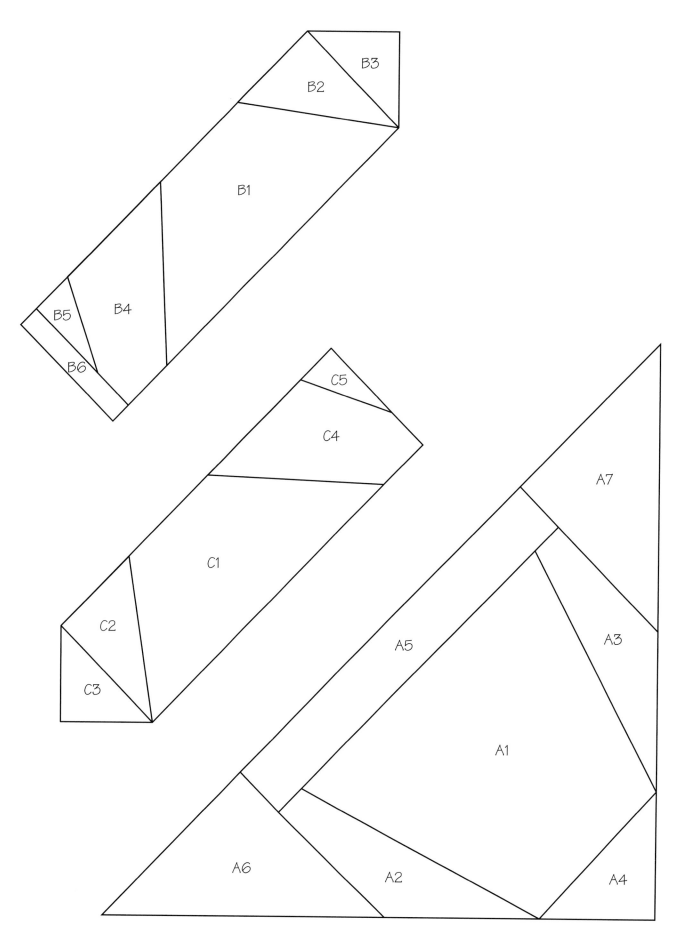

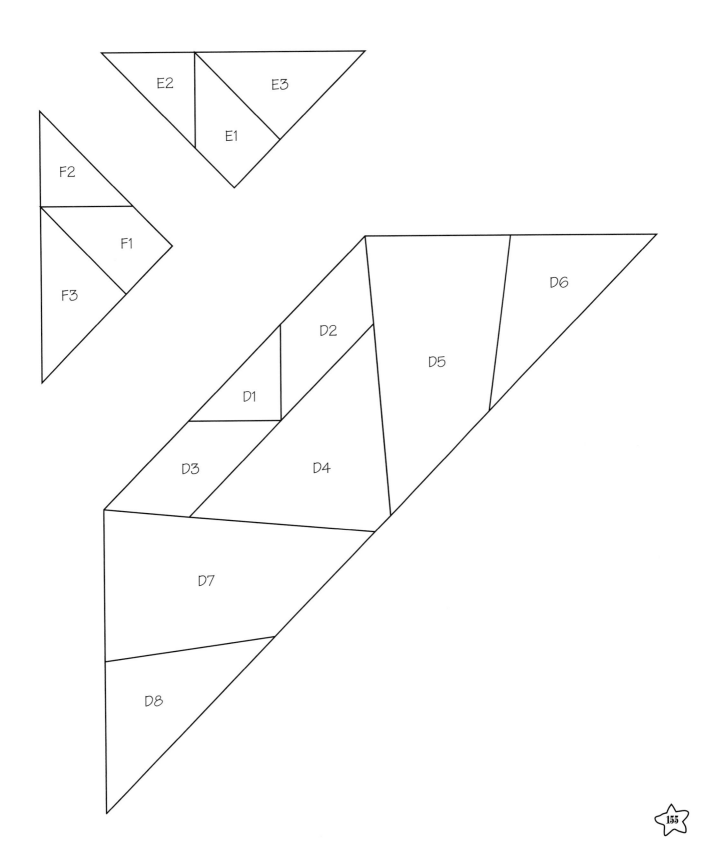

Little Baskets

Fabric scraps, thread spools, our best scissors and thimble...baskets are beautiful containers for all our favorite things. And some of our favorite baskets are right here on this charming chairback cover and tie-on napkin ring. Maybe you'd like to make a table set for each season simply by changing the fabric colors!

Chairback Cover, page 160; Napkin Ring, page 161.

Perfect with a setting of flowers and lace, the basket block design on this wall hanging is so sweet in shades of pink.

Little Baskets Wall Hanging, page 158.

LITTLE BASKETS WALL HANGING
(shown on pg. 157)

Finished size: 29"x43"
Block size: 5" square

FABRICS
• assorted brown prints for baskets – about 2-yds total
• assorted tan prints – about 2-yds total
• assorted pink prints for block backgrounds – about 2-yds total
• pink print for setting squares – ³/₄-yd
• dark pink print for inner border and binding – ²/₃-yd
• brown print for outer border – ¹/₂-yd
• backing – 1¹/₃-yds
Other supplies
• batting – 33"x47"

*Refer to **Wall Hanging Diagram**, pg. 160, as needed. See **Quilter's Basics** (pg. 241) for more in-depth basic instructions.*

CUTTING FOR _EACH_ OF 15 BLOCKS
One brown print:
• Cut one 1⁷/₈" strip. From this, cut:
    • 12 C's – Cut six 1⁷/₈" squares, then cut each in half once diagonally into 2 triangles.
• Cut 1 A – Cut one 2⁷/₈" square, then cut in half once diagonally into 2 triangles. Discard 1 triangle.
One tan print:
• Cut one 1⁷/₈" strip. From this, cut:
    • 4 D's – Cut two 1⁷/₈" squares, then cut each in half once diagonally into 2 triangles.
• Cut 1 B – Cut one 2⁷/₈" square, then cut in half once diagonally into 2 triangles. Discard 1 triangle.
• Cut 1 E – 1¹/₂" square.
One pink print:
• Cut one 1¹/₂"w strip. From this, cut:
    • 2 H's – 1¹/₂"x3¹/₂"
    • 1 G – 1¹/₂" square
• Cut one 1⁷/₈" strip. From this, cut:
    • 6 F's – Cut three 1⁷/₈" squares, then cut each in half once diagonally into 2 triangles.
• Cut one I – Cut one 2⁷/₈" square, then cut in half once diagonally into 2 triangles. Discard 1 triangle.

CUTTING FOR REMAINDER OF WALL HANGING
Pink print for setting squares:
• Cut two 5¹/₂"w strips. From these, cut:
    • 8 setting squares – 5¹/₂" square
• Cut one 8¹/₄" strip. From this, cut:
    • 12 side setting triangles – Cut three 8¹/₄" squares, then cut each twice diagonally into 4 triangles.
• Cut one 4³/₈" strip. From this, cut:
    • 4 corner setting triangles – Cut two 4³/₈" squares, then cut each once diagonally into 2 triangles.
Dark pink print:
• Cut four ³/₄"w strips. From these, cut:
    • 2 top/bottom inner borders – ³/₄"x22"
    • 2 side inner borders – ³/₄"x35¹/₂"
Brown print for outer border:
• Cut four 4"w strips. From these, cut:
    • 2 top/bottom borders – 4"x29"
    • 2 side borders – 4"x36"

PIECING EACH BLOCK A (MAKE 6)
1. Sew brown print A and tan print B together to make Unit 1.

Unit 1 – make 1

2. Sew 1 brown print C and 1 tan print D together to make each of 4 Unit 2's.

Unit 2 – make 4

3. Sew Unit 2's and tan print E together to make 1 Unit 3 and 1 Unit 4.

Unit 3 – make 1

Unit 4 – make 1

4. Sew Unit 1, Unit 3, and Unit 4 together to make Unit 5.

Unit 5 – make 1

5. Sew 1 brown print C and 1 pink print F together to make each of 6 Unit 6's.

Unit 6 – make 6

6. Sew Unit 6's and pink print G together to make Unit 7 and Unit 8.

Unit 7 – make 1

Unit 8 – make 1

7. Sew Unit 5, Unit 7, and Unit 8 together to make Unit 9.

Unit 9 – make 1

8. Sew 1 pink print H and 1 brown print C together to make Unit 10 and Unit 11.

Unit 10 – make 1

Unit 11 – make 1

9. Sew Unit 10, Unit 11, and pink print I to Unit 9 to complete Block A. Block should measure 5$\frac{1}{2}$" square.

Block A

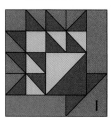

PIECING EACH BLOCK B (MAKE 9)

Follow Block A instructions, changing Units 3-5 to match those shown below.

Unit 3   Unit 4   Unit 5

Block B

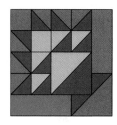

FINISHING

1. Follow **Assembly Diagram** to sew Blocks, setting squares, setting triangles, and corner triangles into diagonal rows. Sew rows together to make wall hanging center. Wall hanging center should measure 21$\frac{1}{2}$"x35$\frac{1}{2}$".

Assembly Diagram

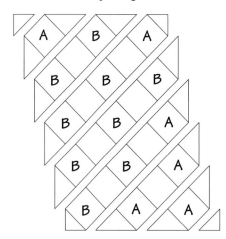

2. Sew side, then top and bottom inner borders to center. Repeat with outer borders to complete wall hanging top.

3. Mark, layer, and quilt using **Quilting Diagram** as a suggestion.

4. Bind wall hanging using 4^1/$_8$-yds of 2^1/$_2$"w bias binding.

Wall Hanging Diagram

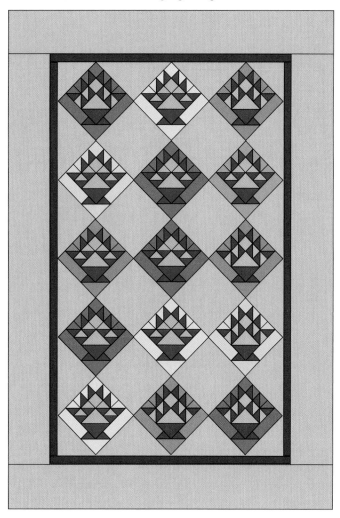

Quilting Diagram

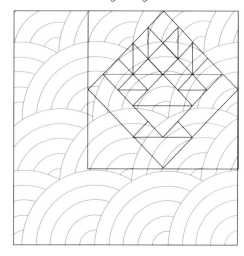

CHAIRBACK COVER
(shown on pg. 156)

Finished size: 11^1/$_2$"w

FABRICS
- brown print – fat quarter
- brown stripe for border and appliqués – fat quarter
- tan print – fat quarter
- pink print for block – fat quarter
- dark pink print for outer border – fat quarter
- maroon print for binding – fat quarter
- dark pink print and pink print for appliqués – scraps
- backing – fat quarter

Other supplies
- batting – 16"x20"
- paper-backed fusible web
- ^{1}/$_4$"w grosgrain ribbon – 1-yd

Refer to **Chairback Cover Diagram** *as needed. See* **Quilter's Basics** *(pg. 241) for more in-depth basic instructions.*

INSTRUCTIONS
1. Follow *Cutting and Piecing Block A* instructions (Little Baskets Wall Hanging, pg. 158) to make 1 Block.

2. For inner border, cut the following from brown stripe: one 1"x5^1/$_2$" strip, two 1"x6" strips, and one 1"x6^1/$_2$" strip. Beginning with shortest strip and working clockwise, sew one strip to each edge of block.

3. For outer border, cut the following from pink print: two 1^1/$_2$"x6^1/$_2$" strips and two 1^1/$_2$"x8^1/$_2$" strips. Sew short strips to opposite sides of block and long strips to remaining sides. Block should measure 8^1/$_2$" square.

4. Cut the following pieces from tan print: one 6^1/$_2$" square and one 8^7/$_8$" square; cut each in half once diagonally to form 2 small and 2 large triangles. Discard 1 large triangle.

5. Sew a small triangle to top left and top right edges of block, then sew large triangle to long edge of pieced area to complete chairback cover top.

6. For flower appliqué, trace patterns (this page) onto paper side of web. Fuse patterns to scraps. Cut out appliqués; fuse to large triangle.

7. Mark, layer, and quilt chairback cover as desired. (We outline quilted around outer edge of inner border, around each appliqué, and down center of leaf appliqués; we then quilted 5 arcs 1/2" apart on each small triangle.)

8. Bind chairback cover using 1 1/4-yds of 1 1/2"w bias binding and a scant 1/4" seam allowance.

9. Press chairback cover in half along long edge of large triangle. Cut ribbon in half. Sew center of 1 ribbon to each top corner of chairback cover.

diagonally (discard 1 triangle); and six 3/4" squares cut in half once diagonally to make 12 small triangles.

3. For base, fuse pink squares (right sides out) together with fleece sandwiched between.

4. Bind edges of base with 1 1/2"w straight-grain binding (see **Binding** instructions, pg. 252).

5. Arrange remaining print pieces on 1 side of base to make basket design; fuse in place. Stitch over all raw edges using clear thread and a narrow zigzag stitch with a medium stitch length.

6. Cut ribbon in half. Sew 1 end of each ribbon to side corners of binding. Sew buttons on top of ribbon ends. Tie ribbon ends around napkin.

Chairback Cover Diagram

Napkin Ring Diagram

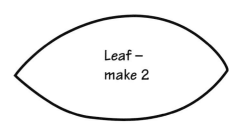

Leaf – make 2

NAPKIN RING

(shown on pg. 156)

Finished size: 4" square

SUPPLIES
- pink print, tan print, brown print — scraps
- red print for binding — 1/8-yd
- fusible craft fleece
- clear nylon thread
- 2 buttons
- 1/4"w grosgrain ribbon — 1/4-yd

INSTRUCTIONS

1. Fuse web to wrong side of pink, tan, and brown prints.

2. Cut the following pieces:
- pink print — two 4" squares
- tan print — one 2 1/4" square
- brown print — one 1 1/2" square cut in half once

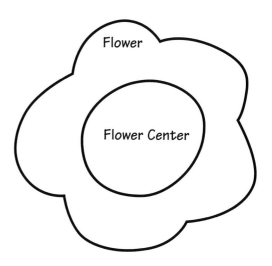

Flower

Flower Center

Picture Perfect Quilts

Kate, Holly and Mary Elizabeth have a terrific idea for remembering all those special occasions…quilted wall hangings…a snap to make with color transfers of photographs and artwork! Choose any subject: an anniversary, the first day of school, a favorite holiday or family vacation.

Make a family photo calendar: Select snapshots for each month of the year and make color copies. You may want to use one photo per month, or you can make a collage for each month. Arrange and glue on a ready-made wall calendar, then fill in family birthdays, anniversaries and events. You can also take your photos to a print shop and let them make a custom-designed calendar for you.

Artwork Wall Hanging, page 164.

Remembered Joys are never past.

— James Montgomery

Anniversary Wall Hanging, page 165.

163

ARTWORK WALL HANGING
(shown on pg. 162)

FABRICS
- white solid
- assorted fabrics for frames
- assorted fabrics for backgrounds
- fabric for inner border
- fabric for outer border
- fabric for backing
- fabric for binding

Other supplies
- batting – 45" x 60"
- child's artwork and/or photographs
- photograph transfer paper — for color copiers **or** for inkjet printers
- desired embellishments

Refer to **Wall Hanging Top Diagram** *as needed. See* **Quilter's Basics** *(pg. 241) for more in-depth basic instructions.*

PIECING
Use $1/4$" seam allowances throughout.

1. Follow manufacturer's instructions to transfer artwork and/or photos to white fabric; trim to desired sizes, allowing $1/4$" seam allowance on each side.

2. To frame each piece of artwork, cut side frame strips the same length as sides of artwork and the desired width. (Our frame strips were cut $1^3/4$"w for a $1^1/4$" finished frame.) Sew frame strips to sides. Cut top and bottom frame strips the length of top and the desired width. Sew frame strips to top and bottom.

3. Working on a flat surface, arrange framed artwork in rows as desired. (**Hint:** The artwork will be easier to work with if the framed artwork in each row is the same height.) Some fabric backgrounds may need to be cut to complete rows. Determine size needed and add seam allowances.

4. Sew framed artwork and backgrounds together to complete rows. Sew rows together to complete center of wall hanging.

5. Embellish as desired. We added our budding artist's photo by sewing frame strips to each side of the photo, pressing under raw edges, and topstitching it in place. We sewed buttons to each corner. She signed her work and drew a perky little flower on one of our fabric backgrounds and we Backstitched over her signature using 3 strands of embroidery floss. Our little artist had experimented with crayon shavings melted between two layers of waxed paper and framed with a construction paper heart. We copied the heart, cut it out, Blanket Stitched it to the wall hanging, and added a ribbon bow and button for just the right finishing touch.

6. Cut inner top and bottom borders as long as the center of the wall hanging and the desired width. (Our borders were cut $1^1/4$"w for a $3/4$" finished border.) Sew borders to top and bottom. Cut inner side borders as long as the center of the wall hanging with borders added and the desired width. Sew borders to sides.

7. Cut outer top and bottom borders as long as the center of the wall hanging with inner borders added and the desired width. (Our borders were cut $2^3/4$"w for a $2^1/4$" finished border.) Sew borders to top and bottom. Cut outer side borders as long as the center of the wall hanging with borders added and the desired width. Sew borders to sides.

FINISHING

1. Mark, layer, and quilt wall hanging. We quilted in the ditch around all artwork, frames, and borders.

2. Follow **Making a Hanging Sleeve**, pg. 254, to attach hanging sleeve to wall hanging.

3. Follow **Binding**, pg. 252, to bind wall hanging using $2^1/2$"w continuous bias binding with mitered corners.

Wall Hanging Top Diagram

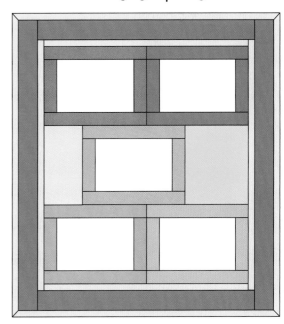

ANNIVERSARY WALL HANGING

(shown on pg. 163)

Finished Size: 39¹/₂" x 39¹/₂"

FABRICS

Yardage is based on 45"w fabric.
- white solid — ¹/₂-yd
- yellow solid — ¹/₄-yd
- small yellow print for outer borders — 1-yd
- yellow floral print — ¹/₂-yd
- light blue print for vines — ⁵/₈-yd
- medium blue print — ⁵/₈-yd
- dark blue print for inner borders — ³/₄-yd
- fabric for backing — 1¹/₄-yds
- fabric for binding — ⁵/₈-yd

Other supplies
- batting – 45" x 60"
- photographs
- photo transfer paper — for color copiers **or** for inkjet printers
- embroidery floss — blue
- black permanent fabric marker
- template plastic

*Refer to **Wall Hanging Top Diagram,** pg. 166, as needed. See **Quilter's Basics** (pg. 241) for more in-depth basic instructions.*

CUTTING
White Solid:
- Cut 10 squares 4¹/₂" x 4¹/₂".
- Cut 4 squares 6" x 6".
Yellow Solid:
- Cut 4 strips 1³/₄"w.
- Cut 2 squares 4" x 4".
Small Yellow Print:
- Cut 2 rectangles 8" x 24".
- Cut 2 rectangles 8" x 39".
Yellow Floral Print:
- Cut 4 strips 1³/₄"w.
- Use patterns, pg. 167, and follow **Preparing Appliqué Pieces**, page 247, to make the following appliqués.
- 8 small leaves
- 4 large leaves

Light Blue Print:
- Refer to **Making Continuous Bias Strip Binding,** pg. 252, to cut 1¹/₂" w strips 4¹/₂ yds long.
Medium Blue Print:
- Cut 4 strips 1³/₄"w.
- Use patterns to make the following appliqués.
  - 12 small flowers
  - 4 large flowers
Dark Blue Print:
- Cut 2 strips 1" x 23".
- Cut 2 strips 1" x 24".

PIECING

1. Follow manufacturer's instructions to transfer photographs to white fabric squares.

2. Sew 2 medium blue print strips and 1 yellow solid strip together to make Strip Set A. Make 2 Strip Set A's. Cut across Strip Sets at 4¹/₄" intervals to make Unit 1's. Make 18 Unit 1's.

Strip Set A

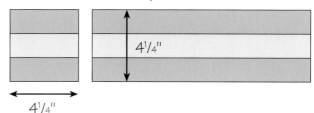

Unit 1 – make 18

3. Sew 2 yellow floral print strips and 1 yellow solid strip together to make Strip Set B. Make 2 Strip Set B's. Cut across Strip Sets at 4¹/₄" intervals to make Unit 2. Make 18 Unit 2's.

Strip Set B

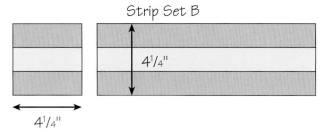

Unit 2 – make 18

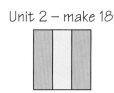

4. Sew 3 Unit 1's and 3 Unit 2's together to make a Row. Make 6 rows.

Row – make 6

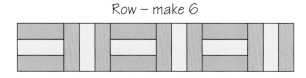

5. Sew Rows together to make Unit 3.

Unit 3

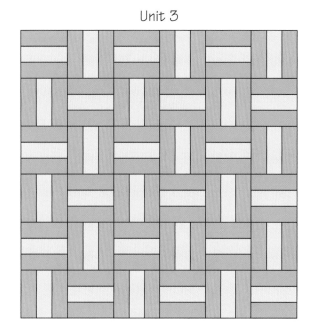

6. Sew dark blue print strips to each side of Unit 3. Sew remaining inner border strips to top and bottom.

7. Sew small yellow print rectangles to each side of Unit 3. Sew remaining outer border strips to top and bottom.

8. Cut 2 4" diameter circles from solid yellow fabric squares. Refer to **Stitch Diagrams**, pgs. 255 – 256, to Chain Stitch year using 3 strands of floss. Scatter French Knots around numbers using 3 strands of floss.

9. Fold bias strip for vine in half lengthwise; stitch ¹/₄" from long raw edges. Press strip with seam allowance centered on 1 side. Cut vine into 4 equal pieces.

10. Cut 3³/₄" circles for small flowers and 5³/₈" circles for large flowers from transferred photos.

11. Follow **Needle-Turn Appliqué**, pg. 248, to appliqué photos to centers of flowers; appliqué vine, leaves, and flowers to border.

FINISHING

1. Mark, layer, and quilt wall hanging. Quilt-in-the-ditch around all rectangles in center, along each side of inner border, and around all flowers, leaves, and vines.

2. Follow **Making a Hanging Sleeve**, pg. 254, to attach hanging sleeve to wall hanging.

3. Follow **Binding,** pg. 252, to bind wall hanging using a 22" square of binding fabric to make 4¹/₂-yds of 2¹/₂"w continuous bias binding with mitered corners.

4. Have friends use black permanent pen to write their sentiments on the solid yellow rectangles of the quilt.

Wall Hanging Top Diagram

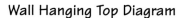

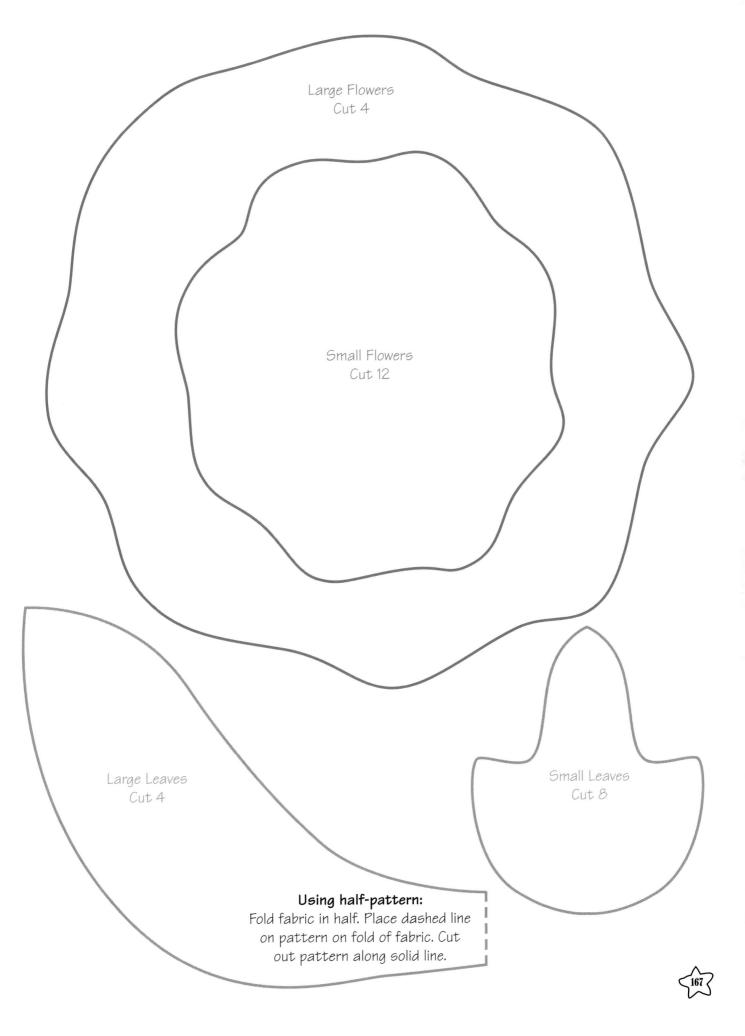

Large Flowers
Cut 4

Small Flowers
Cut 12

Large Leaves
Cut 4

Small Leaves
Cut 8

Using half-pattern:
Fold fabric in half. Place dashed line
on pattern on fold of fabric. Cut
out pattern along solid line.

Cheery Cherry Nursery

*G*reet baby with an "orchard" of appliquéd cherries...Mary Elizabeth's favorite! We combined traditional print fabrics with an open fruit-print plaid for a fresh, cheerful look that's suitable for both girls and boys. The adorable wall hanging features appliquéd blocks alternated with traditional Nine-Patches, and the crib set is easy to piece together.

Cheery Cherry Wall Hanging, page 174.

Cheery Cherry Crib Quilt, page 177; Bumper Pads, page 181.

Favorite Country Friends® baby gifts: A baby's cup, the softest blankie imaginable, personalized "Thank-You" notes printed with baby's name, a keepsake photo frame, a sterling locket engraved with baby's name and birthdate, a collection of classic lullabies on compact disc and a hand-painted toy box.

Babies
are always more
trouble
~than you thought~
and more
Wonderful.
—CHARLES OSGOOD

Mother and baby will be spending a lot of time in the nursery, so make it especially cozy and inviting. Rocking baby will be even more relaxing with a comfy cushion for the rocking chair, and the changing pad cover can be easily removed for washing.

If you just can't bear to pack away baby's extra-special outfits, display them! They can be mounted in a shadowbox frame or clipped on a tiny clothesline…or snippets of worn-out clothes can be pieced together to make a sweet quilt or wall hanging full of memories.

Chair Pad, page 181.

Cheery Cherry Changing Pad Cover, page 183; Cheery Cherry Valance, page 184.

"A child should always say what's true
And speak when he is spoken to,
And behave mannerly at the table:
At least as far as he is able."

— Robert Louis Stevenson

Why buy all-new furniture when you can hand down a treasured piece from your own childhood? It's easy to make everything coordinate! Simply paint the pieces the same color and cover with matching fabric. A colorful throw pillow completes the collection…for a boy, you could omit the ruffle and finish the pillow with a knife-edge, or add welting.

Fabric-Covered Dresser, page 184.

Cheery Cherry Pillow, page 185.

The good things in Life are not to be had SINGLY; but come to us with a MIXTURE.
— anonymous —

Fabric scraps can be used to create a photo frame, and it's oh-so easy! Find a flat, white wooden frame (or paint one), cut fabric strips a little narrower than the frame borders and fuse or glue in place. Glue big, bright buttons to the corners and add a bow, if you like.

"The best way to make children good is to make them happy."

— Oscar Wilde

Start a keepsake collection for a little one. You can use a toy box, trunk, blanket chest…it doesn't matter what you use, what's important is what's inside. Some ideas: Grandma's embroidered hankies, tried & true favorite recipes, a handed-down quilt, scrapbooks, special cards & letters and family photos.

CHEERY CHERRY WALL HANGING

(shown on pg. 168)

Finished Size: 33" x 33"

FABRICS

Yardage is based on 45"w fabric.
- white — 3/8-yd
- pink stripe — 1/4-yd
- pink check — 1/4-yd
- blue polka-dot — 1/4-yd
- pink print — 1/4-yd
- blue plaid — 5/8-yd
- green, dark green, and red fabrics for appliqués
- fabric for backing — 1 1/4-yds
- fabric for binding — 1/2-yd

Other supplies
- batting — 45" x 60"
- paper-backed fusible web

*Refer to **Wall Hanging Diagram**, pg. 175, as needed. See **Quilter's Basics** (pg. 241) for more in-depth basic instructions.*

CUTTING
White:
- Cut 4 squares 7 1/2" x 7 1/2".
- Cut 1 strip 3"w.

Pink Stripe:
- Cut 1 strip 2 3/4"w.

Pink Check:
- Cut 1 strip 2 3/4"w.

Blue Polka-dot:
- Cut 2 strips 2 3/4"w.
- Cut 1 strip 3"w.

Pink Print:
- Cut 4 strips 1 3/4"w. From these strips cut:
  - 2 strips 1 3/4" x 21 1/2".
  - 2 strips 1 3/4" x 24".

Blue Plaid:
- Cut 4 strips 5"w. From these strips cut:
  - 2 strips 5" x 24".
  - 2 strips 5" x 33".

Green, dark green, and red:
- Use patterns, pg. 176, and follow **Preparing Appliqué Pieces**, pg. 247, to make the following appliqués:
  - 8 cherries.
  - 4 cherry stems.
  - 8 leaves.

PIECING

1. Follow manufacturer's instructions to fuse appliqués to white squares.

2. Follow **Satin Stitch Appliqué**, pg. 248, to appliqué cherries, stems, and leaves.

3. To make 9-patch blocks, sew pink stripe strip, 3"w blue polka-dot strip, and pink check strip together to make Strip Set A. Cut 10 2 3/4"w Unit 1's from strip set. Repeat with remaining polka dot strips and white strip to make Strip Set B and cut 5 3"w Unit 2's.

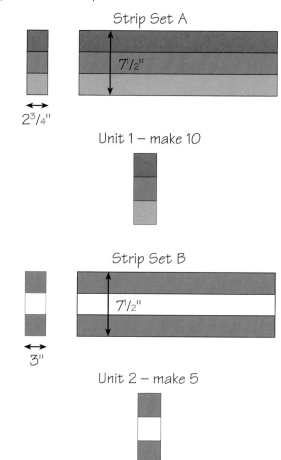

Strip Set A

7 1/2"

2 3/4"

Unit 1 — make 10

Strip Set B

7 1/2"

3"

Unit 2 — make 5

4. Sew 2 Unit 1's and 1 Unit 2 together to make 5 9-patch blocks.

5. Sew 2 9-patch blocks and 1 appliquéd square together to complete Unit 3. Make 2 Unit 3's.

Unit 3 – make 2

6. Sew 2 appliquéd squares and 1 9-patch block together to complete Unit 4.

Unit 4

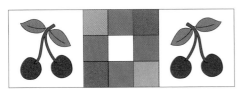

7. Sew Units 3 and 4 together to make Unit 5.

Unit 5

8. Sew pink print strips to sides, then top and bottom of background.

9. Sew plaid strips to sides, then top and bottom of background.

FINISHING

1. Mark, layer, and quilt. Quilt in the ditch on each side of the pink border. Outline quilt $1/8$" from edges of cherry clusters. Echo quilt twice around each cherry cluster $1/4$" apart. Quilt an "X" across each blue polka-dot square in each 9-patch block. Quilt motifs in remaining squares in each 9-patch block. Beginning in center, place curved edge of scallop pattern, pg. 176, along raw edge of border and mark scalloped cutting line along border. Echo quilt marked line 1" apart twice along border.

2. Trim along marked line.

3. Follow **Making Continuous Bias Strip Binding**, pg. 252, and use a 16" square of binding fabric to make $6^{1}/2$-yds of $1^{1}/4$"w continuous bias binding. Press one raw edge of binding $1/4$" to wrong side. Match remaining raw edge to raw edge of quilt top and sew binding around quilt. To sew around scallops, pin binding to one scallop at a time as you sew. Gently ease binding around outer curves, being careful not to stretch it. At junctions between scallops, raise presser foot to turn the corner, keeping the fabric as smooth as possible. Trim batting and backing even with quilt top. Blindstitch binding to quilt backing.

Wall Hanging Diagram

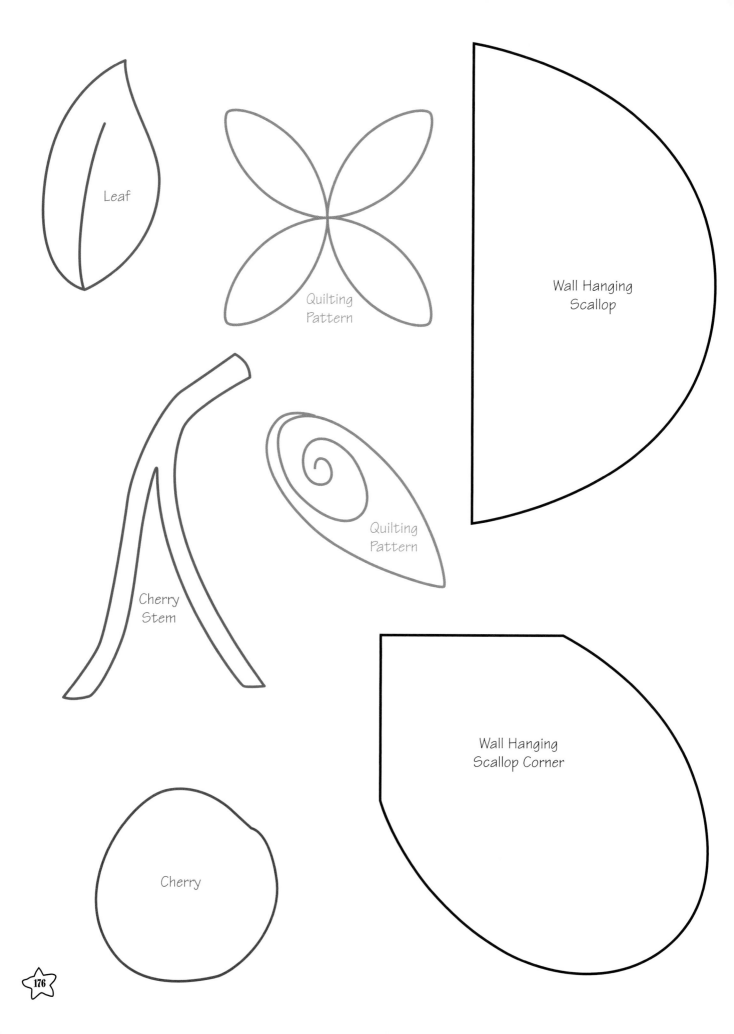

Leaf

Quilting Pattern

Wall Hanging Scallop

Cherry Stem

Quilting Pattern

Wall Hanging Scallop Corner

Cherry

CHEERY CHERRY CRIB QUILT

(shown on pg. 169)

Finished Size: 39¹/₂" x 47¹/₂"

FABRICS

Yardage is based on 45"w fabric.
• white — 1-yd
• pink print — ³/₈-yd
• blue plaid — 1-yd
• green, dark green, and red fabrics for appliqués
• fabric for backing and hanging sleeve — 1¹/₂-yds
• fabric for binding — ¹/₂-yd

Other supplies
• batting — 45" x 60"
• paper-backed fusible web
• embroidery floss — blue
• hot iron transfer pencil
• tracing paper

Refer to **Quilt Top Diagram** *as needed. See* **Quilter's Basics** *(pg. 241) for more in-depth basic instructions.*

CUTTING
White:
• For background, cut 1 rectangle 23" x 31".
Pink Print:
• Cut 4 strips 1³/₄"w. From these strips cut:
  • 2 strips 1³/₄" x 31".
  • 2 strips 1³/₄" x 25¹/₂".
Blue Plaid:
• Cut 4 strips 7¹/₂"w. From these strips cut:
  • 2 strips 7¹/₂" x 33¹/₂".
  • 2 strips 7¹/₂" x 39¹/₂".
Green, dark green, and red:
• Use patterns, pg. 176, and follow **Preparing Appliqué Pieces**, pg. 247, to make the following appliqués:
  • 14 cherries.
  • 7 cherry stems.
  • 10 leaves.

PIECING
1. Follow manufacturer's instructions to fuse appliqués to background.

2. Follow **Satin Stitch Appliqué**, pg. 248, to appliqué cherries, stems, and leaves.

3. Following manufacturer's instructions, use hot iron transfer pencil and patterns, pgs. 178 – 179, to transfer verse to background. Refer to **Stitch Diagram**, pg. 256, to Stem Stitch verse.

4. Sew pink print strips to sides, then top and bottom of background.

5. Sew plaid strips to sides, then top and bottom of background.

FINISHING
1. Mark, layer, and quilt. Quilt in the ditch on each side of the pink border. Outline quilt ¹/₈" from edges of cherry clusters. Echo quilt around each cherry cluster ¹/₄" apart. Beginning in center, place curved edge of scallop patterns, pg. 180, along raw edge of border and mark scalloped cutting line along border. Echo quilt marked line 1" apart twice.

2. Trim along marked line.

3. Follow **Making Continuous Bias Strip Binding**, pg. 252, and use an 18" square of binding fabric to make 7¹/₂-yds of 1¹/₄"w continuous bias binding. Press one raw edge of binding ¹/₄" to wrong side. Match remaining raw edge to raw edge of quilt top and sew binding around quilt. To sew around scallops, pin binding to one scallop at a time as you sew. Gently ease binding around outer curves, being careful not to stretch it. At junctions between scallops, raise presser foot to turn the corner, keeping the fabric as smooth as possible. Trim backing and batting even with edges of quilt top. Blindstitch back of binding to quilt backing.

Quilt Top Diagram

Looking for A for sweet ripe berry

Cheery

cherry

Baby's

merry

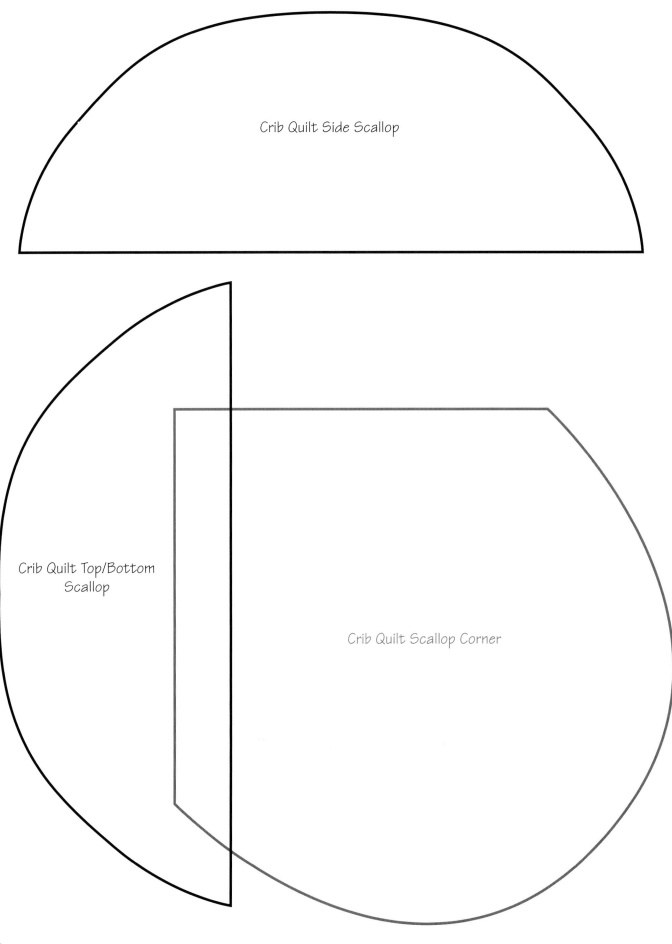

Crib Quilt Side Scallop

Crib Quilt Top/Bottom
Scallop

Crib Quilt Scallop Corner

BUMPER PADS

(shown on pg. 169)

Finished Size: Our bumper pads fit a standard (27" x 52") baby crib.

FABRICS

Yardage is based on 45"w fabric.
• white — 2½-yds
• blue print — 2½-yds
• green, dark green, and red fabrics for appliqués

Other supplies
• 72"w upholstery batting — 2½-yds
• paper-backed fusible web

CUTTING

White:
• For panels, cut 4 rectangles 8" x 80".

Blue Print:
• Cut 8 lengthwise strips 2½"w. From these strips cut:
  • 8 strips 2½" x 80".
• For ties, cut 16 strips 2" x 16".

Green, dark green, and red:
• Use patterns, pg. 176, and follow **Preparing Appliqué Pieces**, pg. 247, to make the following appliqués:
  • 64 cherries.
  • 32 cherry stems.
  • 64 leaves.

Batting:
• Cut 2 rectangles 12" x 80".

PIECING

1. Sew 1 strip each to top and bottom edges of each panel.

2. Fuse 8 clusters of cherries to each panel. Follow **Satin Stitch Appliqué**, pg. 248, to appliqué cherries, stems, and leaves.

3. For ties, press each edge of strip ¼" to wrong side; press strip in half lengthwise. Stitch along long edges. Fold each tie in half.

4. Referring to Fig. 1 (appliqués are not shown), mark each long edge of 2 Panels 26½" from ends. Lightly draw a line between marks across width of panel. Baste folded ends of ties as shown, adjusting location of ties at marks to fit the bed if necessary.

Fig. 1

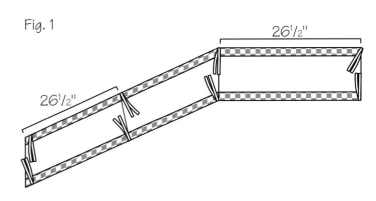

5. Matching right sides and raw edges, place 1 panel with ties together with 1 panel without ties. Place 1 batting rectangle on top of panels; pin all layers together. Using a ½" seam allowance and sewing through all layers, sew panels together, leaving an opening for turning. Trim corners and turn right side out. Whipstitch opening closed.

6. Stitch across width of bumper panels (through all layers) along lines marked in Step 4.

7. Repeat Steps 3-6 to complete remaining pad.

CHAIR PAD

(shown on pg. 170)

Finished Size: 14" x 25"

FABRICS

Yardage is based on 45"w fabric.
• white — ¼-yd
• pink stripe — ¼-yd
• pink check — ¼-yd
• blue polka-dot — ¼-yd
• blue plaid — ¼-yd
• green, dark green, and red fabrics for appliqués
• fabric for backing and ties — ¾-yd
• fabric for binding — ½-yd

Other supplies
• 72"w upholstery batting — ½-yd
• paper-backed fusible web

Refer to **Chair Pad Top Diagram**, pg. 182, as needed. See **Quilter's Basics** (pg. 241) for more in-depth basic instructions.

CUTTING

White:
- Cut square 8" x 8".

Pink Stripe:
- Cut 1 strip 3"w. From this strip, cut:
  - 4 rectangles 3" x 3½".

Pink Check:
- Cut 1 strip 3"w. From this strip, cut:
  - 4 rectangles 3" x 3½".

Blue Polka-dot:
- Cut 1 strip 3½"w. From this strip, cut:
  - 4 squares 3½" x 3½".
- Cut 1 strip 3"w. From this strip, cut:
  - 4 rectangles 3" x 3½".

Blue Plaid:
- Cut 1 strip 6"w. From this strip cut:
  - 2 rectangles 6" x 14".
- For ties, cut 2 strips 2" x 16".

Green, dark green, and red:
- Use patterns, pg. 176, and follow **Preparing Appliqué Pieces**, pg. 247, to make the following appliqués:
  - 2 cherries.
  - 1 cherry stem.
  - 2 leaves.

PIECING

1. Follow manufacturer's instructions to fuse appliqués to white square.

2. Follow **Satin Stitch Appliqué**, pg. 248, to appliqué cherries, stem, and leaves.

3. Beginning and ending with a square, sew 2 polka-dot squares, 1 pink checked rectangle, 1 polka-dot rectangle, and 1 pink striped rectangle together to make Unit 1. Make 2 Unit 1's. Sew 1 pink checked rectangle, 1 blue polka-dot rectangle, and 1 pink striped rectangle together to make Unit 2. Make 2 Unit 2's.

Unit 1 – make 2

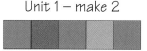

Unit 2 – make 2

4. Sew Unit 2's to each side of appliquéd block to make Unit 3.

Unit 3

5. Sew Unit 1's to Unit 3 to make Unit 4.

Unit 4

6. Sew borders to top and bottom of Unit 4.

FINISHING

1. Mark, layer, and quilt. Outline quilt ⅛" from edges of cherry clusters. Echo quilt twice around each cherry cluster ¼" apart. Quilt in the ditch around appliquéd block. Quilt an "X" across each small square. Quilt straight lines 2" apart on top and bottom borders.

2. For ties, press each edge of strip ¼" to wrong side; press strip in half lengthwise. Stitch along long edges. Fold each tie in half.

3. Referring to **Chair Pad Top Diagram**, baste folded ends of ties to back of chair pad.

4. Refer to **Binding**, pg. 252, to bind wall hanging using a 14" square of binding fabric to make 2¼-yds of 2½"w continuous bias binding with mitered corners.

Chair Pad Top Diagram

CHEERY CHERRY CHANGING PAD COVER

(shown on pg. 171)

Block Size: 10" x 10"

FABRICS

Yardage is based on 45"w fabric.
• white — ⅛-yd
• pink stripe — ⅛-yd **each**
• pink check — ⅛-yd
• blue polka-dot — ⅛-yd
• blue check print for borders, sashing, and
  backing — 1-yd

Other supplies
• changing pad
• safety pins

*See **Quilter's Basics** (pg. 241) for more in-depth basic
instructions.*

CUTTING
White:
• Cut 2 squares 3⅞" x 3⅞".

Pink Prints:
• From each pink print, cut 1 strip 3⅞"w. From each
strip, cut:
  •4 squares 3⅞" x 3⅞".

Blue Polka-dot:
• Cut 1 strip 3⅞"w. From this strip, cut:
  •8 squares 3⅞" x 3⅞".

Blue Check Print:
• Cut 1 sashing strip 3" x 10⅝".
• Cut 2 end borders 10⅝" x 12".

PIECING

1. Sew 2 pink print squares to 1 blue polka-dot square
to make Unit 1. Make 4 Unit 1's.

Unit 1 – make 4

2. Sew 2 blue polka-dot squares to 1 white square to
make Unit 2. Make 2 Unit 2's.

Unit 2 – make 2

3. Sew 2 Unit 1's and 1 Unit 2 together to make Block.
Make 2 Blocks.

Block – make 2

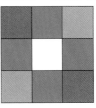

4. Sew 2 end borders, 2 blocks, and 1 sashing strip
together to make Unit 3.

Unit 3

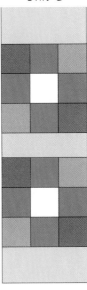

5. Measure width and length of changing pad. **To
determine width of side border strip,** subtract 10⅝"
from width of changing pad. **To determine length of
side border strip,** add 12" to length of changing pad.
Cut 2 side border strips the determined
measurements. Sew side borders to Unit 3.

6. Cut backing same size as changing pad cover top.
Matching right sides and raw edges, sew top to
backing along long sides to form a tube; turn.

7. To hem each end, press raw edge ¼" to wrong side;
press to wrong side again. Sew along folded edges.

8. Place changing pad in tube. Fold ends to back and
pin.

CHEERY CHERRY VALANCE

(shown on pg. 171)

Finished Size: $15\frac{1}{2}$" long

FABRICS

- white
- pink print
- blue plaid

Other supplies

- $\frac{3}{4}$" curtain rod
- tracing paper
- removable fabric marking pen

INSTRUCTIONS

1. To determine size to cut white fabric for scallops:
Mount curtain rod outside window frame. Measure width of window from bracket to bracket. Multiply this measurement by $1\frac{1}{2}$. Find a number slightly more or less that is divisible by $6\frac{3}{4}$.

Example: Window is 38"w. Multiply by $1\frac{1}{2}$. Answer is 57. Find the number closest to 57 that is divisible by $6\frac{3}{4}$ to achieve a whole number. Divide 54 by $6\frac{3}{4}$ to make 8 scallops. Divide $60\frac{3}{4}$ by $6\frac{3}{4}$ to make 9 scallops. Either number of scallops will work. Decide whether you want 8 scallops or 9 scallops. An uneven number usually looks nice.

After deciding measurement, add 1" for seam allowances. Cut 2 strips of white fabric 6"w and the determined length.

2. Cut blue plaid fabric 16"w and the length determined in Step 1. Cut pink print fabric $1\frac{1}{4}$"w and the length determined in Step 1.

3. Trace Crib Quilt Side Scallop pattern, pg. 180, onto tracing paper. On wrong side of 1 white fabric strip draw a line $3\frac{3}{4}$" from 1 long edge. Placing curved edge of pattern along drawn line and allowing $\frac{1}{2}$" on each end for seam allowance, use fabric marking pen to draw scallops end to end on white fabric.

4. Matching right sides and raw edges and sewing $\frac{1}{2}$" from straight edges on each end, sew white strips together along drawn line. Trim $\frac{1}{4}$" from stitching line. Clip curves, turn, and press.

5. Press 1 long edge of pink print fabric $\frac{1}{4}$" to wrong side. Matching wrong side of pink print strip to right side of blue plaid rectangle and aligning lower raw edges, topstitch folded edge of pink print to blue plaid.

6. To hem sides, press short sides of blue plaid rectangle $\frac{1}{4}$" to wrong side; press $\frac{1}{4}$" to wrong side again. Stitch along folded edges.

7. Matching right side of pink print to right side of scallop front, stitch scallop to rectangle using a $\frac{1}{4}$" seam allowance. Press seam allowance toward scallop.

8. Enclosing raw edge of pink print in scallop, whipstitch back of scallop to back of pink print over raw edges.

9. Press remaining edge of blue plaid fabric $\frac{1}{4}$" to wrong side. Press $3\frac{1}{4}$" to wrong side again. Topstitch along lower folded edge. Topstitch $1\frac{3}{8}$" from top edge to form casing.

FABRIC-COVERED DRESSER

(shown on pg. 172)

SUPPLIES

- wooden dresser
- sandpaper
- tack cloth
- primer
- white paint
- paintbrushes
- poster board
- tissue paper
- fabric
- hot glue gun and glue sticks
- awl

INSTRUCTIONS

1. Sand dresser surfaces that are to be painted; wipe with tack cloth. Allowing to dry after each application, apply primer, then two coats of white paint.

2. To cover square or rectangular recessed areas of dresser, simply measure area and cut a piece of poster board slightly smaller. To cover a curved recessed area of dresser, cut pattern from tissue paper slightly smaller than recessed area of dresser. Use pattern to cut shape from poster board. Cut fabric 1" larger on all sides than pattern.

3. Center poster board on wrong side of fabric piece. Folding at corners, easing along curved edges, and pulling fabric taut, hot glue edges of fabric to back of poster board. Hot glue fabric-covered panel in place on dresser.

4. To cover drawer fronts, remove drawer pulls. Measure drawer front. Cut a pattern from tissue paper 1" larger on all sides and mark location for screws. Centering motifs on fabric as desired, use pattern to cut fabric. Center drawer front on wrong side of fabric piece. Folding at corners and pulling fabric taut, hot glue edges of fabric to back of drawer front. Use awl to punch holes in fabric before replacing drawer pulls.

CHEERY CHERRY PILLOW
(shown on pg. 173)

Finished Size: 13¹/₂" square without ruffle

FABRICS

Yardage is based on 45"w fabric.
• white — ⁷/₈-yd
• pink print — ¹/₈-yd
• blue check print — ⁵/₈-yd
• green, dark green, and red fabrics for appliqués

Other supplies
• pillow form — 14" square
• paper-backed fusible web

*Refer to **Pillow Top Diagram** as needed. See **Quilter's Basics** (pg. 241) for more in-depth basic instructions.*

CUTTING
White:
• For background, cut 1 square 7¹/₂" x 7¹/₂".
• For backing, cut 1 square 14" x 14".
• For ruffle, cut 4 strips 3¹/₂"w. From these strips cut:
  •4 strips 3¹/₂" x 34".
Pink Print:
• Cut 1 strip 1¹/₂"w. From this strip cut:
  •2 strips 1¹/₂" x 7¹/₂".
  •2 strips 1¹/₂" x 9¹/₂".
Blue Check Print:
• Cut 2 strips 2³/₄"w. From these strips cut:
  •2 strips 2³/₄" x 9¹/₂".
  •2 strips 2³/₄" x 14".
• For ruffle trim, cut 4 strips 2"w. From these strips cut:
  •4 strips 2" x 34".

Green, dark green, and red:
• Use patterns, pg. 176, and follow **Preparing Appliqué Pieces**, pg. 247, to make the following appliqués:
  •2 cherries.
  •1 cherry stem.
  •2 leaves.

PIECING
1. Follow manufacturer's instructions to fuse appliqués to background.

2. Follow **Satin Stitch Appliqué**, pg. 248, to appliqué cherries, stem, and leaves.

3. Sew pink print strips to sides, then top and bottom of background.

4. Sew blue check print strips to sides, then top and bottom of background.

FINISHING
1. Sew ruffle strips together end to end to form a circle. Sew ruffle trim strips together end to end to form a circle. Press long edges of ruffle trim strip ¹/₂" to wrong side. Press strip in half. Placing 1 long edge of ruffle in fold of fabric, sew ruffle trim to ruffle, close to folded edges.

2. Use trimmed ruffle and follow **Adding Ruffle To Pillow Top**, pg. 255, to make a ruffled pillow.

Pillow Top Diagram

APPLE GOODNESS

Bright-red, crispy-crunchy and oh-so sweet...the country goodness of apples makes them a natural choice for this kitchen collection! Their delicious aroma will draw the whole family to the room when you stir up a batch of old-fashioned apple butter; while it's simmering, you can get started on our perky appliquéd wall hanging.

The Manner of giving is worth More than the gift.
—Pierre Corneille

Apple Butter Jar, page 192.

DAD'S SPICED APPLE BUTTER

This is an easy slow-cooker recipe that is good served on biscuits or muffins.

8 to 10 Rome, Braeburn or
   Granny Smith apples, peeled
   and quartered
1/2 c. apple juice or water
2 T. lemon juice
3/4 c. sugar
1 t. cinnamon
1/8 t. ground cloves
1/8 t. salt
1/8 t. ground allspice
1/8 t. nutmeg

Place apples in a slow cooker; add juice or water and lemon juice. Combine remaining ingredients in a small bowl; stir until blended. Add to apples; stir. Cover and cook on low 8 hours or on high 3 to 4 hours. Stir and mash apples occasionally throughout cooking time. When desired thickness, ladle apple butter into 6 hot, sterilized half-pint jars. Add lid and tighten down ring. Cool jars. Store in refrigerator.

Dayna Hansen
Junction City, OR

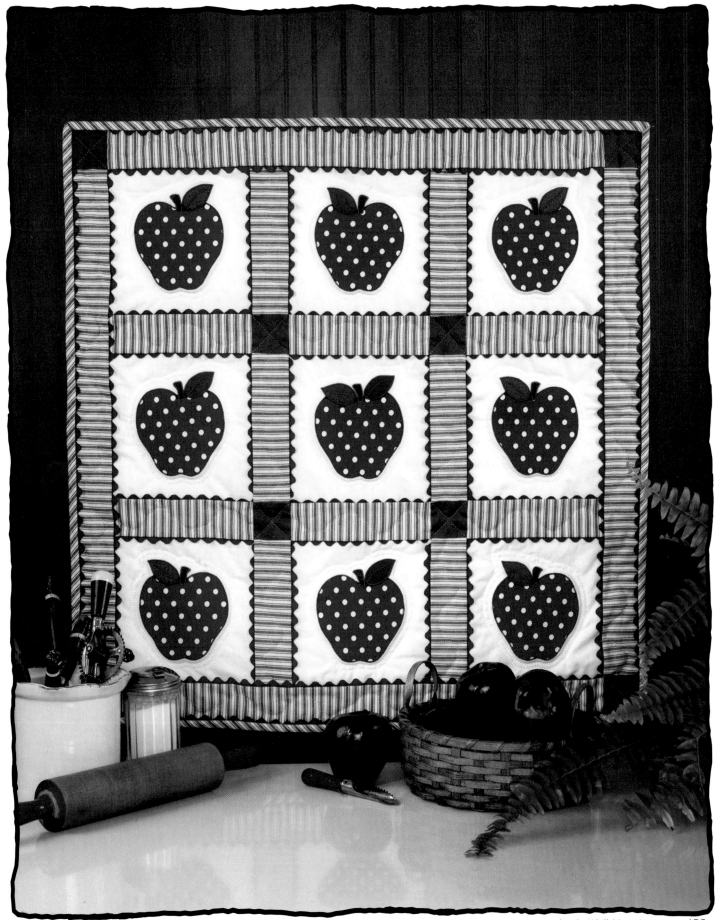

Apple Wall Hanging, page 192.

Dress up your breakfast table! The stem on the apple-shaped place mat is actually a clever holder for the napkin "leaves." For a cheery centerpiece, fill a napkin-lined basket with an assortment of plump soft-sculpture apples.

During your next autumn bonfire, enjoy a warm and tasty apple treat! Slide an apple on a metal skewer and roast until warmed throughout. Slice and enjoy with caramel sauce or sprinkled with cinnamon and sugar.

Baked squash is delicious stuffed with a mixture of chopped apples, raisins, brown sugar and butter!

Soft-Sculpture Apples, page 194.

Apple Place Mat and Napkin, page 195.

APPLE CRUNCH MUFFINS
A delicious fall treat for breakfast at home or on the run!

1¹/₂ c. all-purpose flour
¹/₂ c. sugar
2 t. baking powder
¹/₂ t. salt
¹/₂ t. cinnamon
¹/₄ c. shortening
¹/₂ c. milk
1 egg, slightly beaten
1 c. Granny Smith apples,
    peeled and diced

TOPPING
¹/₄ c. brown sugar, packed
¹/₄ c. chopped walnuts
¹/₂ t. cinnamon

Apple Bread Cloth, page 195.

Sift flour, sugar, baking powder, salt and cinnamon in mixing bowl. Cut in shortening until fine crumbs form. Combine milk and egg. Add to dry ingredients along with apples. Stir just until moistened. Spoon batter into muffin cups, filling two-third full. For topping, mix ingredients together. Sprinkle topping over batter. Bake at 375 degrees for 20 minutes or until golden. Makes 12.

I was 32 when I started cooking; up until then, I just ATE. — JULIA CHILD

190

Make a family trip to an apple orchard ~ a picking expedition is a memory-maker.

Green and red apples in a bowl are a beautiful sight to behold.

Mary Elizabeth's kids love this harvest treat: Core an apple, fill it with peanut butter and top it with raisins.

Ticking dish towels and a checked bread cloth appliquéd with apples add a colorful, retro feel to any kitchen. Set out a basket of moist, spicy muffins for snacking!

Appliquéd Apple Hand Towels, page 197.

APPLE BUTTER JAR

(shown on pg. 186)

SUPPLIES

- glass jar with lid
- sheer fabric — 5¹/₂" square
- tag — 1³/₈" x 2³/₄"
- alphabet rubber stamps — ³/₈" tall
- black rubber stamp ink pad
- white string
- printed paper — slightly larger than tag
- craft glue

INSTRUCTIONS

1. Stamp "APPLE BUTTER" on tag. Glue tag to printed paper. Trim paper ¹/₄" larger than tag on all sides. Attach string to tag.

2. Place sheer fabric over jar lid. Tie string around lid.

APPLE WALL HANGING

(shown on pg. 187)

Finished Size: 30¹/₂" x 30¹/₂"

FABRICS

Yardage is based on 45"w fabric.
- white — ¹/₂-yd
- red print — ¹/₂-yd
- variety of green prints to total ¹/₄-yd
- brown print — ¹/₈-yd
- green stripe — ⁵/₈-yd
- fabric for backing and hanging sleeve — 1¹/₄-yds
- fabric for binding — ⁵/₈-yd

Other supplies
- red jumbo rick rack — 12¹/₂-yds
- batting — 45" x 60"
- paper-backed fusible web

*Refer to **Wall Hanging Top Diagram**, pg. 193, as needed. See **Quilter's Basics** (pg. 241) for more in-depth basic instructions.*

CUTTING

White:
- Cut 2 strips 8"w. From these strips, cut:
  - 9 blocks 8" x 8".

Red Print:
- Use pattern, pg. 194, and follow **Preparing Appliqué Pieces**, pg. 247, to make 9 apple appliqués.

Green Print:
- Use pattern, pg. 194, to make 10 leaf appliqués.
- Cut 1 strip 2¹/₂"w. From this strip, cut:
  - 8 sashing squares 2¹/₂" x 2¹/₂".

Green Stripe:
- Cut 3 strips 2¹/₂"w. From these strips, cut:
  - 12 sashing strips 2¹/₂" x 8".
- Cut 4 strips 2¹/₂"w. From these strips, cut:
  - 4 border strips 2¹/₂" x 27".

Brown Print:
- Use pattern, page 194, to make 9 stem appliqués.

PIECING

1. Follow manufacturer's instructions to fuse appliqués to each white block.

2. Follow **Satin Stitch Appliqué**, pg. 248, to appliqué apples, leaves, and stems.

3. Cut 24 8" lengths of rick rack. Centering rick rack along ¹/₄" seamline, baste rick rack to blocks as follows:

Block 1 — bottom and right side edges

Block 2 — bottom and side edges

Block 3 — bottom and left side edges

Block 4 — top, bottom, and right side edges

Block 5 — all sides

Block 6 — top, bottom, and left side edges

Block 7 — top and right side edges

Block 8 — top, left, and right side edges

Block 9 — top and left side edges

. Sew Blocks 1, 2, and 3 and 2 sashing strips ogether to make Unit 1. Repeat with Blocks 4, 5, and and Blocks 7, 8, and 9 to make 3 Unit 1's. Press eam allowances towards sashing strips.

Unit 1 – make 3

. Sew 3 sashing strips and 2 sashing squares ogether to make Unit 2. Press seam allowances owards sashing strips. Make 2 Unit 2's.

Unit 2 – make 2

. Sew Unit 1's and Unit 2's together to complete nit 3.

Unit 3

. Cut 4, 27" lengths of rick rack. Centering rick rack long 1/4" seamline, baste 1 length to each edge of nit 3.

. Sew 1 border strip to right and left sides of Unit 3.

. Sew 1 sashing square to each end of remaining order strips. Sew border strips to top and bottom of nit 3.

FINISHING

1. Mark, layer, and quilt wall hanging, outline quilting 1/4" from edges of each appliqué; outline quilt 1/4" from previous line of stitching. Quilt two diagonal lines across each sashing square to make an "X". Quilt a wavy line in each sashing strip and border strip.

2. Follow **Making a Hanging Sleeve**, pg. 254, to attach hanging sleeve to wall hanging.

3. Cut 4 31" lengths of rick rack. Centering rick rack along 1/4" seamline, sew 1 length to each edge of wall hanging top.

4. Follow **Binding**, pg. 252, to bind wall hanging using a 19 1/2" square to make 2 1/2"w continuous bias binding with mitered corners.

Wall Hanging Top Diagram

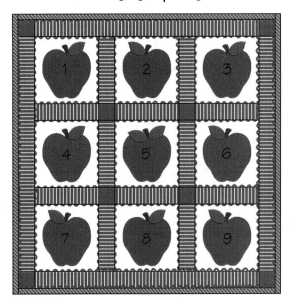

SOFT-SCULPTURE APPLES

(shown on pg. 188)

Finished Size: Approximately 9" diameter

SUPPLIES FOR EACH APPLE
• red print — scraps
• green solid — scraps
• green embroidery floss
• polyester fiberfill
• cinnamon stick — about 2" long and ¼" diameter

INSTRUCTIONS
Use 3 strands of floss for embroidery unless otherwise indicated.

1. Trace apple section pattern onto tracing paper; cut out.

2. Use pattern to cut 6 sections from red print fabric.

3. Matching side edges and leaving straight edges unstitched, sew 3 sections together to make a unit. Repeat with remaining sections. Sew the units together. Do not clip curves. Turn and stuff with fiberfill.

4. Fold straight edge of opening to inside of apple. Hand baste along folded edge, leaving long thread ends.

5. Refer to **Stitch Diagram**, pg. 256, to stitch long Straight Stitches for veins in leaf.

6. Glue cinnamon stick into opening. Knot basting thread tightly around stick. Glue leaf to apple.

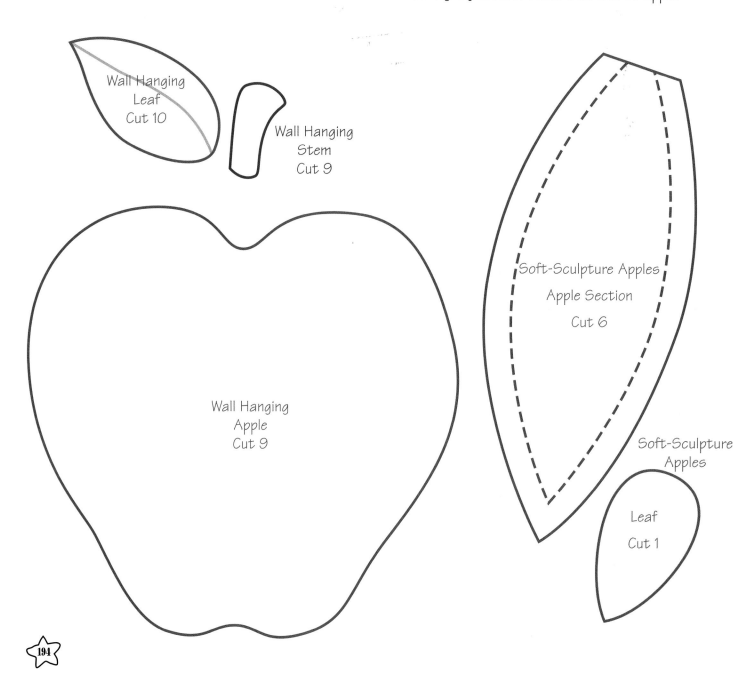

Wall Hanging Leaf Cut 10

Wall Hanging Stem Cut 9

Wall Hanging Apple Cut 9

Soft-Sculpture Apples Apple Section Cut 6

Soft-Sculpture Apples Leaf Cut 1

APPLE PLACE MAT AND NAPKIN

(shown on pg. 189)

Finished Size: 17" X 14¹/₂" with 14" square napkin

FABRICS FOR 1 PLACE MAT AND NAPKIN

Yardage is based on 45"w fabric.
- red solid — 1-yd
- green print — ¹/₂-yd
- scrap of brown print for stem

Other supplies
- fleece — 18" x 30"
- tracing paper

INSTRUCTIONS

1. Cut red solid fabric in two 18" x 15¹/₂" pieces. Place 1 piece right side down on a flat surface. Layer fleece, then remaining fabric piece on top, gently smoothing any wrinkles; pin layers together.

2. Spacing lines 1" apart, sew diagonal lines across the layered pieces. Repeat to stitch diagonal lines in the opposite direction across the layered pieces.

3. Trace patterns, pg. 196, onto tracing paper, matching dashed lines and turning paper as needed to make a complete half-pattern; cut out.

4. Use pattern to cut an apple shape from quilted fabric.

FINISHING

1. For loop, cut a 2" x 4¹/₂" piece of brown print fabric. Press each long edge ¹/₂" to wrong side; press piece in half lengthwise. Stitch together along folded edges. Matching raw edges, sew end of loop to top center of place mat front using a ³/₈" seam allowance.

2. Follow **Binding**, pg. 252, to cut 1¹/₂-yds of 2¹/₂"w continuous bias binding. Sew binding to front of place mat. Matching raw edges, sew remaining end of loop to top center of place mat back using a ³/₈" seam allowance. Folding binding over to back of place mat, blindstitch binding to back, taking care not to stitch through to front of place mat.

3. For napkin, cut a 15" square from green print fabric. To hem, press one edge ¹/₄" to wrong side; press to wrong side again. Stitch along inside folded edge. Repeat for remaining edges.

APPLE BREAD CLOTH

(shown on pg. 190)

Finished Size: 19¹/₂" square

FABRICS

Yardage is based on 45"w fabric.
- red print — ⁵/₈-yd
- scraps for apple and leaf

INSTRUCTIONS

1. Cut a 20" square of red print fabric.

2. For hem, press edges ¹/₄" to wrong side; press ¹/₄" to wrong side again. Stitch along inside folded edge.

3. Use patterns, below, and follow **Preparing Appliqué Pieces,** pg. 247, to make apple and leaf appliqués.

4. Follow manufacturer's instructions to fuse appliqués to corner of bread cloth.

5. Follow **Satin Stitch Appliqué**, pg. 248, to appliqué apple and leaves. Machine satin stitch the stem.

Leaf
Cut 2

Apple
Cut 1

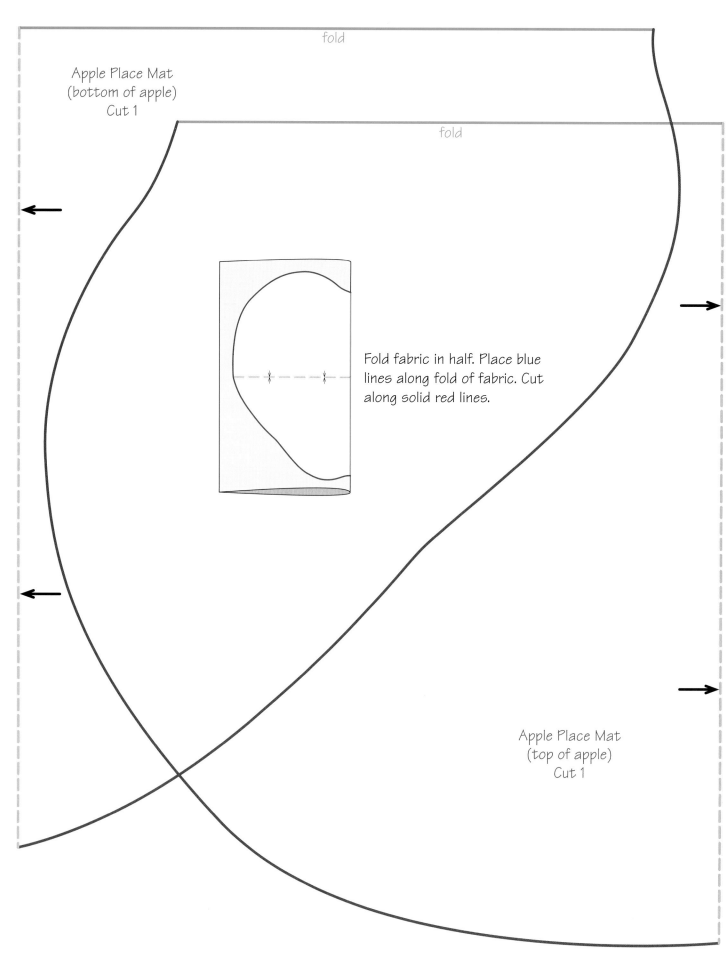

fold

Apple Place Mat
(bottom of apple)
Cut 1

fold

Fold fabric in half. Place blue
lines along fold of fabric. Cut
along solid red lines.

Apple Place Mat
(top of apple)
Cut 1

196

APPLIQUÉD APPLE HAND TOWELS

(shown on pg. 191)

Finished Size: 17" x 24"

FABRICS FOR 1 HAND TOWEL

Yardage is based on 45"w fabric.
• green stripe — ⁵⁄₈-yd
• scraps for apple, leaf, and stem

Other supplies
• jumbo rickrack — 17" length

INSTRUCTIONS

1. Cut a 17¹⁄₂" x 24¹⁄₂" piece of green stripe fabric.

2. Stitch length of rick rack 1¹⁄₂" above 1 short edge.

3. For hem, press edges ¹⁄₄" to wrong side; press ¹⁄₄" to wrong side again. Stitch along inside folded edge.

4. Use patterns, this page, and follow **Preparing Appliqué Pieces,** pg. 247, to make apple, leaf, and stem appliqués.

5. Follow manufacturer's instructions to fuse appliqués to hand towel.

6. Follow **Satin Stitch Appliqué**, pg. 248, to appliqué apple, leaf, and stem.

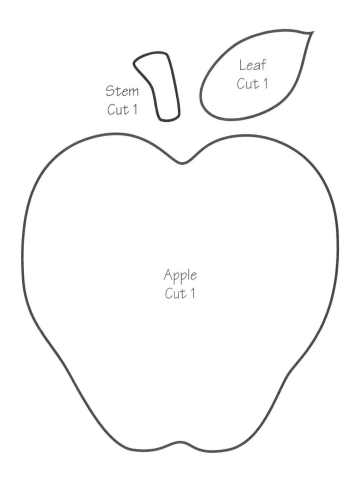

Stem
Cut 1

Leaf
Cut 1

Apple
Cut 1

Friendship Gifts

The Country Friends® love to surprise each other with thoughtful handmade gifts! Kate and Mary Elizabeth know that Holly collects buttons, so they stitched up a pretty button basket wall hanging and pillow for her birthday. Wouldn't someone you know enjoy a treat like that? Turn the page for more neat gifts to make.

Button Wall Hanging, page 202.

Button Pillow, page 204.

DETAILS, DETAILS!

When you're making button crafts, you may want to experiment using the buttons **with** and **without** thread in the holes. Please your eye ⌐ does it look better to have a snazzy shot of colored thread running through the design, or does the beauty of the button stand alone?

Beauty is in the eye of the beholder.
—OLD SAYING

In the late 1880's, young girls in the United States were crazy for "charm strings," long chains of buttons collected one by one and sewn together. The goal was to amass 1,000 buttons...it was said that Prince Charming would arrive after the 999th button was sewn on!

Liberty Pouch, page 204.

"I pledge allegiance to the flag of the United States of America and to the Republic for which it stands, one Nation under God, indivisible, with Liberty and Justice for all."

★ Public school children have been reciting that simple pledge since 1892.

Bee Project Keeper, page 206; Bee Needle Case, page 207.

Add patriotic flair to a tiny purse with a homespun flag, or delight a crafty friend with the "bee-utiful" project pouch and needle case. Our simple wall hanging shares a loving sentiment.

Nothing is better than a Loyal friend.

~EURIPIDES

FRIENDS ARE LIFE'S BLESSINGS

"Friends" Wall Hanging, 208.

BUTTON WALL HANGING
(shown on pg. 198)

Finished Size: $9^1/2$" x $12^1/2$"

FABRICS

Yardage is based on 45"w fabric.
- cream solid for background — $^1/4$-yd
- 4 assorted plaids for borders — $^1/8$-yd of each
- fabric for backing and hanging sleeve — $^3/8$-yd

Other Supplies
- batting — 13" x 16"
- 5" dia. doily
- embroidery floss — brown, yellow, gold
- hot-iron transfer pen
- tracing paper
- fabric marking pen
- rick rack
- assorted buttons

CUTTING

All measurements include a $^1/4$" seam allowance.

Cream Solid:
- Cut 1 rectangle 8" x 10" for background.

Assorted Plaids:
- Cut 2 short side borders $2^1/2$" x $8^1/2$".
- Cut 1 top border $2^1/2$" x $10^1/2$".
- Cut 1 bottom border $3^1/2$" x $10^1/2$".

Backing and Hanging Sleeve Fabric:
- Cut 1 piece 10" x $4^1/2$" for hanging sleeve.
- Cut 1 piece $10^1/2$" X $13^1/2$" for backing.

PIECING

1. Trace basket pattern, pg. 203, onto tracing paper. Follow manufacturer's instructions and use hot-iron transfer pencil to transfer pattern to background fabric.

2. Refer to **Stitch Diagrams**, pgs. 255 – 256, to Stem Stitch basket. For flowers within handle, use marking pen to draw around various buttons. Remove button and Blanket Stitch along drawn line, varying the length of the stitches. Sew buttons to basket and within handle.

3. Cutting lower edge $^1/4$" below base of basket, trim background to $6^1/2$" x $8^1/2$".

4. To complete wall hanging top, sew side borders to background. Sew top border to background. Cut doily in half. Matching raw edges and centering doily along 1 long edge of border, baste doily to border. Sew bottom border to background. Whipstitch loose edge of doily in place.

5. Follow **Making a Hanging Sleeve**, pg. 254, to sew hanging sleeve to one short edge of backing piece.

6. Cut 2 $10^1/2$" lengths and 2 $13^1/2$" lengths of rick rack. Centering rick rack along $^1/4$" seamline, baste 1 length to each edge of wall hanging top.

7. Matching right sides and raw edges, place backing and top on a flat work surface; lay batting on top. Sew around 4 sides, leaving an opening for turning; turn. Sew opening closed.

butth

butth

why?'

pit

the

butth

Words

Basket

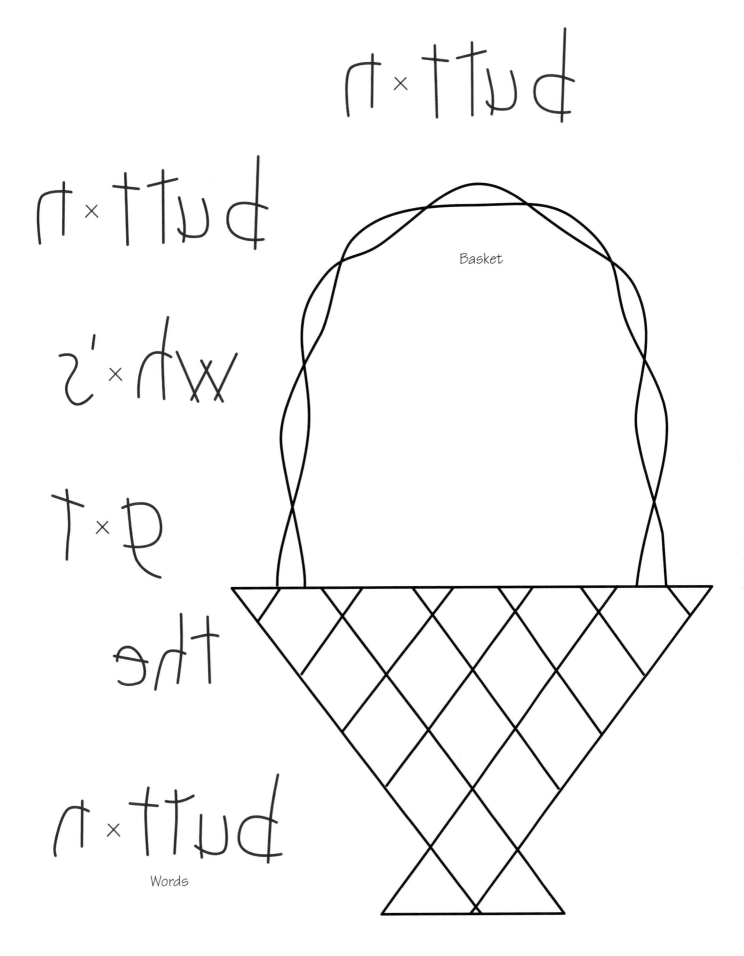

BUTTON PILLOW

(shown on pg. 199)

Finished Size: 12" square

FABRICS

Yardage is based on 45"w fabric.
- cream solid — 1/8-yd
- assorted plaids — scraps of each
- fabric for backing — 3/8-yd

Other Supplies
- 12" pillow form **or** polyester fiberfill
- 2 5" dia. cotton doilies
- embroidery floss — brown
- hot-iron transfer pen
- tracing paper
- black rick rack — 1 1/2-yds
- assorted buttons
- tea bag

CUTTING

All measurements include a 1/4" seam allowance.

Cream Solid:
- Cut 6 rectangles 4" x 6".
- Cut 4 corner squares 2 3/4" x 2 3/4".

Assorted Plaids:
- Cut 4 borders 2 3/4" x 8".
- Cut 12 strips 1 3/4"w and various lengths.

Backing Fabric:
- Cut 1 square 12 1/2" x 12 1/2".

PIECING

1. Steep 1 tea bag in 2 cups of hot water; allow to cool. Immerse cream fabric and doilies into tea. Soak until desired color is achieved. Remove from tea and allow to dry. Press if desired.

2. Trace each word pattern, pg. 203, onto tracing paper. Follow manufacturer's instructions and use hot-iron transfer pencil to transfer one word pattern to each cream rectangle.

3. Refer to **Stitch Diagram**, pg. 256, to Stem Stitch words.

4. Centering word, trim each "word" rectangle to 1 3/4"w and 1/2" longer than length of word.

5. Sew 1 plaid strip to each short side of each "word" rectangle. Staggering placement of "word" rectangle as desired, sew strips together along long sides. Trim sides of design to form a 7 1/2" square.

6. Cut doilies in half. Matching raw edges and centering 1 doily piece along 1 long edge of 1 side border, sew side border to center square. Whipstitch loose edge of doily in place. Repeat for remaining side border.

7. Sew 1 corner square to each end of remaining borders. Matching raw edges and centering 1 doily piece along 1 long edge of 1 border, sew top border to center square. Whipstitch loose edge of doily in place. Repeat for bottom border.

8. Sew buttons to centers of corner squares. Sew buttons to doilies. For each "o", sew button to each "word" rectangle.

9. Cut 4 12 1/2" lengths of rick rack. Centering rick rack along 1/4" seamline, baste 1 length to each edge of pillow top.

10. Refer to **Pillow Finishing**, pg. 255, to complete knife-edge pillow.

LIBERTY POUCH

(shown on pg. 200)

Finished Size: 6 1/2" X 9"

FABRICS

Yardage is based on 45"w fabric.
- blue solid — 3/8-yd
- ticking stripe — 3/8-yd
- red, blue, cream, and gold wool — scraps

Other Supplies
- buttons — one 3/8", two 9/16", one 11/16", and one 1 1/8"
- embroidery floss — black, cream, gold, and navy
- tracing paper
- sew-on Velcro® dot closure

CUTTING

All measurements include a 1/4" seam allowance.

Blue Solid:
- For pouch front, cut 1 rectangle 7" x 9".
- For pouch back, cut 1 rectangle 7" x 16".
- For strap, cut 2 strips 2" x 27" (pieced if necessary).

Ticking Stripe:
- For lining front, cut 1 rectangle 7" x 9".
- For lining back, cut 1 rectangle 7" x 16".
- For inside pocket, cut 1 rectangle 7" x 7".
- For outside pocket, cut 2 rectangles 3 3/4" x 5 1/4".
- For binding, cut 1 strip 1" x 25 1/2".

Red wool:
- Cut 3 stripes 1/2" x 4 3/4".

Blue wool:
• Cut 1 piece 1½" x 3¼".
Cream wool:
• Cut 4 stripes ½" x 4¾".
Gold wool:
• Use patterns to cut 2 stars.

INSTRUCTIONS
Use 2 strands of floss for all embroidery.

1. Fold tracing paper in half. Placing folded edge of tracing paper along dashed line of pattern, trace Flap pattern. Remove tracing paper from pattern. Turn traced pattern over. Trace drawn line on other side of tracing paper; open. Placing rounded end of pattern on 1 short side, use pattern to cut flap on pouch back and lining back.

2. For inside pocket, press 1 side ¼" to wrong side; press ¼" to wrong side again. Sew along folded edge.

3. Refer to **Stitch Diagrams**, pgs. 255 – 256, to Blanket Stitch star to 1 outside pocket piece using gold floss.

4. For outside pocket, match right sides and raw edges and sew around all sides, leaving opening for turning; turn. Press and sew opening closed.

5. With top of pocket 1" from 1 short edge and with pocket centered, topstitch outside pocket to pouch front. Sew loop side of Velcro® closure 1¼" below pocket.

6. For pouch, match right sides and raw edges and sew pouch front to pouch back along 3 straight sides; turn.

7. Blanket Stitch red stripes to flap of pouch using black floss. Blanket Stitch cream stripes to flap using cream thread. Blanket Stitch blue piece to flap using black floss. Blanket Stitch gold star to flap using gold floss.

8. Use blue floss to Feather Stitch a line above and below flag. Nesting buttons, sew ⅜", ¹¹/₁₆", and 1⅛" buttons to point of flap.

9. For strap, sew short ends together. Press long edges of strip ½" to wrong side. Press strip in half lengthwise. Topstitch along folded edges. Press raw edges under. Sew ends to pouch back piece approximately ¼" below fold of flap. Sew remaining buttons over ends of strap.

10. For lining, with raw edges of inside pocket sandwiched in between, match right sides and raw edges of lining front and back and sew 3 straight sides together. Do **not** turn. Sew hook side of Velcro® closure ¾" below point of lining back.

11. Place lining inside pouch. Matching raw edges, baste around top of pouch.

12. Sew short ends of binding together. Press 1 long edge ¼" to wrong side. Matching raw edges, sew binding to pouch opening. Fold binding to inside; whipstitch in place over seamline.

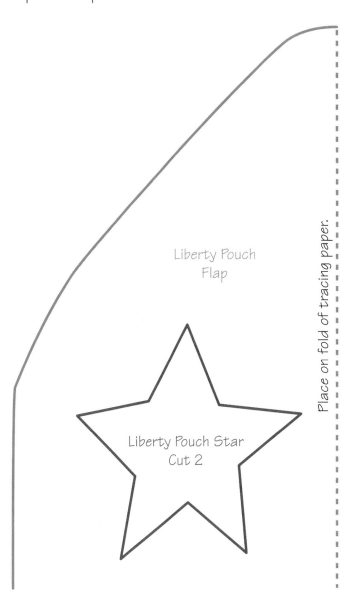

Liberty Pouch Flap

Liberty Pouch Star Cut 2

Place on fold of tracing paper.

BEE PROJECT KEEPER

(shown on pg. 200)

Finished Size: 10½" tall and 8" diameter

FABRICS

Yardage is based on 45"w fabric.
- black wool — ⅜-yd
- red wool — ¼-yd
- gold wool — ⅛-yd
- light gold wool — ⅛-yd
- dark green wool — ⅛-yd
- green wool — ⅛-yd
- small scrap of tan tweed
- green plaid flannel — ½-yd

Other Supplies
- embroidery floss — black and yellow
- paper-backed fusible web
- large safety pin

CUTTING

All measurements include a ½" seam allowance.

Black Wool:
- Cut 1 rectangle 25½" x 11" for bag sides.
- Use patterns, pg. 207, to cut:
  - 1 base.
  - 3 top bee stripes.
  - 3 bottom bee stripes.

Red Wool:
- Use pattern, pg. 207, to cut 5 flowers.

Gold Wool:
- Use pattern, pg. 207, to cut 5 flower bases.

Light Gold Wool:
- Use pattern, pg. 207, to cut 3 bees.

Dark Green Wool:
- Use pattern, pg. 207, to cut 5 stems.

Green Wool:
- Use pattern, pg. 207, to cut 5 leaves.

Tan Tweed:
- Use pattern, pg. 207, to cut 3 wings.

Green Plaid Flannel:
- Cut 1 rectangle 25½" x 11¾" for lining.
- Cut 1 base for lining.
- Cut 1 rectangle 2" x 24" for tie channel.
- Cut 1 rectangle 2½" x 42" for tie.

INSTRUCTIONS

1. Press long raw edges of tie channel ¼" to wrong side ¼"; press short ends 1" to wrong side.

2. Place channel 1½" from 1 long side (top). Topstitch along long edges of channel.

3. Follow **Preparing Appliqué Pieces**, pg. 247, and refer to **Appliqué Placement Diagram** to prepare and fuse appliqué pieces onto bag sides.

4. Refer to **Stitch Diagrams**, pgs. 255 – 256, to Blanket stitch appliqués using 2 strands of black embroidery floss. Running Stitch "bee trail" using 2 strands of yellow embroidery floss.

5. With right sides together, use a ½" seam allowance to sew short ends of bag sides together to form a tube.

6. With right sides together, use a ½" seam allowance to sew black wool base to sides. Clip seam allowance as needed.

7. Repeat Steps 5 and 6 to make lining from green plaid flannel.

8. Press raw edge of lining ¼" to wrong side. Matching wrong sides, place lining into bag with side seams together. Fold the pressed edge of lining to outside to cover raw edge of bag. Topstitch lining to bag to form trim.

9. For tie, press long raw edges to wrong side ¼". Fold in half lengthwise and topstitch along folded edges. Pin large safety pin to one end of tie, and thread it through channel. Tie overhand knot at both ends of tie.

Appliqué Placement Diagram

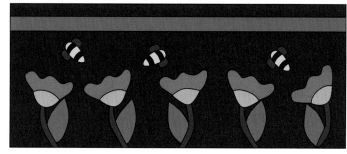

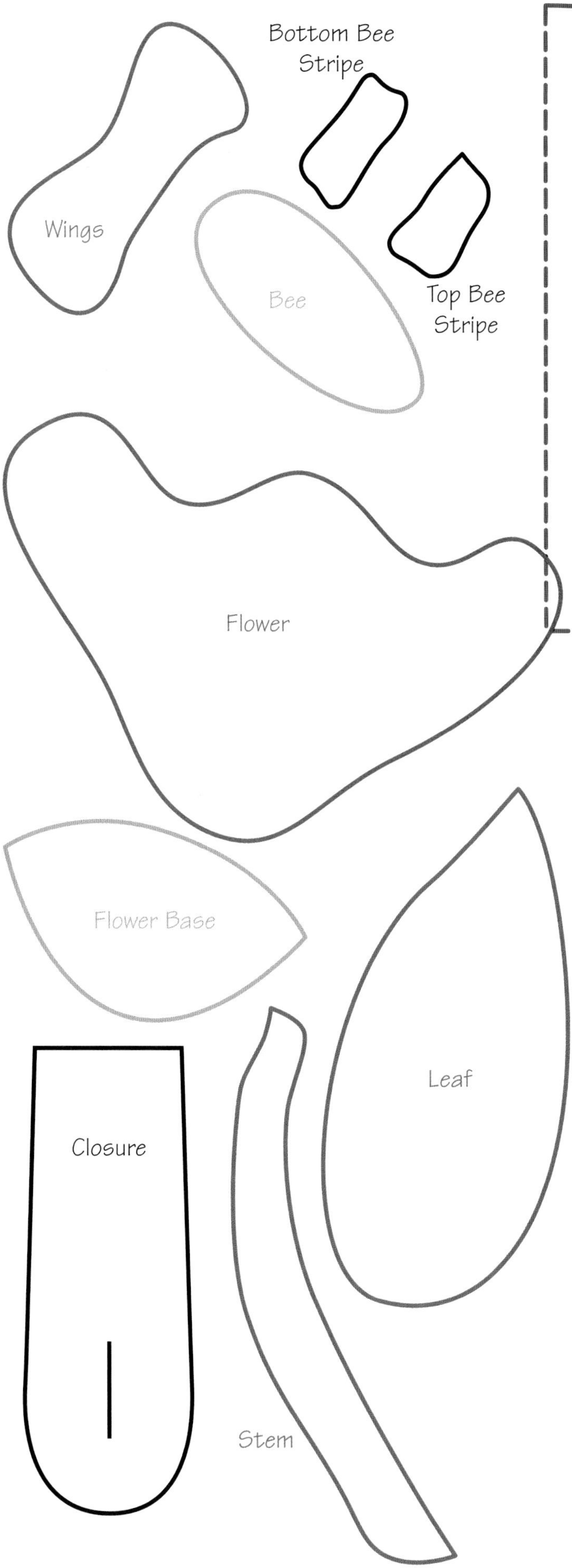

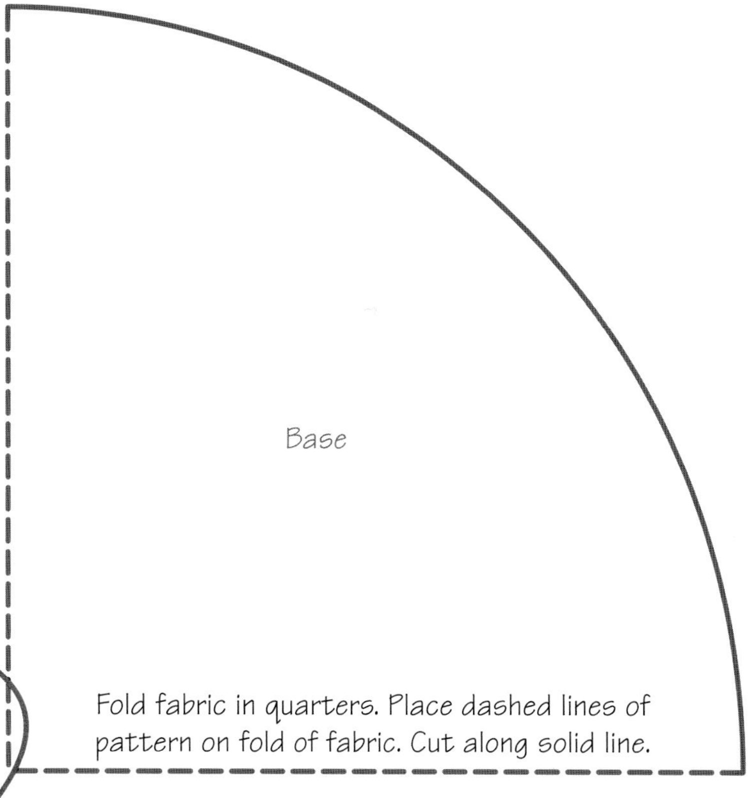

Wings

Bottom Bee Stripe

Bee

Top Bee Stripe

Base

Flower

Fold fabric in quarters. Place dashed lines of pattern on fold of fabric. Cut along solid line.

BEE NEEDLE CASE
(shown on pg. 200)

Finished Size: 5" square

FABRICS

Yardage is based on 45"w fabric.
- black wool — $\frac{1}{4}$-yd
- red wool — scrap
- gold plaid wool — scrap
- yellow wool — scrap
- green tweed — scrap
- green plaid — scrap
- dark green wool — scrap
- cotton fabric — $\frac{1}{4}$-yd

Other Supplies
- embroidery floss — black
- paper-backed fusible web
- $\frac{5}{8}$" diameter button

CUTTING
All measurements include a $\frac{1}{4}$" seam allowance.

Black Wool:
- Cut 1 rectangle $5\frac{1}{2}$" x $10\frac{1}{2}$" for front.
- Use pattern to cut closure.
- Use patterns to cut bee stripes.

Red Wool:
- Use pattern to cut flower.

Flower Base

Leaf

Closure

Stem

Gold Plaid Wool:
• Use pattern to cut flower base.
Yellow Wool:
• Use pattern to cut bee.
Green Tweed:
• Use pattern to cut wings.
Green Plaid:
• Use pattern to cut 2 leaves.
Dark Green Wool:
• Use pattern to cut stem.
• Cut 1 rectangle $5^1/2$" x $2^3/4$" for pocket.
Cotton Fabric:
• Cut 1 rectangle $5^1/2$" x $10^1/2$" for lining.

INSTRUCTIONS

1. Follow **Preparing Appliqué Pieces**, pg. 247, and refer to **Appliqué Placement Diagram**, to prepare and fuse appliqué pieces to 1 end of front.

2. Refer to **Stitch Diagram,** pg. 256, to Blanket stitch appliqués using 2 strands of black embroidery floss.

3. Blanket Stitch along 1 long edge of pocket. Matching short raw edges, baste wrong side of pocket to right side of lining.

4. Matching right sides, sew lining to front, leaving an opening for turning; turn. Sew opening closed. Blanket Stitch around all sides of needle case.

5. Sew button to front. Cut a small slit in end of closure to fit over button. Blanket Stitch along edges of slit. Blanket Stitch along edges of closure, securing approximately 1" of end of closure to front as you stitch.

Appliqué Placement Diagram

"FRIENDS" WALL HANGING
(shown on pg. 201)

Finished Size: $14^1/2$" X 17"

FABRICS

Yardage is based on 45"w fabric.
• cream solid— $3/8$-yd
• green polka dot— $1/4$-yd

• green floral— $1/2$-yd
• fabric for backing — $1/2$-yd
Other Supplies
• embroidery floss — black, lavender, gold, green
• batting — 45" x 60"
• hot-iron transfer pen
• tracing paper

CUTTING
All measurements include a $1/4$" seam allowance.
Cream Solid:
• Cut 1 rectangle $9^1/2$" x 12" for background.
Green Polka Dot
• Cut 2 2" x 12" side inner borders.
• 2" x $11^1/2$" top/bottom inner borders.
Green Floral
• Cut 2 3" x 14" side outer borders.
• Cut 2 3" x $15^1/2$" top/bottom outer borders.
Backing Fabric:
• Cut 1 piece 3" x $15^1/2$" for hanging sleeve.
• Cut 1 piece $18^1/2$" x 21" for backing.

INSTRUCTIONS
Use 3 strands of floss for all embroidery. Use $1/4$" seam allowances for sewing.

1. Trace pattern, pg. 209, onto tracing paper. Follow manufacturer's instructions and use hot-iron transfer pencil to transfer design to background.

2. Refer to **Stitch Diagrams**, pgs. 255 – 256, to Stem Stitch words and trellis using black floss. Stem Stitch stems and leaves using green floss. Stem Stitch flowers using lavender floss. Straight Stitch flower centers using gold floss.

3. Sew side, then top and bottom inner borders to background.

4. Sew side, then top and bottom outer borders to complete wall hanging top.

5. Layer backing (right side up), wall hanging top (right side down), then batting. Stitch all layers together $1/4$" from outer edges leaving an opening for turning. Turn wall hanging right side out and slipstitch opening closed.

6. Use long quilting stitches and quilting thread to outline quilt $1/4$" around outer edges of linen and polka dot fabric, and $1/2$" from outer edge of wall hanging.

7. Steep 1 tea bag in 2 cups of hot water; allow to cool. Immerse wall hanging in tea. Soak until desired color is achieved. Remove from tea and allow to dry. Press if desired.

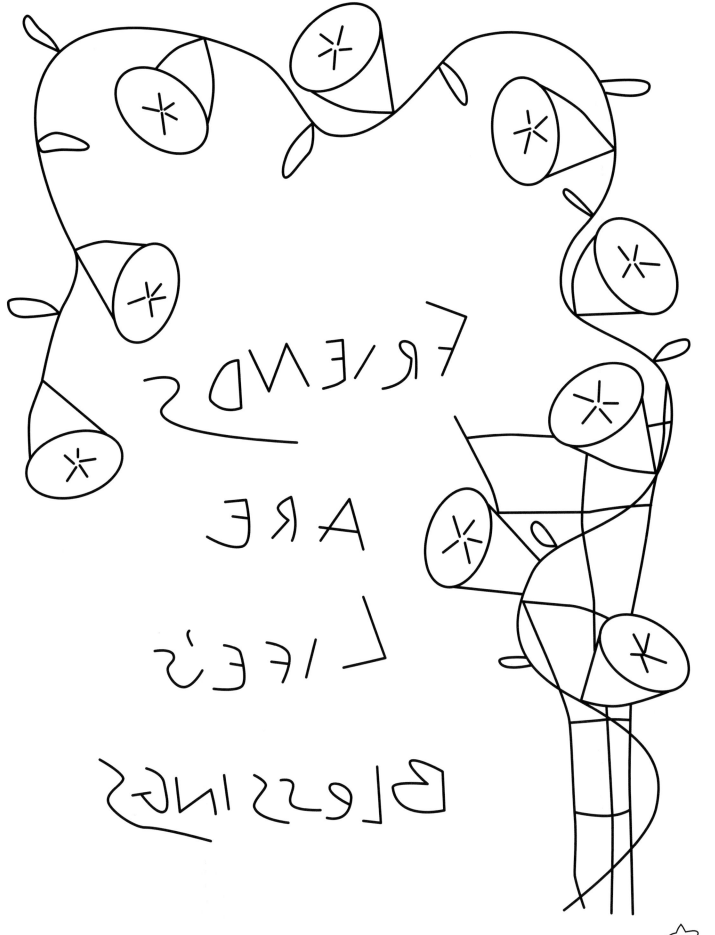

FRIENDS ARE LIFE'S BLESSINGS

How Charming

Like our ABC's and 123's, Teddy bears and rag dolls are childhood companions we never outgrow. Pair them with patchwork pieces such as our embroidered sampler and doll-size quilt and you have a whimsical recipe for charm!

"For You and Me" Embroidery, page 221.

Make new friends but keep the old~ those are silver, these are gold.

Charming Doll Quilt, page 214; Rag Doll, page 219.

"If Friends Were Flowers" Embroidery, page 221.

Quick & Easy JIFFY QUILT

...a great beginner's project!

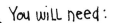

You will need:

★ FABRIC SQUARES in coordinating fabrics
★ FABRIC FOR BACK (solid or print)
★ BIAS BINDING
★ POLYESTER BATTING
★ THREAD
★ EMBROIDERY FLOSS
★ DARNING NEEDLE

— FLOSS TIES

— BIAS BINDING

1. Sew together fabric squares to form a patchwork fabric in the desired fabric size.

2. Lay materials together like so:

← PATCHWORK FABRIC
← BATTING
← BACKING FABRIC

3. Stitch all layers together around all four sides. Finish edges by sewing bias binding around quilt.

4. Sew floss ties at patch corner points, going completely through batting. Tie floss in knot; leave strings long if you wish, or clip short.

Idea! Sew a bright button on each corner as you tie your floss knots!

Yo-Yo Mini Quilt, page 218; Sock Monkey, page 216.

Priceless playmates, sock monkeys and yo-yo's have been "toying" with our affections for generations. Capture the playful spirit of these timeless treasures in our Yo-Yo Mini Quilt and framed embroidery.

CHARMING DOLL QUILT

(shown on pg. 211)

Finished size: 23"x29½"
Block size: 6½" square

FABRICS
• red plaid for border – ⅜-yd
• 48 different light prints – scraps
• 48 different dark prints – scraps
• backing – ⅞-yd
• binding – ⅝-yd

Other supplies
• Easy Angle™ rotary cutting ruler (made by EZ Quilting® by Wright's®)
• batting – 28"x34"

Refer to **Quilt Top Diagram** *as needed. See* **Quilter's Basics** *(pg. 241) for more in-depth basic instructions.*

CUTTING
Red plaid:
• Cut four 2"w strips. From these, cut:
   • 2 side borders – 2"x26½"
   • 2 top/bottom borders – 2"x23

Light and dark print scraps:
• Cut one triangle from each scrap for a total of 48 light and 48 dark triangles as follows:

1. Refer to *Fig. 1* to line up left edge of Easy Angle ruler with straight grain of 1 fabric scrap. Cut along bottom and left edges of ruler.

Fig. 1

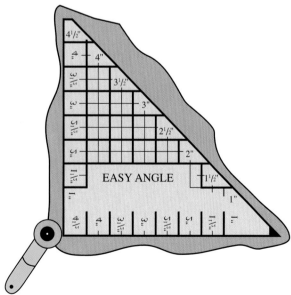

2. Referring to *Fig. 2*, line up bottom edge of ruler with bottom cut edge of fabric; slide ruler to left until 3¾" line (shown in pink) is aligned with left cut edge of fabric. Cut along angled edge of ruler to complete triangle.

Fig. 2

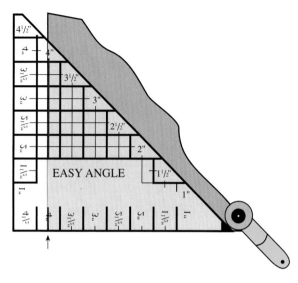

PIECING

1. Sew 1 light and 1 dark triangle together to make each of 48 triangle-squares.

triangle-square – make 48

2. Sew 4 triangle-squares together to make each of 12 Blocks.

Block – make 12

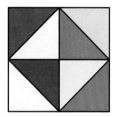

3. Sew 3 Blocks together to make each of 4 Rows.

Row – make 4

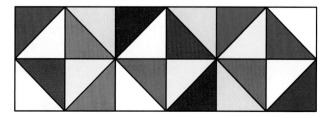

4. Sew Rows together to make quilt top center.

5. Sew side, then top and bottom borders to center to complete quilt top.

FINISHING

1. Mark, layer, and quilt using **Quilting Diagram** as a suggestion.

2. Bind quilt using 3¼-yds of 2½"w bias binding.

Quilting Diagram

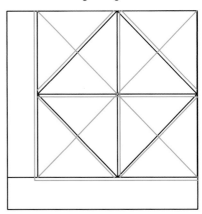

Quilt Top Diagram

SOCK MONKEY

(shown on pg. 213)

Size: 19" high

SUPPLIES
• 2 Red Heel socks
• embroidery floss – black and brown
• 2 black buttons – ½"
• tracing paper
• polyester fiberfill
• red pom-pom – 1"
• red plaid fabric – scrap

Use a ¼" seam allowance and a medium-short stitch length. When whipstitching, fold raw edges of pieces to inside as you stitch.

BODY

1. Turn one sock wrong side out. Start 3" from white heel and sew two seams ⅜" apart in center of sock, curving at ends to make legs (*Fig. 1*).

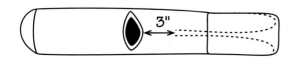

Fig. 1

2. Cut sock between seams to within 1½" of white heel (*Fig. 2*). This leaves opening for stuffing.

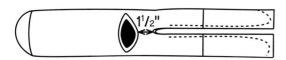

Fig. 2

3. Turn sock right side out and stuff (*Fig 3*). Whipstitch opening closed.

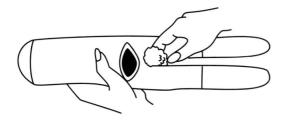

Fig. 3

4. To shape head, tie an 18" length of brown floss (all 6 strands) around sock to form neck (*Fig. 4*).

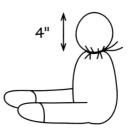

Fig. 4

CUTTING SECOND SOCK

1. Trace ear pattern (pg. 217) onto tracing paper; cut out.

2. Follow **Cutting Diagram** (pg. 217) to cut tail, 2 arms, muzzle, 4 ear pieces, and hat from sock.

FINISHING

1. Fold tail in half lengthwise, right sides together. Sew as shown in *Fig. 5*; turn right side out and stuff. Repeat for arms.

Fig. 5

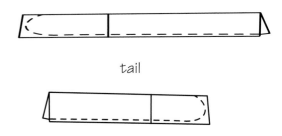

tail

arm

2. Whipstitch tail to body at center of red heel. Whipstitch each arm to body about 1" below neck.

3. Whipstitch muzzle to lower part of face, 2" down

from white area, stuffing muzzle before finishing stitching.

4. Sew each pair of ear pieces together, leaving opening on straight edge. Turn right side out. Whipstitch to head, curving and forming ear shape as you sew.

5. Sew buttons to head for eyes.

6. Using 3 strands of black floss, make straight stitches for eyelashes, mouth, and nostrils. Make one **French Knot** (pg. 256) at each end of mouth.

7. Place hat on head. Stitch in place along edge of white area, allowing brown edge to roll up. Stitch pom-pom to top of hat.

8. For bow tie, cut a 3½"X6" piece from red plaid. Press long edges under 1". Overlap short edges of piece, then tie an 18" length of black floss around center of overlapped area to gather center of tie. Tie

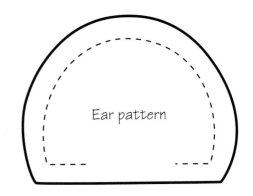

Ear pattern

Cutting Diagram

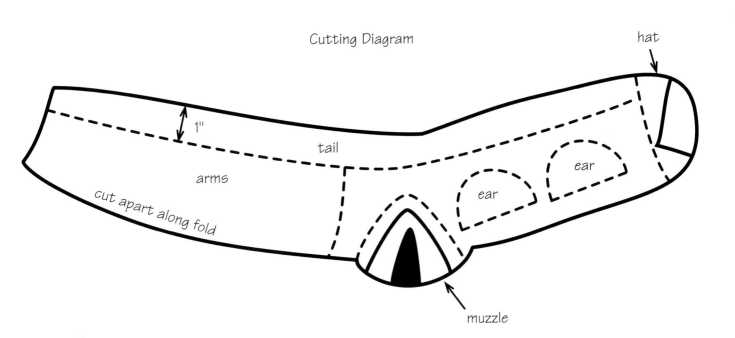

hat

1"

tail

arms

cut apart along fold

ear

ear

muzzle

YO-YO MINI QUILT

(shown on pg. 213)

Finished size: 12"x15"

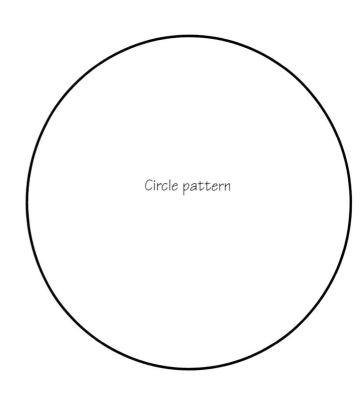

Circle pattern

FABRICS
• assorted fabric scraps — about 1-yd total
Other supplies
• template plastic

INSTRUCTIONS

1. Trace circle pattern onto template plastic and cut out. Use pattern to cut 80 circles from fabric scraps.

2. To make each yo-yo, fold raw edge of one fabric circle $\frac{1}{4}$" to wrong side and work small running stitches around entire circle through the folded area.

3. With right side of the fabric facing out, pull thread to tightly gather fabric; knot thread to secure.

4. Following **Mini Quilt Diagram**, arrange yo-yo's into 8 rows of 10 yo-yo's each. Use a couple of small stitches to stitch each yo-yo to its neighbors.

Mini Quilt Diagram

RAG DOLL

(shown on pg. 211)

Size: 22"H

SUPPLIES

- tracing paper
- iron-on transfer pen
- 22"H muslin doll body
- acrylic paint – red, white, and black
- paintbrushes
- black permanent fine-point marker
- polyurethane semi-gloss varnish
- red cotton knit doll hair loops
- $1^1/_2$"x16" torn fabric strip
- red striped fabric – $^1/_4$-yd
- glue gun
- plaid fabric for dress – $^3/_4$-yd
- small snaps
- muslin for apron – $^5/_8$-yd
- paper-backed fusible web
- fabrics for appliqués – scraps
- 3 buttons

Refer to photo and use a $^1/_4$" seam allowance.

1. Trace doll face pattern (pg. 220) onto tracing paper. Use transfer pen to transfer face to doll's head. Paint nose red. Mix red and white paints together to make a very pale pink. Paint cheeks pink. Draw over remaining face details using black marker.

2. For shoes, paint doll's feet black. Apply varnish over painted area.

3. For hair, hand sew centers of hair loops to head.

4. For each stocking, cut an 8" square from striped fabric. Press edges under $^1/_4$". Wrap square around leg, lining up overlapped edge with seam at back of leg. Catching leg in stitching, blindstitch stocking in place along overlapped edge.

5. For dress bodice, trace bodice pattern (pg. 220) onto tracing paper; cut out. Cut a 10"x21" piece of plaid fabric. Fold in half, matching long edges, then fold in half again, matching short edges. Place pattern on fabric along folds as noted. Cut out bodice. For back opening, unfold bodice and cut down center back. Hem back opening using a $^1/_4$"w double hem.

6. For neck ruffle, cut a 2"x24" plaid fabric strip. Press ends under $^1/_4$"; press in half lengthwise. Baste $^1/_4$" from long raw edge, then pull thread ends to gather to fit bodice neck opening. Stitch in place. Press seam allowance to wrong side. Topstitch along bodice close to ruffle seamline.

7. Hem sleeves using a $^1/_4$"w double hem.

8. For skirt, cut a 10"x45" plaid fabric piece. Hem one long edge (skirt hem) using a $^1/_2$"w double hem. Hem short edges (back opening) using a $^1/_4$"w double hem. Baste $^1/_4$" from remaining raw edge, then pull thread ends to gather skirt to fit bottom edge of bodice. Stitch in place.

9. Sew snaps along back of dress opening. Place dress on doll.

10. From muslin, cut a 17"x20 apron skirt. Press short edges under $^1/_4$". Sew long edges together (top). Turn right side out and press. Topstitch along side edges. Baste $1^1/_2$" from top edge of apron skirt.

11. For embroidery on apron, trace "ABC x 123" from embroidery pattern on pg. 222 onto tracing paper. Use transfer pen to transfer design along apron skirt, repeating as needed. Using 3 strands of floss and straight stitches, stitch design.

12. From muslin, cut one $2^1/_2$"x42" apron tie and two $2^1/_2$"x6" shoulder straps. Press edges of each piece under $^1/_4$". Matching wrong sides, press each in half lengthwise. Topstitch along pressed edges.

13. Pull thread ends to gather top of apron skirt to $7^1/_2$"w. Center apron ties over gathers on right side of apron skirt, then topstitch ties in place. Place apron on doll to determine shoulder strap placement. Sew straps to wrong sides of apron and ties.

14. Sew buttons to apron.

15. For hair bow, tear a 1"x12" strip from remaining dress fabric. Tie into a bow. Glue a button to center of bow. Glue bow to hair.

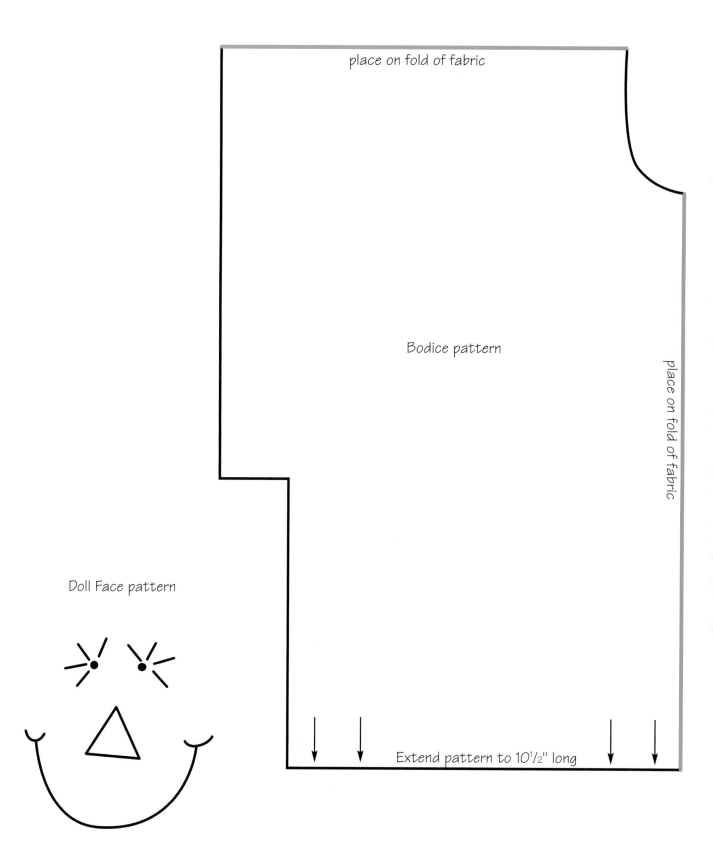

place on fold of fabric

Bodice pattern

place on fold of fabric

Extend pattern to 10¹/₂" long

Doll Face pattern

220

"FOR YOU AND ME" EMBROIDERY

(shown on pg. 210)

SUPPLIES

tracing paper
iron-on transfer pen
unbleached muslin — 12"x15"
embroidery floss — red, blue, yellow, brown, green, pink, dark brown
paper-backed fusible web
frame with 8"x10" opening
assorted buttons
assorted fabric scraps
glue gun

Stitch Diagrams are on pgs. 255 – 256.

INSTRUCTIONS

1. Trace pattern (pg. 222) onto tracing paper. Use transfer pen to transfer design to center of muslin.

2. Referring to photo and pattern, embroider design using 3 strands of floss for words and 2 strands for all other stitching.

3. Fuse web to wrong side of scrap fabrics.

4. Cut 4 strips of fabric to fit around edges of embroidered design; fuse in place. Frame design, using small pieces of cardboard between frame and design to create a shadow box effect

5. Fuse strips of fabric to frame, overlapping as needed.

6. Glue buttons to design and frame.

"IF FRIENDS WERE FLOWERS" EMBROIDERY

(shown on pg. 212)

SUPPLIES

• tracing paper
• iron-on transfer pen
• unbleached muslin — 12"x15"
• embroidery floss — red, blue, yellow, brown, green, pink, dark brown
• frame (painted brown) with 8"x10" opening
• frame (painted red) with 9"x12" opening
• jute
• assorted buttons
• assorted fabric scraps
• glue gun

Stitch Diagrams are on pgs. 255 – 256.

INSTRUCTIONS

1. Trace pattern (pg. 223) onto tracing paper. Use transfer pen to transfer design to center of muslin.

2. Referring to photo and pattern, embroider design using 3 strands of floss for words, dashes, and X's. Use 2 strands for all other stitching.

3. Frame design in 8"x10" frame.

4. Follow *Making Yo-Yo's* (pg. 246) to make 12 desired size yo-yo's from fabric scraps.

5. Glue smaller frame to larger frame. Glue jute around edge of smaller frame. Glue yo-yo's and buttons to frame.

for you and me

ABC×123×Teddy Bears

ABC×123×Teddy Bears

for you and me

222

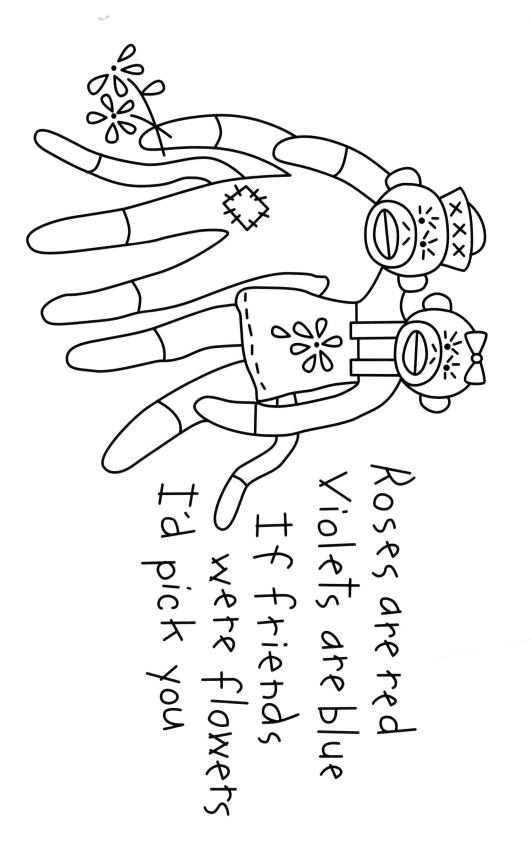

Roses are red
Violets are blue
If friends were flowers
I'd pick you

Button Button

Break out that button collection, or get one started, and make a buttoned work of art! There's something in this collection for almost every room of the house, plus a great dress to wear. Why not start with this easy-to-love sampler of country hearts? And when you use tie-tacking to quilt it, it's easy to finish, too!

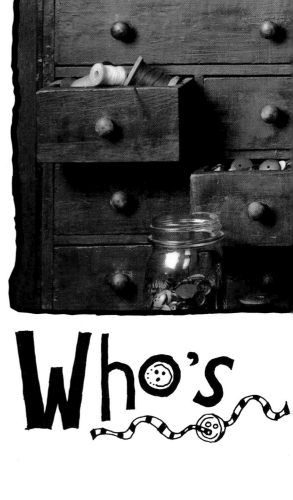

Who's

Friendship Button Wall Quilt, page 237.

got the button?

Display your treasures…wooden spools, a pottery crock full of buttons and a patchwork frame holding a photo of two dear friends. And don't forget these…a batch of cute and delicious cookies nestled in a bread cover blooming with yo-yo flowers!

Patchwork Frame, page 239.

Yo-Yo Flower Bread Cover, page 239.

Button Cookies

…Yummy and, well, cute as a button!

3/4 c. butter, softened
1 c. powdered sugar
1 egg
1 t. almond extract
2·½ c. all-purpose flour
¼ t. salt

Cream butter and sugar; beat in egg and almond extract. Sift together flour and salt; add to butter mixture and mix well. Divide in half and chill one hour.

Roll out half of dough ¼-inch thick ∽ cut with 2-inch round cookie cutter. Place cookies on greased cookie sheet. Make indentation in center of each cookie with the top of a small 1·½ inch diameter drinking glass. Make four holes in center of each cookie with a drinking straw. Bake at 350 degrees for 7 to 9 minutes or until bottoms are lightly browned. Cool on wire racks. Repeat with remaining dough. Makes about 3·¼ dozen cookies.

Floral Pins, page 238.

Rooster Pincushion, page 236.

With a few embroidery stitches and bright buttons, little scraps of felt become pretty lapel pins. And just look at the fine wool "feathers" on our rooster pincushion! You won't believe how easy it is to customize a country dress with yo-yo posies and homespun trims.

10 IDEAS from the BUTTON BOX

1. GLUE BUTTONS TO THE TOP OF A BOX FOR A PRETTY BUTTON BOX OF YOUR OWN. COVER THE SIDES WITH A FAVORITE CALICO OR HOMESPUN.

2. MAKE SWEET SACHETS BY SEWING UP SMALL FABRIC BAGS TO FILL WITH LAVENDER. TIE SHUT WITH TORN FABRIC RAG ⌣ AND GLUE A NEAT BUTTON ON THE KNOT.

3. A BRIGHT IDEA: decorate a boring lampshade with a collection of mismatched buttons!

4. SEW BUTTONS ON A VEST OR OLD JACKET TO GIVE IT A NEW LIFE.

5. SPELL OUT "BUTTONS" ON A WOODEN SIGN WITH... WHAT ELSE? <u>BUTTONS</u>! GET OUT YOUR HOT GLUE GUN AND START SPELLING!

6. STITCH A SAMPLER WITH "I LOVED TO PLAY IN GRANDMA'S BUTTON BOX."

7. FRAME YOUR SAMPLER IN A WOODEN FRAME EMBELLISHED WITH GLUED-ON BUTTONS.

8. A length of elastic band with pretty buttons sewn on makes a snazzy bracelet.

9. TEENY BUTTONS ARE CUTE ON A CLAY POT RIM... OR ON A...

10. ...CLEAR GLASS VOTIVE CANDLE CUP RIM!

Patchwork Blues Pillows, page 235.

Birdhouse Wall Hanging, page 232.

These are the kinds of blues we don't mind getting! Button-topped pillows and a little birdhouse wall hanging will make your favorite room extra cozy.

BIRDHOUSE WALL HANGING

(shown on pg. 231)

Finished size: 25"x29"

FABRICS
- cream stripe – ³/₈-yd
- blue print – ³/₈-yd
- tan stripe – ³/₈-yd
- blue stripe – ¹/₂-yd
- blue check – ¹/₈-yd
- assorted blue prints and plaids – ¹/₄-yd total
- assorted cream prints and plaids – ¹/₄-yd total
- backing – 1-yd
- binding – ⁵/₈-yd

Other supplies
- batting – 26"x30"
- paper-backed fusible web
- clear nylon thread
- assorted white buttons

*Refer to **Wall Hanging Diagram** as needed. See **Quilter's Basics** (pg. 241) for more in-depth basic instructions.*

CUTTING
Cream stripe:
- Cut one background – 9"x13"

Blue print:
- Cut one 2"w strip. From this, cut:
    - 16 A's – 2" square
- Cut one piece for triangle-squares – 11" square

Tan stripe:
- Cut one piece for triangle-squares – 11" square

Blue stripe:
- Cut three 3¹/₂"w strips. From these, cut:
    - two side borders – 3¹/₂"x22¹/₂"
    - two top/bottom borders – 3¹/₂"x18¹/₂"
- Cut two 1¹/₄"w strips. From these, cut:
    - two top/bottom inner borders – 1¹/₄"x13"
    - two side inner borders – 1¹/₄"x10¹/₂"

Blue check:
- Cut one 3¹/₂" strip. From this, cut:
    - 8 B's – 3¹/₂" square

One blue plaid:
- Cut 4 E's – 2¹/₂" square

Assorted blue prints and plaids:
- Cut a total of 12 C's – 2¹/₂" square

Assorted cream prints and plaids:
- Cut a total of 16 D's – 2¹/₂" square

APPLIQUÉING

1. Trace patterns (pg. 234) onto paper side of web. Referring to photo, fuse patterns to wrong sides of remaining fabrics and scraps; cut out.

2. Arrange appliqués on background piece; fuse in place. Stitch around edges of appliqués using clear nylon thread and a medium zigzag stitch with a medium stitch length.

PIECING

1. To make triangle-squares, use blue print and tan stripe squares and follow **Making Triangle-Squares** (pg. 243) to make 32 triangle-squares.

Fig. 1

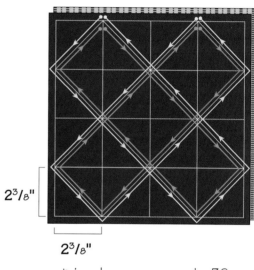

2³/₈"

2³/₈"

triangle-square – make 32

2. Sew 2 triangle-squares together to make each of 16 Unit 1's.

Unit 1 – make 16

3. Sew 2 blue print A's and 1 Unit 1 together to make each of 8 Unit 2's.

Unit 2 – make 8

4. Sew 2 Unit 1's and 1 blue check B together to make each of 4 Unit 3's.

Unit 3 – make 4

5. Sew 2 Unit 2's and 1 Unit 3 together to make each of 4 Star Blocks. Blocks should measure 6$\frac{1}{2}$" square.

Star Block – make 4

6. Sew 4 assorted blue C's and 5 assorted tan D's together to make each of 2 Nine-Patch Blocks. Blocks should measure 6$\frac{1}{2}$" square.

Nine-Patch Blocks – make 2

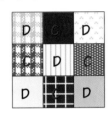

7. Sew 3 assorted cream D's and 2 assorted blue C's together to make each of 2 Unit 4's.

Unit 4 – make 2

8. Sew top, bottom, then side inner borders to background; then add 1 Unit 4 to each side edge to make Row A.

Row A – make 1

9. Sew 2 Star Blocks and 1 Nine-Patch Block together to make each of 2 Row B's.

Row B – make 2

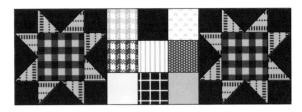

10. Sew Rows together to make wall hanging center.

11. Sew side borders to edges of wall hanging center. Sew 1 blue plaid E to each end of each top/bottom border. Sew borders to wall hanging center to complete wall hanging top. Wall hanging should measure 24$\frac{1}{2}$"x28$\frac{1}{2}$".

FINISHING

1. Mark, layer, and quilt wall hanging, using **Quilting Diagram**, pg. 234, as a suggestion.

2. Bind wall hanging using 3$\frac{1}{4}$-yds of 2$\frac{1}{2}$"w bias binding.

3. Sew buttons to wall hanging.

Wall Hanging Diagram

Quilting Diagram

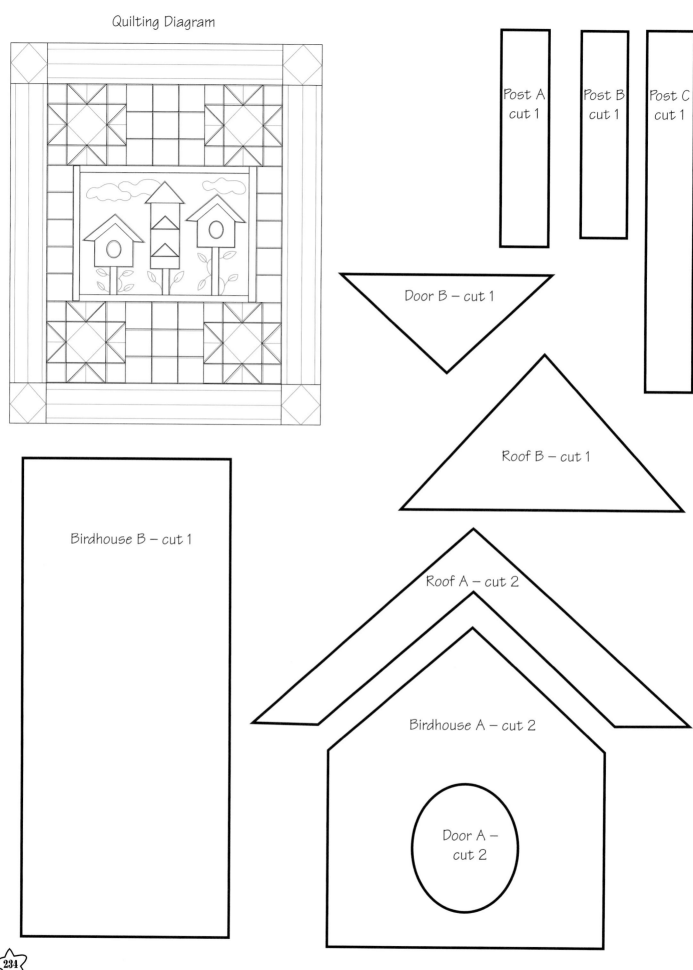

Post A
cut 1

Post B
cut 1

Post C
cut 1

Door B – cut 1

Roof B – cut 1

Roof A – cut 2

Birdhouse B – cut 1

Birdhouse A – cut 2

Door A –
cut 2

PATCHWORK BLUES PILLOWS

(shown on pg. 230)

STAR BLOCK PILLOW
Finished size: 14"x18"
Block size: 6" square

FABRICS
- blue plaid – $^1/_8$-yd
- blue print – $^3/_8$-yd
- white print – $^7/_8$-yd

Other supplies
- 12" pillow form
- six $^3/_4$" buttons

Refer to **Star Block Pillow Diagram** *as needed. See* **Quilter's Basics** *(pg. 241) for more in-depth basic instructions.*

CUTTING
Blue plaid:
- Cut one 3$^1/_2$"w strip. From this, cut:
  - 4 B's – 3$^1/_2$" square

White print:
- Cut one 1$^1/_2$"w strip. From this, cut:
  - 2 top/bottom borders – 1$^1/_2$"x12$^1/_2$"
- Cut two 6$^1/_2$" strips. From these, cut:
  - 2 side borders – 6$^1/_2$"x28$^1/_2$"
- Cut one piece for triangle-squares – 11" square
- Cut one pillow back – 12$^1/_2$"x14$^1/_2$"

Blue print:
- Cut one 2"w strip. From this, cut:
  - 16 A's – 2" square
- Cut one piece for triangle-squares – 11" square

PIECING
1. Follow Steps 1- 5 of **Piecing** (Birdhouse Wall Hanging, pgs. 232 – 233) to make 4 Star Blocks.

2. Sew blocks together; sew top and bottom borders to blocks to complete pillow top.

3. Sew backing to pillow top along top and bottom edges only. Turn and press.

4. Sew short edges of each side border together to form two tubes. Press tubes in half, matching wrong sides and raw edges.

5. Place one side border over each side edge of pillow and backing, matching raw edges. Stitch in place. Turn and press.

6. Work 3 evenly spaced buttonholes on front of each side border. Sew buttons to inside back of each side border.

7. Slip pillow form into pillow. Button to secure.

Star Block Pillow Diagram

NINE-PATCH PILLOW

Finished size: 14"x18"
Block size: 6" square

FABRICS
• 3 different blue plaids for blocks – fat quarter each
• blue plaid for borders, blocks, and backing – 1-yd
• 5 different cream prints – fat quarter each

Other supplies
• 12" pillow form
• six ³/₄" buttons

*Refer to **Nine-Patch Pillow Diagram** as needed. See **Quilter's Basics** (pg. 241) for more in-depth basic instructions.*

CUTTING
Each blue plaid fat quarter:
• Cut one 2¹/₂"w strip. From this, cut:
    • 4 A's – 2¹/₂" square
Blue plaid for borders, blocks, and backing:
• Cut one 2¹/₂"w strip. From this, cut:
    • 4 A's – 2¹/₂" square
• Cut one 1¹/₂"w strip. From this, cut:
    • 2 top/bottom borders – 1¹/₂"x12¹/₂"
• Cut two 6¹/₂"w strips. From these, cut:
    • 2 side borders – 6¹/₂"x28¹/₂"
• Cut 1 pillow back – 12¹/₂"x14¹/₂"
Each cream print:
• Cut one 2¹/₂"w strip. From this, cut:
    • 4 B's – 2¹/₂" square

PIECING
1. Sew 4 A's and 5 B's together to make each of 4 Nine-Patch Blocks.

Nine-Patch Block – make 4

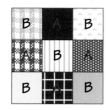

2. Follow Steps 2 – 7 of **Piecing** (Star Block Pillow, pg. 235) to complete pillow.

Nine-Patch Pillow Diagram

ROOSTER PINCUSHION
(shown on pg. 228)

Finished size: 5¹/₂"h

SUPPLIES
• red, grey, tan, and gold wool fabric – scraps
• polyester fiberfill
• wooden thread spool – 1"-diameter
• 2 small buttons for eyes

INSTRUCTIONS
1. Use pattern (pg. 240) to cut 2 rooster pieces from red wool.

2. Using a ¹/₄" seam allowance, sew pieces together, leaving bottom edge open. Turn right side out.

3. Baste along bottom raw edge of rooster.

4. Stuff rooster to within ³/₄" of opening. Insert spool halfway into opening. Pull thread ends to gather fabric around spool; knot ends.

6. Cut three ³/₈"x 6" grey, tan, and gold wool strips. Stack strips together and fold in half. Sew folded area to top of tail to form tail feathers.

7. Sew buttons to head for eyes.

FRIENDSHIP BUTTON WALL QUILT

(shown on pg. 225)

Finished size: 23"x26"
Block size: 3" square

FABRICS
• assorted plaids and stripes – about ³/₄-yd total (ours uses 15 different fabrics)
• muslin – ¹/₂-yd
• plaid for border – ¹/₃-yd
• plaid for binding – ¹/₂-yd
• backing – ³/₄-yd
Other supplies
• batting – 27"x30"
• paper-backed fusible web
• fine-tip permanent pen
• assorted buttons
• assorted embroidery floss

*Refer to **Wall Quilt Diagram** as needed. See **Quilter's Basics** (pg. 241) for more in-depth basic instructions.*

CUTTING
Assorted plaids and stripes:
• Cut a total of 30 A's – 3¹/₂" square
Muslin:
• Cut two 1¹/₄"w strips. From these, cut:
  • 2 top/bottom inner borders – 1¹/₄"x15¹/₂"
  • 2 side inner borders – 1¹/₄"x20"
Plaid for border:
• Cut three 3¹/₂"w strips. From these, cut:
  • 2 top/bottom borders – 3¹/₂"x17"
  • 2 side borders – 3¹/₂"x 26"

HEART APPLIQUÉS
1. Fuse web to remaining muslin. Cut out 30 freehand hearts of various sizes to fit on A squares.

2. Have each friend sign a heart using permanent pen.

PIECING
1. Sew 5 A's together to make each of 6 rows. Sew rows together to make wall quilt center.

2. Arrange 1 heart on each A; fuse in place.

3. Sew top, bottom, then side inner borders to wall hanging center. Repeat with outer borders to complete wall hanging top.

FINISHING
1. Write desired message on inner border using permanent pen.

2. Layer backing, batting, and wall hanging top together. Tie quilt with embroidery floss, slipping buttons onto some ties before making final knots. Our wall hanging is tied at the top of each heart, at intersections of A seamlines, and at random intervals on outer border.

3. Bind quilt using 3¹/₄-yds of 2¹/₂"w bias binding.

Wall Quilt Diagram

YO-YO DRESS

(shown on pg. 229)

SUPPLIES

- cotton long-sleeved dress with straight sleeves, pockets, and stand-up collar
- green plaid for pockets – ¼-yd
- large red plaid – ⅓-yd
- small red plaid – ½-yd
- fabrics for appliqués and yo-yo's – scraps
- paper-backed fusible web
- buttons
- button-covering kit (size to replace dress buttons)
- yellow embroidery floss
- pinking shears

Use a ½" seam allowance. **Stitch Diagrams** *are on pgs. 255 – 256.*

INSTRUCTIONS

1. For pockets, fuse web to wrong side of green plaid. Use pinking shears to cut pieces the same size as pockets; fuse in place.

2. For bias trim, cut 1"w bias strips from small red plaid. Press long edges under ¼". Pin trim along collar, hem, and ½" from side and bottom edges of pockets, piecing as necessary and folding ends under. Stitch in place using 3 strands of floss and a herringbone stitch.

3. For each sleeve cuff, cut 1 large red plaid piece on the bias 7"w x 1" longer than circumference of sleeve opening. Sew 7" ends together to form a tube. Matching wrong sides and raw edges, press tube in half; pink raw edge. Insert pinked edge about 1½" into sleeve. Sew sleeve and cuff together. Fold cuff back over sleeve.

4. For trim at top of each pocket, cut 1 large red plaid piece 4½"w x 1" longer than top of pocket. Press ends under ¼". Sew long raw edges together, turn, and press flat. Hand-stitch cuff to top edge of pocket.

5. Make 6 yo-yo's (see **Making Yo-Yo's**, pg. 246) from scraps, using 2½"-3¼" circles.

6. For appliqués, trace basket and leaf patterns (pg. 240) onto paper side of web. Fuse web to wrong sides of fabrics; cut out pieces. Fuse pieces to dress. Stitch over basket edges using 3 strands of floss and herringbone stitch. Use 3 strands of floss to work a running stitch on leaves.

7. Sew assorted buttons and yo-yo's to dress.

8. Replace dress buttons with covered buttons.

FLORAL PINS

(shown on pg. 228)

SUPPLIES

- ecru felt – scraps
- 3 red buttons for oval pin
- 3 assorted buttons for heart pin
- ecru and green floss
- polyester fiberfill
- red fabric scrap for heart pin
- 1" pin back
- hot glue

Oval Pin

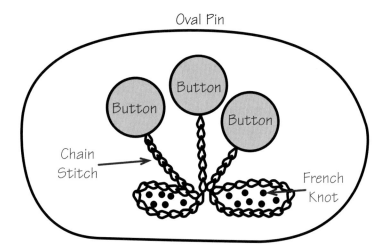

Heart Pin

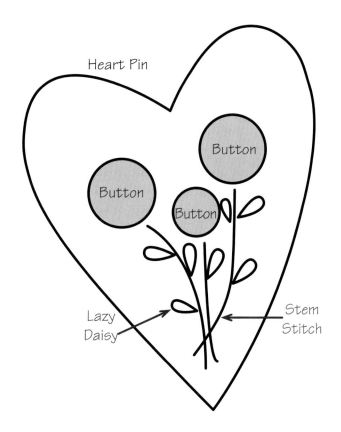

Stitch Diagrams are on pgs. 255 – 256.

INSTRUCTIONS (FOR EACH)

1. Use pattern (pg. 238) to cut 2 pin backgrounds from felt.

2. Refer to pattern to lightly freehand draw embroidery design onto 1 felt piece. Use 1 strand of green floss to work leaves and stems as noted on pattern.

3. Sew buttons to felt piece.

4. Sew felt pieces together using 2 strands of ecru floss and a blanket stitch, stuffing lightly with fiberfill before ending stitching.

5. For heart pin, tie a knot in a $1/2$"w fabric scrap; trim ends. Glue to pin.

6. Glue pin back to pin.

YO-YO FLOWER BREAD COVER
(shown on pg. 227)

Finished size: 18" square

SUPPLIES
• 18" square napkin
• red plaid – $1/2$-yd
• green plaid for appliqués – scrap
• assorted plaids for yo-yo's – scraps
• assorted buttons
• embroidery floss
• $1/2$"w fusible web tape
• paper-backed fusible web – scrap

INSTRUCTIONS

1. For bias trim, cut four 1"x20" bias strips from red plaid. Press under long edges $1/4$". Use web tape to fuse strips 1" from napkin edges, folding ends under and trimming as needed.

2. Use 2 strands of floss to work a herringbone stitch (see **Stitch Diagrams**, pgs. 255 – 256) over bias trim.

3. Follow **Making Yo-Yo's** (pg. 246) to make 4 yo-yo's from $3^1/4$" plaid scrap circles and 8 yo-yo's from 2" plaid scrap circles.

4. Trace each leaf pattern (pg. 240) 8 times onto paper side of web. Fuse to wrong side of green fabric. Cut out leaves.

5. Arrange 3 yo-yo's and 6 leaves on each corner of the bread cloth. Fuse leaves in place. Sew each yo-yo in place with a button.

PATCHWORK FRAME
(shown on pg. 226)

Finished size: 6" square with 3" opening

SUPPLIES
• craft knife
• $1/4$" thick foam board
• poster board
• glue gun
• blue plaid – fat quarter
• paper-backed fusible web
• cream plaid – 8" square
• 4 small buttons

INSTRUCTIONS

1. Use craft knife to cut a 6" square of foam board for frame. Cut a 3" square opening from the center. Cut a 1"x5" foam board piece for stand. Cut a 6" square of poster board for backing.

2. Cut blue plaid fabric larger than backing. Cover backing with fabric, folding excess fabric to the back and using hot glue to secure. Repeat for stand and frame, but do not cut out fabric over frame opening.

3. Trace star pattern (pg. 240) onto paper side of web, turning web as needed to make a complete design. Fuse web to wrong side of cream fabric. Cut out. Fuse star to frame front.

4. At center of frame, use craft knife to cut an "X" through fabrics; extend cuts to corners of opening. Fold and glue fabric to back of frame.

5. Glue backing to frame along side and bottom edges. Fold stand 1" from one end. Glue small folded area to back of frame so that frame will stand. Glue buttons to frame front.

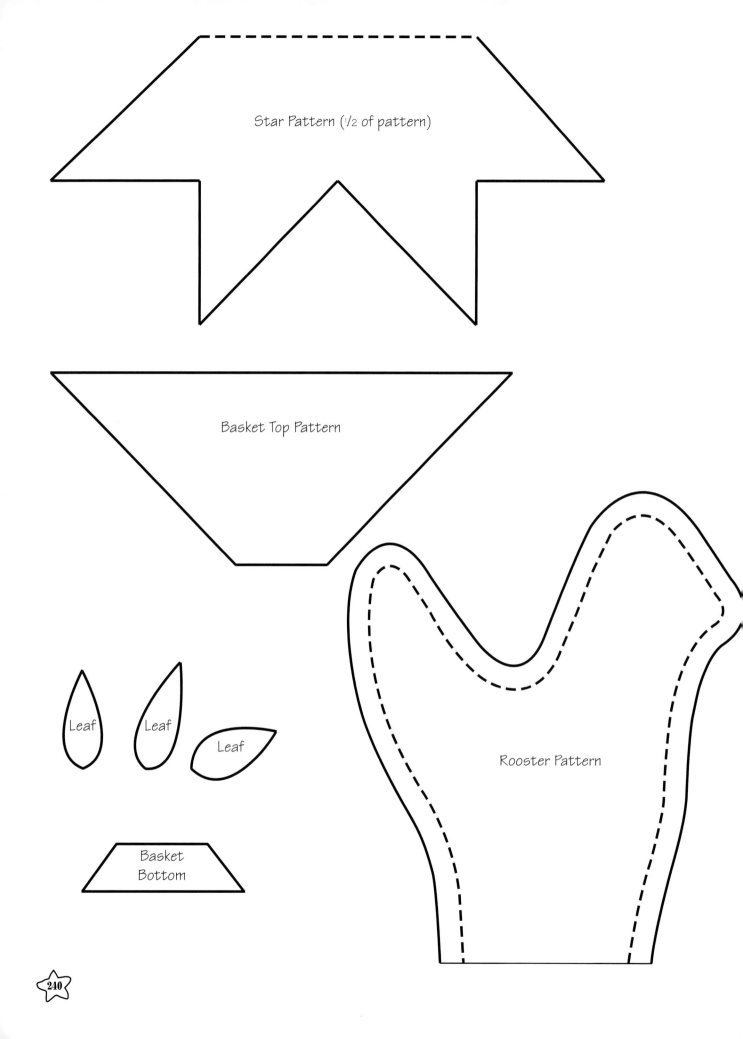

Star Pattern (½ of pattern)

Basket Top Pattern

Leaf

Leaf

Leaf

Rooster Pattern

Basket
Bottom

QUILTER'S BASICS

All yardage amounts listed are based on 45"w 100% cotton fabric with a "usable width" of 42" after washing and trimming selvages. When sewing, match right sides and raw edges and use an accurate 1/4" seam allowance unless otherwise specified.

BASIC TOOLS
ROTARY CUTTING:
18" x 24" rotary cutting mat
6" x 24" rotary cutting ruler with 45° marking
rotary cutter – 45mm size
right-angle triangle

MACHINE-PIECING:
sewing machine
straight pins
scissors
all-purpose sewing thread in neutral color
seam ripper

PRESSING:
steam iron

APPLIQUÉING:
template plastic
hand-sewing needles – sharps
all-purpose sewing thread to match
each appliqué fabric

HAND QUILTING:
Quilting needles – betweens
Quilting thread
Quilting hoop or frame

MACHINE QUILTING:
large brass safety pins
walking foot or even-feed foot for
sewing machine

ROTARY CUTTING

Observe safety precautions when using the rotary cutter since it is extremely sharp. Develop a habit of retracting the blade guard just before making a cut and closing it immediately afterward, before laying down the cutter.

1. Wash, dry, and press fabrics.

2. Refold each piece of fabric lengthwise (as it was on the bolt) with wrong sides together and matching selvages. If necessary adjust fabric slightly at selvages so that fold lies flat; press.

3. Cut all strips from the selvage-to-selvage width of the fabric unless otherwise indicated in project instructions. Place fabric on the cutting mat with the fold of the fabric toward you (Fig. 1). To straighten the uneven fabric edge, make the first "squaring up" cut by placing the right edge of the rotary cutting ruler over the left raw edge of the fabric. Place right-angle triangle (or another rotary cutting ruler) with the lower edge carefully aligned with the fold and the left edge against the ruler (Fig. 1). Hold the ruler firmly with your left hand, placing your little finger off the left edge to anchor the ruler. Remove the triangle, pick up the rotary cutter, and retract the blade guard. Using a smooth downward motion, make the cut by running the blade of the rotary cutter firmly along the right edge of the ruler (Fig. 2). Always cut in a direction away from your body and immediately close the blade guard after each cut.

Fig. 1

Fig. 2

4. To cut each of the strips required for a project, place the ruler over the cut edge of the fabric, aligning desired marking on the ruler with the cut edge (Fig. 3); make the cut. When cutting several strips from a single piece of fabric, check frequently that cuts remain at a perfect right angle to the fold.

Fig. 3

5. To square up selvage ends of a strip before cutting pieces, refer to Fig. 4 and place folded strip on a mat with selvage ends to your right. Aligning a horizontal marking on ruler with 1 long edge of strip, then trim selvage to make end of strip square and even (Fig. 4). Turn strip (or entire mat) so that cut end is to your left before making further cuts.

Fig. 4

6. Pieces such as rectangles and squares can now be cut from strips. Usually strips remain folded, and pieces are cut in pairs after ends of strips are squared up. To cut squares or rectangles from a strip, place ruler over left end of strip, aligning desired marking on ruler with cut end of strip. To ensure perfectly square cuts, align a horizontal marking on ruler with 1 long edge of strip (Fig. 5) before making the cut.

Fig. 5

7. To cut 2 triangles from a square, cut square the size indicated in the project instructions. Cut square once diagonally to make 2 triangles (Fig. 6).

Fig. 6

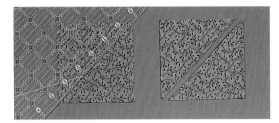

8. To cut 4 triangles from a square, cut square the size indicated in the project instructions. Cut square twice diagonally to make 4 triangles (Fig. 7).

Fig. 7

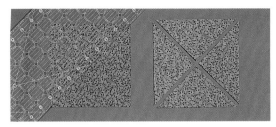

9. In some cases, strips will be sewn together into strip sets before being cut into smaller units. When cutting a strip set, align a seam in strip set with a horizontal marking on the ruler to maintain square cuts (Fig. 8).

Fig. 8

TEMPLATE CUTTING

Our full-sized piecing template patterns have 2 lines – a solid cutting line and a dashed line showing the $1/4$" seam allowance. Patterns for appliqué templates do not include seam allowances.

1. To make a template from a pattern, use a permanent fine-point pen to carefully trace pattern onto template plastic, making sure to transfer all alignment and grain line markings. Cut out template along inner edge of drawn line. Check template against original pattern for accuracy.

2. To use a template, place template on wrong side of fabric (unless otherwise indicated in project instructions), aligning grain line on template with straight grain of fabric. Use a sharp fabric-marking pencil to draw around template. Transfer all alignment markings to fabric. Cut out fabric piece using scissors or rotary cutting equipment.

PIECING

Set sewing machine stitch length for approximately 11 stitches per inch. Use a new, sharp needle suited for medium-weight woven fabric. Use a neutral-colored general-purpose sewing thread (not quilting thread) in the needle and in the bobbin.

Using an accurate $1/4$" seam allowance is essential. On many sewing machines, the measurement from the needle to the outer edge of the presser foot is $1/4$". If this is not the case with your machine, measure $1/4$" from the needle and mark throat plate with a piece of masking tape. Special presser feet that are exactly $1/4$" wide are also available for most sewing machines.

When piecing, always place pieces right sides together and match raw edges; pin if necessary.

SEWING STRIP SETS

When sewing several strips into a strip set, first sew the strips together into pairs, then sew the pairs together to form the strip set. To help avoid distortion, sew 1 seam in 1 direction and then sew the next seam in the opposite direction (Fig. 9).

Fig. 9

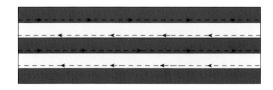

SEWING ACROSS SEAM INTERSECTIONS

When sewing across the intersection of 2 seams, place pieces right sides together and match seams exactly, making sure seam allowances are pressed in opposite directions (Fig. 10).

Fig. 10

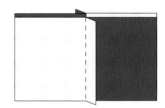

SEWING BIAS SEAMS

Care should be used in handling and stitching bias edges since they stretch easily. After sewing the seam, carefully press seam allowance to 1 side, making sure not to stretch fabric.

SEWING SHARP POINTS

To ensure sharp points when joining triangular or diagonal pieces, stitch across the center of the "X" (shown in pink) formed on the wrong side by previous seams (Fig. 11).

Fig. 11

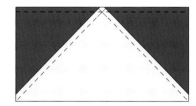

STITCH-AND-FLIP METHOD

Bias seams can be sewn with little distortion using this method. Place pieces (noted in project instructions) right sides together, matching edges. Stitch diagonally across the small piece (Fig. 12). Trim both fabrics 1/4" from stitching line (Fig. 13). Press open top piece, pressing seam allowance toward darker fabric (Fig. 14). Repeat with additional pieces, if needed (Figs. 15 – 17).

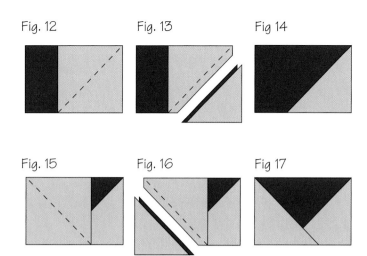

Fig. 12   Fig. 13   Fig 14

Fig. 15   Fig. 16   Fig 17

MAKING TRIANGLE-SQUARES

The grid method for making triangle-squares is faster and more accurate than cutting and sewing individual triangles. Stitching before cutting the triangle-squares apart also prevents stretching the bias edges.

1. Follow project instructions to cut rectangles or squares of fabric for making triangle-squares. Place the indicated pieces right sides together and press.

2. On the wrong side of the lighter fabric, draw a grid of squares similar to that shown in Fig. 18. The size and number of squares will be given in the project instructions. Following the example given in the project instructions, draw 1 diagonal line through each square in the grid (Fig. 19).

Fig. 18   Fig. 19

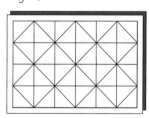

3. Stitch 1/4" on each side of all diagonal lines, drawing stitching lines ahead of time if needed. Project instructions include a diagram similar to Fig. 20, which shows stitching lines and the direction of the stitching.

Fig. 20

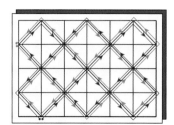

4. Cut along all drawn lines of the grid. Each square of the grid will yield 2 triangle-squares (Fig. 21).

Fig. 21

5. Carefully press triangle-squares open, pressing seam allowances toward darker fabric.

TRIMMING SEAM ALLOWANCES

When sewing with diamond or triangle pieces, some seam allowances may extend beyond the edges of the sewn pieces. Trim away "dog ears" that extend beyond the edges of the sewn pieces (Fig. 22).

Fig. 22

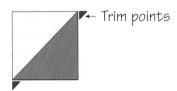

← Trim points

SETTING IN SEAMS

1. When sewing 2 diamond-shaped pieces together, place pieces right sides together, carefully matching edges; pin. Mark a small dot 1/4" from corner of 1 piece (Fig. 23). Stitch pieces together in the direction shown, stopping at center of dot and backstitching.

Fig. 23

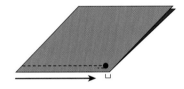

2. Mark corner of each piece to be set in with a small dot (Fig. 24).

Fig. 24

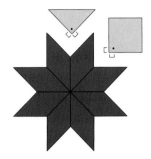

3. To sew first set-in seam, pin the triangle (or corner square) to the diamond on the left. Stitch seam from the outer edge to the dot, backstitching at dot; clip threads (Fig. 25).

Fig. 25

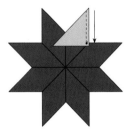

4. To sew second set-in seam, pivot the added triangle (or corner square) to match raw edges of next diamond. Beginning at dot, take 2 or 3 stitches, then backstitch, making sure not to backstitch into the previous seam allowance. Continue stitching to outer edge (Fig. 26).

Fig. 26

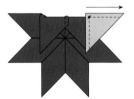

PRESSING

Use a steam iron set on "Cotton" for all pressing. Press as you sew, taking care to prevent small folds along seamlines. Seam allowances are usually pressed to one side, usually toward the darker fabric. However, to reduce bulk it may occasionally be necessary to press seam allowances toward the lighter fabric or even to press them open. To prevent a dark fabric seam allowance from showing through a light fabric, trim the darker seam allowance slightly narrower than the lighter seam allowance. To press long seams, such as those in long strip sets, without curving or other distortion, lay strips across the width of the ironing board.

FOUNDATION PIECING

PREPARING YOUR SEWING MACHINE

To prepare your sewing machine for foundation piecing, insert a 90/14 needle. This needle will help perforate your paper to make the needle-punch foundations. This needle should then be reserved exclusively for the use on foundation work, as paper will dull needles quickly.

Set your machine to a short straight stitch (18 stitches per inch). It is helpful to use an open-toe foot.

MAKING NEEDLE-PUNCH PAPER FOUNDATIONS

Using a fine-point marker and leaving at least a 1" space around design, trace desired pattern.

To make needle-punch foundations, place up to eight pieces of foundation paper (notebook paper will do) under traced pattern and secure with pins. With your needle in your machine but no thread, sew precisely on the drawn lines. The punched holes serve as your sewing guide.

Cut out leaving at least 1" around the design.

If applicable, transfer pattern labels to paper foundation.

PIECING

Place your original pattern nearby as a guide. If you wish, transfer numbers to your needle-punched foundations.

Thread your machine with a neutral-colored thread. Follow project instructions to place and sew fabric.

Rough cut a piece of fabric at least ¹/₂" larger on all sides than area 1 on the foundation.

Center fabric piece right side up on back of foundation; completely cover area 1 with fabric.

Fold foundation on line between area 1 and area 2. Trim fabric ¹/₄" from fold (Fig. 27). Unfold foundation.

Fig. 27

6. Rough cut a piece of fabric in the same manner for area 2 on foundation. Matching trimmed edge, place piece #2 right sides together on piece #1, making sure fabric extends beyond outer seamlines (Fig. 28). Turn foundation over to front and pin.

Fig. 28

7. Sew along punched line between areas 1 and 2, extending sewing a few stitches beyond beginning and end of line (Fig. 29).

Fig. 29

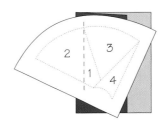

8. Open out piece #2; press. Pin piece #2 to foundation (Fig. 30).

Fig. 30

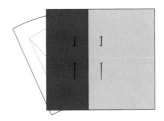

9. Repeat adding pieces in same manner until foundation is covered.

10. Trim fabric and foundation ¹/₄" outside punched lines.

11. When removing paper from fabric, score the seams with the eye of a large needle or use tweezers to gently remove small pieces.

PAPER-PIECING FOR LOG CABIN BLOCKS

This method uses strips precut to the correct "log" width, but helps you piece very precisely. The figures below show a paper-pieced Pineapple Variation block, but the same process is used for any Log Cabin-style block.

1. Determine which fabric strip will be used for the center square (labeled as "1" on the pattern) of the block. Place square right-side up over center square area on numbered side of foundation; pin in place (Fig. 31). Hold foundation up to a light to make sure enough fabric extends beyond the center square outline (sewing line) for seam allowance.

Fig. 31

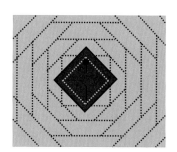

2. To cover area 2 on foundation, choose the correct-colored fabric strip. Refer to Fig. 32 to place strip wrong-side up on center square. Turn foundation over to paper side and sew directly on top of sewing line between areas 1 and 2, extending stitching a few stitches beyond beginning and end of line. Turn foundation back over to fabric side (Fig. 32).

Fig. 32

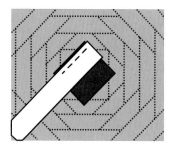

3. Trim strip even with ends of stitching. Open out strip and press. Make sure enough fabric extends beyond adjacent seamlines for seam allowance. (On Pineapple Variation block, you will need to trim off corners of pieces to correlate with seamlines.)

4. Repeat Steps 2 and 3 for areas 3, 4, and 5 (Fig. 33), then continue until entire foundation is covered.

Fig. 33

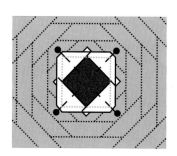

5. When piecing is complete, turn foundation to paper side and use a long stitch to baste along the outer seamline. Trim foundation and fabric to exactly 1/4" from basted line for seam allowance.

6. Tear away paper.

MAKING YO-YO'S

1. Cut a circle pattern from template plastic or heavy paper. To determine size of pattern, double the desired finished size of the yo-yo and add $^1/_2$". (use a $4^1/_2$" circle pattern to make a finished 2" yo-yo.)

2. Use pattern to cut circle from fabric.

3. Fold raw edge of fabric circle $^1/_4$" to wrong side and work small running stitches around entire circle through the folded area (Fig. 34).

Fig 34.

4. With right side of the fabric facing out, pull thread to tightly gather fabric; knot thread to secure.

5. Flatten yo-yo so that gathered circle is at the center (Fig. 35).

Fig. 35

APPLIQUÉ

PREPARING APPLIQUÉ PIECES

Patterns are printed in reverse to enable you to use our speedy method of preparing appliqués. This method can be used when securing appliqués with Invisible Appliqué, Satin Stitch Appliqué, or Mock Hand Appliqué. White or light-colored fabrics may need to be lined with fusible interfacing before applying fusible web to prevent darker fabrics from showing through.

1. Place paper-backed fusible web, web side down, over appliqué pattern. Use a pencil to trace pattern onto paper side of web as many times as indicated in project instructions for a single fabric. Repeat for additional patterns and fabrics.

2. Follow manufacturer's instructions to fuse traced patterns to wrong side of fabrics. Do not remove paper backing. (Note: Some pieces may be given as measurements, such as a 2" x 4" rectangle, instead of drawn patterns. Fuse web to wrong side of the fabrics indicated for these pieces.)

3. Use scissors to cut out appliqué pieces along traced lines; use rotary cutting equipment to cut out appliqué pieces given as measurements. Remove paper backing from all pieces.

INVISIBLE APPLIQUÉ

This machine appliqué method uses clear nylon thread to secure the appliqué pieces. Transparent monofilament (clear nylon) thread is available in 2 colors: clear and smoke. Use clear on white or very light fabrics and smoke on darker colors.

1. Referring to diagram and/or photo, arrange prepared appliqués on the background fabric and follow manufacturer's instructions to fuse in place.

2. Pin a stabilizer, such as paper or any of the commercially available products, on wrong side of background fabric before stitching appliqués in place.

3. Thread sewing machine with transparent monofilament thread; use general-purpose thread that matches background fabric in bobbin.

4. Set sewing machine for a very narrow width (approximately ¹⁄₁₆") zigzag stitch and a short stitch length. You may find that loosening the top tension slightly will yield a smoother stitch.

5. Begin by stitching 2 or 3 stitches in place (drop feed dogs or set stitch length at 0) to anchor thread. Most of the zigzag stitch should be done on the appliqué with the right edges of the stitch falling at the very outside edge of the appliqué. Stitch over all exposed raw edges of appliqué pieces.

6. (Note: Dots on Figs. 36-41 indicate where to leave needle in fabric when pivoting.) For outside corners, stitch just past the corner, stopping with the needle in background fabric (Fig. 36). Raise presser foot. Pivot project, lower presser foot, and stitch adjacent side (Fig. 37).

Fig. 36   Fig. 37

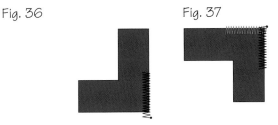

7. For **inside corners**, stitch just past the corner, stopping with the needle in **appliqué** fabric (Fig. 38). Raise presser foot. Pivot project, lower presser foot, and stitch adjacent side (Fig. 39).

Fig. 38   Fig. 39

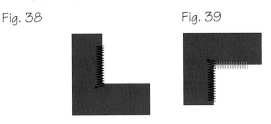

8. When stitching **outside** curves, stop with needle in **background** fabric. Raise presser foot and pivot project as needed. Lower presser foot and continue stitching, pivoting as often as necessary to follow curve (Fig. 40).

Fig. 40

9. When stitching **inside** curves, stop with needle in **appliqué** fabric. Raise presser foot and pivot project as needed. Lower presser foot and continue stitching, pivoting as often as necessary to follow curve (Fig. 41).

Fig. 41

10. Do not backstitch at end of stitching. Pull threads to wrong side of background fabric; knot thread and trim ends.

11. Carefully tear away stabilizer.

NEEDLE-TURN APPLIQUÉ

In this traditional hand appliqué method, the needle is used to turn the seam allowance under as you sew the appliqué to the background fabric using a Blind Stitch, page 255. When stitching, match the color of thread to the color of appliqué to disguise your stitches. Appliqué each piece starting with the ones directly on the background fabric. It is not necessary to appliqué areas that will be covered by another appliqué. Stitches on the right side of fabric should not show. Stitches on the edge of an appliqué and on background fabric should be equal in length. Clipped areas should be secured with a few extra stitches to prevent fraying.

1. Follow **Template Cutting**, pg. 242, Step 1 to cut templates from template plastic.

2. Place template on right side of appliqué fabric. Use a pencil to lightly draw around template, leaving at least 1/2" between shapes; repeat for number of shapes specified in project instructions.

3. Cut out shapes approximately 3/16" outside drawn line. Clip inside curves and points up to, but not through, drawn line. Arrange shapes on background fabric and pin or baste in place.

4. Thread a sharps needle with a single strand of general-purpose sewing thread; knot one end.

5. Pin center of appliqué to right side of background fabric. Begin on as straight an edge as possible and use point of needle to turn under a small amount of seam allowance, concealing drawn line on appliqué. Hold seam allowance in place with thumb of your non-sewing hand (Fig. 42).

Fig. 42

6. To stitch, bring needle up through background fabric at 1, even with turned edge of appliqué (Fig. 43).

Fig. 43

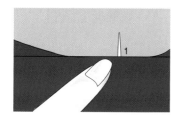

7. Insert needle into turned edge at 2, directly across from 1. Bring needle out of folded edge at 3 (Fig. 44). Insert needle into background fabric at 4, even with edge of appliqué and directly across from 3. Bring needle up through background fabric at 5, forming a small stitch on wrong side of fabric (Fig. 45).

Fig. 44

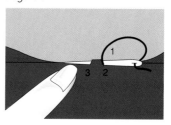

Fig. 45

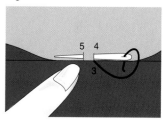

8. Continue needle-turning method to completely secure appliqué, referring to information below about stitching outward points and bias strips.

Stitching Outward Points: Appliqué long edge of shape until you are about 1/2" from the point (Fig. 46). Turn seam allowance under at point (Fig. 47). Turn remainder of seam allowance between stitching and point, using non-stitching thumb to hold allowance in place. Stitch to point, taking 2 or 3 stitches at top of point to secure. Turn under small amount of seam allowance past point and resume stitching.

Fig. 46

Fig. 47

Stitching Pressed Bias Strips: Since seam allowances have already been stitched or pressed under during preparation of bias strips used as appliqués, simply baste bias strip to background fabric, then stitch in place along edges using the same blindstitch used in needle-turning.

SATIN STITCH APPLIQUÉ

A good satin stitch is a thick, smooth, almost solid line of zigzag stitching that covers the exposed raw edges of appliqué pieces.

1. Place a stabilizer, such as paper or any of the commercially available products, on wrong side of background fabric before stitching appliqués in place.

2. Thread needle of sewing machine with general-purpose thread. Use thread that matches the background fabric in the bobbin for all stitching. Set sewing machine for a medium width zigzag stitch (approximately ⅛") and a very short stitch length. Set upper tension slightly looser than for regular stitching.

3. Beginning on as straight an edge as possible, position fabric so that most of the satin stitch will be on the appliqué piece. Do not backstitch; hold upper thread toward you and sew over it two or three stitches to anchor thread. Following Steps 6–9 of **Invisible Appliqué**, pg. 247, for stitching corners and curves, stitch over exposed raw edges of appliqué pieces, changing thread color as necessary.

4. Do not backstitch at end of stitching. Pull threads to wrong side of background fabric; knot thread and trim ends. Remove paper and stabilizer.

MOCK HAND APPLIQUÉ

This technique uses the blindstitch on your sewing machine to achieve a look that closely resembles traditional hand appliqué. Using an updated method, appliqués are prepared with turned-under edges and then machine stitched to the background fabric. For best appliqué results, your sewing machine must have blindstitch capability with a variable stitch width. If your blindstitch width cannot be adjusted, you may still wish to try this technique to see if you are happy with the results. Some sewing machines have a narrower blindstitch width than others.

1. Follow project instructions to prepare appliqué pieces.

2. Thread needle of sewing machine with transparent monofilament thread; use general-purpose thread in bobbin in a color to match background fabric.

3. Set sewing machine for narrow blindstitch (just wide enough to catch 2 or 3 threads of the appliqué) and a very short stitch length (20 - 30 stitches per inch).

4. Arrange appliqué pieces on background fabric as described in project instructions. Use pins or hand baste to secure.

5. (Note: Follow Steps 6 - 9 of **Invisible Appliqué**, page 247, for needle position when pivoting.) Sew around edges of each appliqué so that the straight stitches fall on the background fabric very near the appliqué and the "hem" stitches barely catch the folded edge of the appliqué (Fig. 48)

Fig. 48

6. It is not necessary to backstitch at the beginning or end of stitching. End stitching by sewing ¼" over the first stitches. Trim thread ends close the fabric.

BORDERS

Borders cut along the lengthwise grain will lie flatter than borders cut along the crosswise grain. In most cases, our instructions for cutting borders for bed-size quilts include an extra 2" of length at each end for "insurance"; borders will be trimmed after measuring completed center section of quilt top.

ADDING SQUARED BORDERS

1. Mark the center of each edge of quilt top.

2. Our borders are most often added to the side edges, then the top and bottom edges of a quilt top. To add side borders, measure center of quilt top to determine length of borders (Fig. 49). Trim side borders to the determined length.

Fig. 49

3. Mark center of 1 long edge of side border. Matching center marks and raw edges, pin border to quilt top, easing in any fullness; stitch. Repeat for remaining side border.

4. Measure center of quilt top, including attached borders, to determine length of top and bottom borders. Trim borders to the determined length. Repeat Step 3 to add borders to quilt top (Fig. 50).

Fig. 50

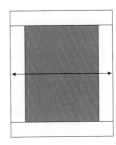

ADDING MITERED BORDERS

1. Mark the center of each edge of quilt top.

2. Mark center of 1 long edge of top border. Measure across center of quilt top (see Fig. 49). Matching center marks and raw edges, pin border to center of quilt top edge. Beginning at center of border, measure ½ the width of the quilt top in both directions and mark. Match marks on border with corners of quilt top and pin. Easing in any fullness, pin border to quilt top between center and corners. Sew border to quilt top, beginning and ending seams exactly ¼" from each corner of quilt top and backstitching at beginning and end of stitching (Fig. 51).

Fig. 51

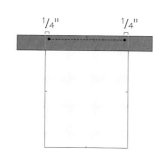

3. Repeat Step 2 to sew bottom, then side borders, to center section of quilt top. To temporarily move first 2 borders out of the way, fold and pin ends as shown in Fig. 52.

Fig. 52

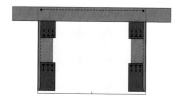

4. Fold 1 corner of quilt top diagonally with right sides together and matching edges. Use ruler to mark stitching line as shown in Fig. 53. Pin borders together along drawn line. Sew on drawn line, backstitching at beginning and end of stitching (Fig. 53).

Fig. 53   Fig. 54

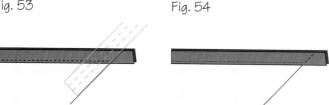

5. Turn mitered corner right side up. Check to make sure corner will lie flat with no gaps or puckers.

6. Trim seam allowances to ¼"; press to 1 side.

7. Repeat Steps 4 - 6 to miter each remaining corner.

QUILTING

Quilting holds the 3 layers (top, batting, and backing) of the quilt together and can be done by hand or machine. Our project instructions tell you which method is used on each project. Because marking, layering, and quilting are interrelated and may be done in different orders depending on circumstances, please read the entire **Quilting** section, pages 250 – 252, before beginning the quilting process on your project.

TYPES OF QUILTING
In-The-Ditch-Quilting
Quilting very close to a seamline or appliqué is called "in-the-ditch" quilting. This type of quilting does not need to be marked. When quilting in the ditch, quilt on the side **opposite** the seam allowance.

Outline Quilting
Quilting approximately ¼" from a seam or appliqué is called "outline" quilting. Outline quilting may be marked, or you may place ¼"w masking tape along seamlines and quilt along the opposite edge of the tape. (Do not leave tape on quilt longer than necessary, since it may leave an adhesive residue.)

Ornamental Quilting
Quilting decorative lines or designs is called "ornamental" quilting. This type of quilting should be marked before you baste quilt layers together.

MARKING QUILTING LINES
Fabric marking pencils, various types of chalk markers, and fabric marking pens with inks that disappear with exposure to air or water are readily available and work well for different applications. Lead pencils work well on light-color fabrics, but marks may be difficult to remove. White pencils work well on dark-color fabrics, and silver pencils show up well on many colors. Since chalk rubs off easily, it's a good choice if you are marking as you quilt. Fabric marking pens make more durable and visible markings, but the marks should be carefully removed according to manufacturer's instructions. Press down only as hard as necessary to make a visible line.

When you choose to mark your quilt, whether before or after the layers are basted together, is also a factor in deciding which marking tool to use. If you mark with chalk or a chalk pencil, handling the quilt during basting may rub off the markings. Intricate or ornamental designs may not be practical to mark as you quilt; mark these designs before basting using a more durable marker.

To choose marking tools, take all these factors into consideration and **test** different markers **on scrap fabric** until you find the one that gives the desired result.

CHOOSING AND PREPARING THE BACKING

To allow for slight shifting of the quilt top during quilting, the backing should be approximately 4" larger on all sides for a bed-size quilt top or approximately 2" larger on all sides for a wall hanging. Yardage requirements listed for quilt backings are calculated for 45"w fabric. If you are making a bed-size quilt, using 90"w or 108"w fabric for the backing may eliminate piecing. To piece a backing using 45"w fabric, use the following instructions.

1. Measure length and width of quilt top; add 8" (4" for a wall hanging) to each measurement.

2. If quilt top is 76"w or less, cut backing fabric into 2 lengths slightly longer than the determined length measurement. Trim selvages. Place lengths with right sides facing and sew long edges together, forming a tube (Fig. 55). Match seams and press along 1 fold (Fig. 56). Cut along pressed fold to form a single piece (Fig. 57).

Fig. 55   Fig. 56   Fig. 57

  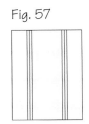

3. If quilt top is more than 76"w, cut backing fabric into 3 lengths slightly longer than the determined width measurement. Trim selvages. Sew long edges together to form a single piece.

4. Trim backing to correct size, if necessary, and press seam allowances open.

CHOOSING AND PREPARING THE BATTING

Choosing the right batting will make your quilting job easier. For fine hand quilting, choose a low-loft batting in any of the fiber types described here. Machine quilters will want to choose a low-loft batting that is all cotton or a cotton/polyester blend because the cotton helps "grip" the layers of the quilt. If the quilt is to be tied, a high-loft batting, sometimes called extra-loft or fat batting, is a good choice.

Batting is available in many different fibers. Bonded polyester batting is one of the most popular batting types. It is treated with a protective coating to stabilize the fibers and to reduce "bearding," a process in which batting fibers work their way out through the quilt fabrics. Other batting options include cotton/polyester batting, which combines the best of both polyester and cotton battings; all-cotton batting, which must be quilted more closely than polyester batting; and wool and silk battings, which are generally more expensive and usually only dry-cleanable.

Whichever batting you choose, read the manufacturer's instructions closely for any special notes on care or preparation. When you're ready to use your chosen batting in a project, cut batting the same size as the prepared backing.

ASSEMBLING THE QUILT

1. Examine wrong side of quilt top closely; trim any seam allowances and clip any threads that may show through the front of the quilt. Press quilt top.

2. If quilt top is to be marked before layering, mark quilting lines (see Marking Quilting Lines).

3. Place backing **wrong** side up on a flat surface. Use masking tape to tape edges of backing to surface. Place batting on top of backing fabric. Smooth batting gently, being careful not to stretch or tear. Center quilt top **right** side up on batting.

4. If hand quilting, begin in the center and work toward the outer edges to hand baste all layers together. Use long stitches and place basting lines approximately 4" apart (Fig. 58). Smooth fullness or wrinkles toward outer edges.

Fig. 58

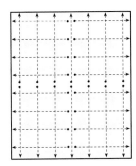

5. If machine quilting, use 1" rustproof safety pins to "pin-baste" all layers together, spacing pins approximately 4" apart. Begin at the center and work toward the outer edges to secure all layers. If possible, place pins away from areas that will be quilted, although pins may be removed as needed when quilting.

HAND QUILTING

The quilting stitch is a basic running stitch that forms a broken line on the quilt top and backing. Stitches on the quilt top and backing should be straight and equal in length.

1. Secure center of quilt in hoop or frame. Check quilt top and backing to make sure they are smooth. To help prevent puckers, always begin quilting in the center of the quilt and work toward the outside edges.

2. Thread needle with an 18" - 20" length of quilting thread; knot 1 end. Using a thimble, insert needle into quilt top and batting approximately ½" from where you wish to begin quilting. Bring needle up at the point where you wish to begin (Fig. 59); when knot catches on quilt top, give thread a quick, short pull to "pop" knot through fabric into batting (Fig. 60).

Fig. 59

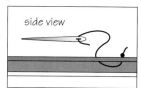

Fig. 60

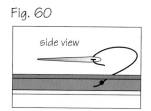

3. Holding the needle with your sewing hand and placing your other hand underneath the quilt, use thimble to push the tip of the needle down through all layers. As soon as needle touches your finger underneath, use that finger to push the tip of the needle only back up through the layers to top of quilt. (The amount of the needle showing above the fabric determines the length of the quilting stitch.) Referring to Fig. 61, rock the needle up and down, taking 3 - 6 stitches before bringing the needle and thread completely through the layers. Check the back of the quilt to make sure stitches are going through all layers. When quilting through a seam allowance or quilting a curve or corner, you may need to make 1 stitch at a time.

Fig. 61

4. When you reach the end of your thread, knot thread close to the fabric and "pop" knot into batting; clip thread close to fabric.

5. Stop and move your hoop as often as necessary. You do not have to tie a knot every time you move your hoop; you may leave the thread dangling and pick it up again when you return to that part of the quilt.

MACHINE QUILTING
The following instructions are for straight-line quilting, which requires a walking foot or even-feed foot. The term "straight-line" is somewhat deceptive, since curves (especially gentle ones) as well as straight lines can be stitched with this technique.

1. Wind your sewing machine bobbin with general-purpose thread that matches the quilt backing. Do not use quilting thread. Thread the needle of your machine with transparent monofilament thread if you want your quilting to blend with your quilt top fabrics. Use decorative thread, such as a metallic or contrasting-color general-purpose thread, when you want the quilting lines to stand out more. Set the stitch length for 6 - 10 stitches per inch and attach the walking foot to sewing machine.

2. After pin-basting, decide which section of the quilt will have the longest continuous quilting line, oftentimes the area from center top to center bottom. Leaving the area exposed where you will place your first line of quilting, roll up each edge of the quilt to help reduce the bulk, keeping fabrics smooth. Smaller projects may not need to be rolled.

3. Start stitching at beginning of longest quilting line, using very short stitches for the first ¼" to "lock" beginning of quilting line. Stitch across project, using one hand on each side of the walking foot to slightly spread the fabric and to guide the fabric through the machine. Lock stitches at end of quilting line.

4. Continue machine quilting, stitching longer quilting lines first to stabilize the quilt before moving on to other areas.

BINDING
Binding encloses the raw edges of your quilt. Because of its stretchiness, bias binding works well for binding projects with curves or rounded corners and tends to lie smooth and flat in any given circumstance. It is also more durable than other types of binding. Binding may also be cut from the straight lengthwise or crosswise grain of the fabric. You will find that straight-grain binding works well for projects with straight edges.

MAKING CONTINUOUS BIAS STRIP BINDING
Bias strips for binding can simply be cut and pieced to the desired length. However, when a long length of binding is needed, the "continuous" method is quick and accurate.

1. Cut a square from binding fabric the size indicated in the project instructions. Cut square in half diagonally to make 2 triangles.

2. With right sides together and using a ¼" seam allowance, sew triangles together (Fig. 62); press seam allowance open.

Fig. 62

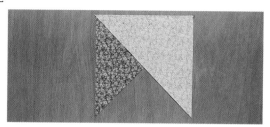

3. On wrong side of fabric, draw lines the width of the binding as specified in the project instructions, usually 2¹/²" (Fig. 63). Cut off any remaining fabric less than this width.

Fig. 63

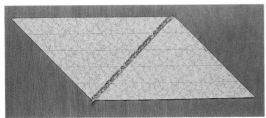

4. With right sides inside, bring short edges together to form a tube; match raw edges so that first drawn line of top section meets second drawn line of bottom section (Fig. 64).

Fig. 64

5. Carefully pin edges together by inserting pins through drawn lines at the point where drawn lines intersect, making sure the pins go through intersections on both sides. Using a ¹/⁴" seam allowance, sew edges together. Press seam allowance open.

6. To cut continuous strip, begin cutting along first drawn line (Fig. 65). Continue cutting along drawn line around tube.

Fig. 65

7. Trim ends of bias strip square.

8. Matching wrong sides and raw edges, press bias strip in half lengthwise to complete binding.

MAKING STRAIGHT-GRAIN BINDING

1. To determine length of strip needed if attaching binding with mitered corners, measure edges of the quilt and add 12".

2. To determine lengths of strips needed if attaching binding with overlapped corners, measure each edge of quilt; add 3" to each measurement.

3. Cut lengthwise or crosswise strips of binding fabric the determined length and the width called for in the project instructions. Strips may be pieced to achieve the necessary length.

4. Matching wrong sides and raw edges, press strip(s) in half lengthwise to complete binding.

ATTACHING BINDING WITH MITERED CORNERS

1. Press 1 end of binding diagonally (Fig. 66).

Fig. 66

2. Beginning with pressed end several inches from a corner, lay binding around quilt to make sure that seams in binding will not end up at a corner. Adjust placement if necessary. Matching raw edges of binding to raw edge of quilt top, pin binding to right side of quilt along 1 edge.

3. When you reach the first corner, mark ¹/⁴" from corner of quilt top (Fig. 67).

Fig. 67

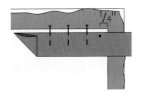

4. Using a ¹/⁴" seam allowance, sew binding to quilt, backstitching at beginning of stitching and when you reach the mark (Fig. 68). Lift needle out of fabric and clip thread.

Fig. 68

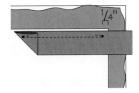

5. Fold binding as shown in Figs. 69 and 70 and pin binding to adjacent side, matching raw edges. When you reach the next corner, mark ¹/⁴" from edge of quilt top.

Fig. 69   Fig. 70

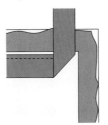 

6. Backstitching at edge of quilt top, sew pinned binding to quilt (Fig. 71); backstitch when you reach the next mark. Lift needle out of fabric and clip thread.

Fig. 71

7. Repeat Steps 5 and 6 to continue sewing binding to quilt until binding overlaps beginning end by approximately 2". Trim excess binding.

8. If using 2¹⁄₂"w binding (finished size ¹⁄₂"), trim backing and batting a scant ¹⁄₄" larger than quilt top so that batting and backing will fill the binding when it is folded over to the quilt backing. If using narrower binding, trim backing and batting even with edges of quilt top.

9. On 1 edge of quilt, fold binding over to quilt backing and pin pressed edge in place, covering stitching line (Fig. 72). On adjacent side, fold binding over, forming a mitered corner (Fig. 73). Repeat to pin remainder of binding in place.

Fig. 72   Fig. 73

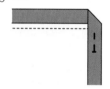

10. Follow **Stitch Diagram**, pg. 255 to Blindstitch binding to backing, taking care not to stitch through to front of quilt.

ATTACHING BINDING WITH OVERLAPPED CORNERS

1. Matching raw edges and using a ¹⁄₄" seam allowance, sew a length of binding to top and bottom edges on right side of quilt.

2. If using 2¹⁄₂"w binding (finished size ¹⁄₂"), trim backing and batting from top and bottom edges a scant ¹⁄₄" larger than quilt top so that batting and backing will fill the binding when it is folded over to the quilt backing. If using narrower binding, trim backing and batting even with edges of quilt top.

3. Trim ends of top and bottom binding even with edges of quilt top. Fold binding over to quilt backing and pin pressed edges in place, covering stitching line (Fig. 74); blindstitch binding to backing.

Fig. 74

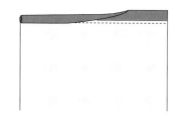

4. Leaving approximately 1¹⁄₂" of binding at each end, stitch a length of binding to each side edge of quilt. Trim backing and batting as in Step 2.

5. Trim each end of binding ¹⁄₂" longer than bound edge. Fold each end of binding over to quilt backing (Fig. 75); pin in place. Fold binding over to quilt backing and blindstitch in place, taking care not to stitch through to front of quilt.

Fig. 75

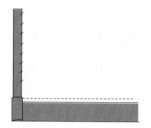

MAKING A HANGING SLEEVE

Attaching a hanging sleeve to the back of your wall hanging or quilt before the binding is added allows you to display your completed project on a wall.

1. Measure the width of the wall hanging or quilt top and subtract 1". Cut a piece of fabric 7"w by the determined measurement.

2. Press short edges of fabric piece ¹⁄₄" to wrong side; press edges ¹⁄₄" to wrong side again and machine stitch in place.

3. Matching wrong sides, fold piece in half lengthwise to form a tube.

4. Follow project instructions to sew binding to quilt top and to trim backing and batting. Before blindstitching binding to backing, match raw edges and stitch hanging sleeve to center top edge on back of wall hanging.

5. Finish binding wall hanging, treating the hanging sleeve as part of the backing.

6. Blindstitch bottom of hanging sleeve to backing, taking care not to stitch through to front of quilt.

7. Insert dowel or slat into hanging sleeve.

PILLOW FINISHING

If desired, you may add welting and/or a ruffle to the pillow top before sewing the pillow top and back together.

ADDING WELTING TO PILLOW TOP

1. To make welting, use bias strip indicated in project instructions. (Or measure edges of pillow top and add 4". Measure circumference of cord and add 2". Cut a bias strip of fabric the determined measurement, piecing if necessary.)

2. Lay cord along center of bias strip on wrong side of fabric; fold strip over cord. Using a zipper foot, machine baste along length of strip close to cord. Trim seam allowance to the width you will use to sew pillow top and back together (see Step 2 of **Making A Knife-Edge Pillow**).

3. Matching raw edges and beginning and ending 3" from ends of welting, baste welting to right side of pillow top. To make turning corners easier, clip seam allowance of welting at pillow top corners.

4. Remove approximately 3" of seam at 1 end of welting; fold fabric away from cord. Trim remaining end of welting so that cord ends meet exactly (Fig. 76).

Fig. 76

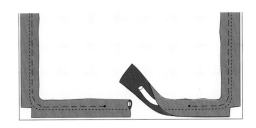

5. Fold short edge of welting fabric 1/2" to wrong side; fold fabric back over area where ends meet (Fig. 77).

Fig. 77

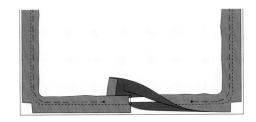

6. Baste remainder of welting to pillow top close to cord (Fig. 78).

Fig. 78

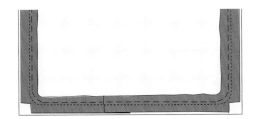

7. Follow Making A Knife-Edge Pillow to complete pillow.

ADDING RUFFLE TO PILLOW TOP

1. To make ruffle, use fabric strip indicated in project instructions.

2. Matching right sides, use a 1/4" seam allowance to sew short edges of ruffle together to form a large circle; press seam allowance open. To form ruffle, fold along length with wrong sides together and raw edges matching; press.

3. To gather ruffle, place quilting thread 1/4" from raw edge of ruffle. Using a medium-width zigzag stitch with medium stitch length, stitch over quilting thread, being careful not to catch quilting thread in stitching. Pull quilting thread, drawing up gathers to fit pillow top.

4. Matching raw edges, baste ruffle to right side of pillow top.

5. Follow **Making A Knife-Edge Pillow** to complete pillow.

MAKING A KNIFE-EDGE PILLOW

1. For pillow back, cut a piece of fabric the same size as pillow top.

2. Place pillow back and pillow top right sides together. The seam allowance width you use will depend on the construction of the pillow top. If the pillow top has borders on which the finished width of the border is not crucial, use a 1/2" seam allowance for durability. If the pillow top is pieced so that a wider seam allowance would interfere with the design, use a 1/4" seam allowance. Using the determined seam allowance (or stitching as close as possible to welting), sew pillow top and back together, leaving an opening at bottom edge for turning.

3. Turn pillow right side out, carefully pushing corners outward. Stuff with polyester fiberfill or pillow form and sew final closure by hand.

STITCH DIAGRAMS

BLIND STITCH

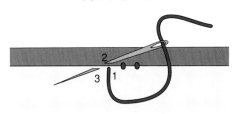

SATIN STITCH

STEM STITCH

BACK STITCH

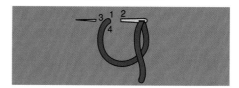

RUNNING STITCH

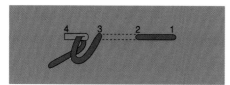

FRENCH KNOT

BLANKET STITCH

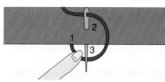 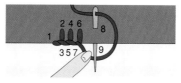

STRAIGHT STITCH

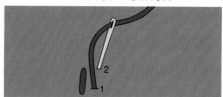

FEATHER STITCH

CROSS STITCH

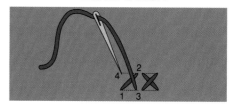

CHAIN STITCH

Credits

To the talented designers who helped create the following projects,
we extend a special word of thanks:

- Christina Tiano Myers and Cindy Tiano Jones: *Anniversary Wall Hanging*, shown on page 163.
  - Country Threads: *Pumpkin Pillow*, shown on page 24; *Autumn Harvest Wall Hanging*,
    shown on page 25; *Soft-Sculpture Pumpkins*, shown on page 27; *Hen House* collection,
  shown on pages 36-37; *Santa Wall Hanging*, shown on page 100. • Holly Witt: *"For You and Me"*
  Embroidery, shown on page 210; *"If Friends Were Flowers" Embroidery*, shown on page 212.
  - Katy Jones: Hand-drawn artwork for *Artwork Wall Hanging*, shown on page 162.
- Marie Henry: *Cabin Fever Wall Quilt*, shown on page 75; *Pineapple Variation Wall Hanging*,
  shown on page 77; *Falling Timbers Wall Hanging*, shown on page 84; *Farmhouse Christmas
  Wall Quilt*, shown on page 99; *Little Baskets Wall Hanging*, shown on page 157.
- Merrilyn Fedder: *Scaredy-Cats*, shown on page 26; *Rooster Pincushion*, shown on page 228.
- Pat Sloan: *Fireside Quilts* section, shown on pages 6-11; *Friendship Gifts* section, shown on
  pages 198-201. • Patricia Eaton: *Wild Rose Wall Hanging*, shown on page 127; *Tiny Tulips
  Wall Quilt* collection, shown on pages 126-129; *Friendship Button Wall Quilt*, page 225.
  - Wilma Gilbert: *Cozy Cabin Pillow*, shown on page 74.